The Armchair Traveller Series

About the Author

PAUL HYLAND is the author of two previous travel books, a spy thriller and an award-winning poetry collection. He is the recipient of several grants from the Arts Council of Great Britain, and lives with his wife in North Devon.

THE BLACK HEART

A Voyage into Central Africa

by

PAUL HYLAND

PARAGON HOUSE
New York

First paperback edition, 1990
Published in the United States by
Paragon House Publishers
90 Fifth Avenue
New York, NY 10011

See page six for permissions

Library of Congress Cataloging-in-Publication Data

Hyland, Paul.
The black heart : a voyage into central Africa / by Paul
Hyland.
    p.   cm. — (The Armchair traveller series)
        ISBN 1-55778-323-3 : $10.95
1. Zaire—Description and travel—1981-   2. Congo River-
Description and travel.   3. Hyland, Paul—Journeys—
Zaire.   4. Crawford, Daniel, 1870–1926.   5. Conrad,
Joseph, 1857–1924.   6. Casement, Roger, Sir, 1864–1916.
            I. Title.   II. Series.
        [DT647.5.H95   1990]
    916.75104′3—dc20   90-6916   CIP

This book is printed on acid-free paper
Manufactured in the United States of America
10   9   8   7   6   5   4   3   2   1

If I'd known that you are the enemy of man
Night
I'd have said to Africa:
Keep the treasure of your tales,
Don't surrender your soul to the night.
SÉBASTIEN NGONSO

It has practically ruined me, this Congo business.
ROGER CASEMENT

Before the Congo I was just a mere animal.
JOSEPH CONRAD

Sons of the dust! When I die this land is Crawford's.
M'SIRI

ACKNOWLEDGEMENTS

Many thanks are due to those who have assisted my travels and research: my wife, Noëlle, for her companionship, for providing literal translations from the French and for compiling the index; H.E. Citoyen Mukamba Kadiata Nzemba, Zaïrian Ambassador to the UK; Citoyen Conseiller Ndimba Muanda; H.E. Patrick H. C. Eyers, H.M. Ambassador to Zaïre, Mrs Heidi Eyers and Sophie Eyers; Robin Bradshaw; Kalomo Bambanday; Kelekele Ofeka Kama; the late Dr John F. Carrington; Keith and Senga Lake; May Montgomery; Esther Sinclair; Bev Turner; Kit Taylor; Dr Lyn and Carol Bulkeley; Susan Evans; Revd Andrew and Margaret Gandon; Revd Lunkebila Kanda; Joan Parker; the late Dr Arthur Wright and Elizabeth Wright; Peter W. and Ann Scott; Mairi Hedderwick; Père Cyrille Bouillon; Bumba-Meli Edo; Lumeto lua Lumeto; Gata Lebo Kete; Nestor Seeuws; Badi-Banga Ne-Mwine; Ron and Doris Weeks; Benkt Bryngelson; Lomboto-Botolokele Ilolo; François and Danielle Seneque; Dose Lebeke; Victor Abrantes; Simon Houghton; Omango Ngonkoli; Ndebe-An-Nzibir; Murray and Joy Stevenson; Gwen Hunter; Vumuka-ku-Nanga; Botomba Elonda-Lolika; Jane Raffloer; Shoaib and Romina Alavi; Alan and Janice Brown; Kyungu Lenge; Julie Rollison; Rebecca Pike; Dr Xavier Kurz; Diyaya Lutete; Ngundu La-Botali; Dan Nelson; Dana Whittaker; Père Gustave Hulstaert; Cleland and Helen Weeks; Lennart and Eva Karlsson; Dr Steve and Carolyn Green; Ken Kruse; Maria Salomé Ferro; Cila Symons; and many others, some of whom are mentioned in the text. Out of discretion a number of names have been changed.

I am grateful to the Home Office for granting me access to Roger Casement's papers in the Public Record Office. For permission to quote material in copyright I acknowledge the following: V. S. Naipaul and Aitken & Stone Ltd for quotations from *A Bend in the River* (André Deutsch 1979) and "A New King for the Congo" (*New York Review of Books* 26 June 1975); Graham Greene and the publishers for *In Search of a Character* (The Bodley Head 1961, Viking Penguin) and *The Heart of the Matter* (William Heinemann 1948, The Bodley Head, Viking Penguin); the translation of "On the Congo" by Harry Edmund Martinson from *Friends, You Drank Some Darkness* (Beacon Press) © 1975 by Robert Bly, reprinted with his permission; Harry Brown for his publication *A Missionary in the Making* (1984); Ruth Slade and Oxford University Press for *King Leopold's Congo* (1962); William Kimber & Co. Ltd for *The Exploration Diaries of H. M. Stanley* edited by Richard Stanley and Alan Neame (1961) I am deeply indebted to books listed in the bibliography, especially to biographies of Joseph Conrad, Roger Casement and Dan Crawford, and to the work of Norman Sherry. I also acknowledge assistance from the Arts Council of Great Britain.

P.H.

CONTENTS

CENTRAL AFRIC

REPUBLIC
OF
ZAÏRE

C O N G O

Ubangi

Basank

Mband.

Zaïre

L. Mai-N

BRAZZAVILLE

KINSHASA

Kasa

Boma

Mbanza Ngungu

Matadi

PART I

Kwango

ATLANTIC

OCEAN

LUANDA

Ngunza

A N G O

0   100   200   300 Miles
0   100   200   300 Km.
Railway

Lobito

Benguela

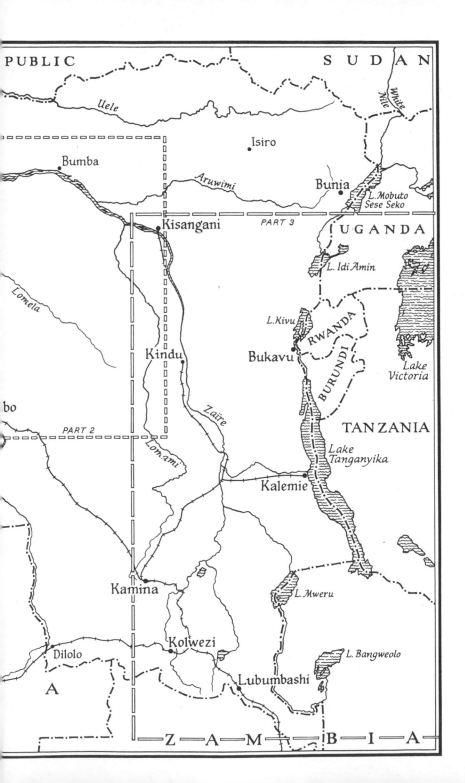

PHOTOGRAPHS

INTRODUCTION

There were no other visitors in the museum of the Lisbon Geographical Society. Noëlle and I were shown into a lecture-room like a banqueting-hall with tiers of galleries. We climbed stairs to balconies holding antiquities gathered from half the world. Our earnest guide displayed her treasures, fast-talking in French and Portuguese, and sent a plump cleaner scuttling from light-switch to light-switch. In a side-room the map of the world lit up to show all the voyages of discovery, a web across the oceans, Portugal in her greatness. Then, in another small room, I found what I was looking for: pillars of stone once planted like way-marks, or claims, on African shores. Back home now, with their carved shields and proud inscriptions, they are memorials in an echoing mausoleum. Portugal has turned her back on ocean and empire; reluctantly, hopefully she faces Spain and Europe.

On his first voyage of discovery in 1482 the explorer Diogo Cão had erected the pillar I wanted to see, the *padrão de São Jorge*, at the mouth of the Congo river. I found nothing more than two fragments preserved by Angolans after a British man-o'-war had battered it for target-practice. I reached out to stroke the wounded stones, half-expecting a spark of static to sting me. The fetishes were lifeless, but the hair bristled on the back of my neck.

At midnight we boarded a Lockheed Tristar, the *Luis de Camões* and flew due south. Noëlle seemed to sleep. Her face was pale and beautiful, her dark hair glinted. Even today, travellers such as Redmond O'Hanlon won't take their wives with them so that it doesn't look too easy. It was my endurance I doubted. I had not stepped outside Europe; Noëlle had been in Africa before and roughed it out East. I filled with tenderness, wondering if our relationship would survive the journey's trials or break. Then I dozed too.

As a child I had a recurring nightmare: the world rolled towards me. It was not a school globe with clear-cut coloured countries but all clouds and oceans and half-hidden continents, massive and ethereal. It spun heavily, rolled onwards, nearer, nearer, never reaching me but always crushing me with horror. Recently I woke from another dream: I am chasing three men into darkness. I follow them into the night and at dawn I am still running. But now they are chasing me. I look over my shoulder; still I can't see them, the sun is behind them, they are back-lit ghosts. I shorten my stride, weary, utterly visible, defenceless against the burning light.

The sun rose over the Sahara. It was a waking dream. The plan I'd been turning over in my mind for months was clear enough in daylight. A century after the foundation of the Congo Free State I and my wife Noëlle wanted to follow Joseph Conrad, Polish mariner turned novelist, and Roger Casement, Irish nationalist and champion of the oppressed, upriver as far as Conrad's "Inner Station", old Stanleyville, now Kisangani. From there, somehow, we hoped to make it up the Lualaba to the Shaba, old Katanga, and the territory of my great-uncle Dan Crawford, extraordinary Scots missionary and explorer. All three men were in Congo in 1890. Conrad visited Casement, and would have met Crawford had he stayed the course of his contract. Journals, letters and books, especially Crawford's *Thinking Black*, Conrad's *Heart of Darkness*, Casement's *Congo Report* and "black diaries", gave me the map for my journey. I had been reared on Congo tales and tempted with gifts — a comb from Katanga, an arrow from Equateur, a drum from Bas-Congo — because relatives had lived in Congo, now Zaïre, from 1889 to 1976. They had loved the country. I wanted to look at the old white myths of the Dark Continent in today's light. I longed to visit the grave of Conrad's Mistah Kurtz, to see where British Consul Casement investigated Congo Free State atrocities, to stay in Crawford's village. The plan was seductive enough. Now Noëlle and I had to live it.

Early on that Sunday morning in May we had our first glimpse of Zaïre through the windows of the *Luis de Camões*: trees, dust, mud-and-grass houses and two tear-shaped islands in a ragged expanse of river. The air seemed to give way beneath us, once, twice, and then we touched down at N'Djili airport. We emerged into heat. It was not so humid, nor was the smell of the soil so strong, as I'd expected. We walked the tarmac. The terminal building was intimidating: few notices and no uniforms, a mass of officials, people claiming to be officials, and men and boys eager to carry bags. We entered the crush and met Simon, our Zaïrian contact, who at what we supposed was Immigration slid our passports through a narrow slit beneath a screen that should have been clear glass but was opaque. It was as if Noëlle and I vanished, sucked with our papers into the continent's maw. After a decent interval, Simon banged on the screen, again, again. Then he went inside. At last he emerged, passports in hand. We waited for a long time in a plain pillared hall, under a portrait of Maréchal Mobutu, hanging jauntily askew. A young woman joined Noëlle on the baggage conveyor, and leaned against her in a companionable way.

Everyone was calm, friendly, curious until the luggage, including our rucksacks, was pushed through a hole in the wall. Importunate pandemonium broke out. Customs men growled "*Ouvrez!*" at us but Simon quelled them with a look. Soon we were speeding along the pot-holed dual-carriageway across the N'Djili river and into Kinshasa. Crazy cars, lorries, *fula-fulas* with boys spread-eagled at the back. Palms, acacias, flame trees, a pelt of dry grass behind straggling markets, *depôts de ciment*, shanty-town shops, *boulangeries*, Golden Lion Bar, Dancing, Lycée du Prince de Liège, shacks. A man in baggy shorts and gaping T-shirt pulling a cart with a band straining at his forehead and a transistor radio for burden. Tinny rhythm belting from the yard of a humble Kimbanguist church, the gracious lines of a white Greek Orthodox edifice, a Catholic hulk, and the monstrous soaring concrete monument to the Heroes of the Revolution with a crane on top of one of its unfinished pillars.

We borrowed money from the Pakistanis in the flat below the one we had been loaned, and went down to Chez Alice, a restaurant of *paillottes*, circular thatched shelters, beside half-finished or half-demolished breeze-block shells. Two men wheeled a hand-cart full of debris through the courtyard. A glossy cockerel and some dowdy hens strutted and scratched in the sand. A straw-coloured pye-dog annoyed them and then lay down to attend to his own vermin. Yellow finches shook the dusty shrubs, and grasses in the roof above us, while a khaki lizard clambered around the shelter's low wall. We laid into spicy chicken, rice, red-hot *pili-pili* and *mpondu*, manioc leaves boiled like spinach. We laid hands on the surface of Africa. Everything was so near and yet so far. The *patron* from Matadi talked to us. I looked into the depths of his eyes — his quick penetrating glance — and saw their brilliance and obscurity. We walked to the Pool and looked across to hazy Brazzaville. The river was vast, hot and lazy. Water hyacinth processed towards the distant roar of rapids. Here was the entrance hall to the interior. Far out, a whale-boat like a floating tea-trolley creased the floor. I tied hopes and fears to its diminishing stern.

We went back and slept. We woke to the sunset and the falling dark. For three days we lived with the languor and energy of Kinshasa; we glimpsed the village life and market economy that persists beneath its high-rise profile; we saw wealth and poverty, warmth and violence; we wondered at the way anarchy was ordered. It was hard sometimes to keep faith with our journey, hard to imagine that we'd ever see through, beyond the vivid opacity of things.

Kinshasa can wait. We made for the coast. American missionaries in a Landcruiser gave us a lift to Kimpese, where my sister and her husband lived through the trauma of Independence in 1960. From there a Swedish pilot flew us in a Cesna to Moanda near the mouth of the river, the beginning of my story.

Part One

TO THE POOL

C

Pointe Noire

C A B I N D A

Isangila

Inga

Palabala

Yelala
Falls

Vista

Moanda

Boma

Matad

Banana

Zaïre

| 0 | 25 | 50 | 75 Miles |

| 0 | 25 | 50 | 75 Km. |

Railway

N G O

Langa-Langa

Zaïre

BRAZZAVILLE

Pool Malebo

KINSHASA

•Kasangulu

Manyanga

Ngombe Lutete

Luila

Inkisi

Lunzadi

Luaza

•Madimba

•Lukunga

Poika

Lukunga

Kwilu

•Inkisi

Manteke

Mbanza Ngungu •

•ionzo

•Kimpese

ngololo

Kibentele

•Sao Salvador do Congo

N G O L A

M.VERITY

THE MOUTH

The endeavour is large and man is small.
I, Diogo Cão, navigator, left behind
This pillar at the edge of the dusky beach
And sailed onward.
FERNANDO PESSOA *Padrão*

I must say when I saw the Congo again — when its vast and gaunt waters broke on my view, and the blaze of its intemperate sun made me close my eyes in sheer physical pain, I felt like turning tail at the mouth of the river.
ROGER CASEMENT *Letter to Sir Martin Gosselin*

Water squirted through two empty rivet holes, wetting my feet, and seeped between flimsy plates each time the metal dinghy slapped the merest swell on the broad and profound face of the Zaïre. I glanced round to see if Noëlle had noticed. She grinned ruefully. Before we launched into this trip, involving a thousand miles of river-travel, she had quite forgotten how afraid she was of water. I echoed Marlow, the narrator of *Heart of Darkness*, "The snake had charmed me". Now we were in the mouth of the serpent that uncoiled from the continent's centre and flickered its silty, freshwater tongue 150 miles into the Atlantic. It seemed unlikely that much of the river's volume, second only to the Amazon's, would come aboard with us; the young Zaïrian boatman was more concerned with nursing the outboard motor and with scanning white light thrown off the water's surface. He made for silhouettes of friends or relatives standing upon their reflections, paddling *pirogues*, dug-out canoes, and spinning their nets out into the water ahead. We made rendez-vous after rendezvous with them, on the fifteen miles breadth of languidly thrusting water between Banana Creek and Diogo's Bay, but news was not good that morning, the dug-outs empty. Fold by fold, flounce by weighted flounce, each fisherman methodically gathered up his net once more and held it between hands and teeth, poised for the next cast.

Oceanwards, a tanker glinted beyond the rivermouth's jaws – the spit of land to the north called Banana Point and, seven miles southwards, Angola and the hooked promontory of Santo Antonio, called Shark Point by the English. Just outside this, Ponta do Padrão shoves its blunt snout at the Atlantic, the point at the mouth of the *rio poderoso*, lusty river, where Diogo Cão planted his pillar of stone.

How hard for that tanker-captain, sitting in the bridge of his vast vessel, or for us, squatting in our dinghy, to take our minds and spirits back half a millenium and understand either Diogo Cão's triumph or his presumption. Imagine the fifteenth-century Portuguese teetering on the edge of Europe; imagine Prince Henry the Navigator building at Sagres his school for mariners hard by the *fim do mundo*, the end of the world at Cape St Vincent. Imagine them plotting, with the latest charts and the great stone compass there — the rose of the winds, a path around that anathema, the Moslem world, to the mythic East and the Kingdom of Prester John. See them edging cape by cape down the north-west coast of Africa until at twenty-six degrees north of the Equator, they came to Cape Bojador on the Saharan coast. Bojador means "jutting", but it was not just another headland. It was the Cape of Fear, a neurotic point beyond which, Arabs and Christians agreed, you fell into the devil's power, your body turned black and anarchic whirlpools threw the waters into primitive chaos: terrors that grew out of the loss, south of that latitude, of their lodestar, the Pole Star. Even the invention of the astrolabe could hardly lay the phantasms in mariners' minds, until Gil Eanes swore he'd die or be damned rather than not sail on through mental darkness. He emerged, rather tamely, into more of the same ocean and on to coasts where men and camels, rather than devils, went about their business. Gil Eanes returned to Portugal with intact white skin, and was ennobled. In *Mar Português*, Fernando Pessoa asks:

Was it worth while? All is worth while
If the spirit is not small.
Whoever would pass beyond Bojador
Must pass beyond pain.
To the sea God gave peril and the abysm
But in it mirrored Heaven.

Nobility of spirit and the lust for gold, ivory and slaves lured the discoverers on around West Africa until, half a century later, Diogo Cão's caravel broached Congo mouth and the Kingdom of the Kongo, whose people called the river *nzadi*. Ironically it was the old Portuguese corruption of this, *Zaïre*, which President Mobutu restored to the river, and applied to the country and the currency, *les trois Z*, in the 1970s' authenticity movement. On my wall at home hangs a map of Africa, published in Amsterdam in 1617, on which the river is labelled both *R. Congo* and *Zaire Rio*. It runs due west from a vast, mythical *Lac Zaire, ubi Tritosnes et Syrenes este discuntur*, whose northern outlet feeds the Nile. For most of the last century the maps still showed a shrunken Congo along with huge white blotches representing the vacuum in the European imagination. It was a vacuum that curious natures abhorred. In *A Personal Record*, Joseph Conrad recalled:

> It was in 1868, when nine years old or thereabouts, that while looking at a map of Africa of the time and putting my finger on the blank space then representing the unsolved mystery of that continent, I said to myself with absolute assurance and an amazing audacity which are no longer in my character now:
> "When I grow up I shall go *there*."

The Portuguese never got *there*. They did not strike far inland from the coast and the navigable reaches of the Lower Congo. But they were *here*, offering their *padroado*, their exclusive patronage, and proud of it. They saw this foothold, Georges Balandier maintains, "as an enlarged version of their own kingdom, a kind of negative to be subjected to that developing agent which was Christian and Lusitanian civilization". When Luis Vaz De Camões wrote his epic *Os Lusiadas* in the 1550s he planted the myth of the Congo in the European mind:

> In that place is the mighty kingdom of Congo,
> Already converted by us to the faith of Christ,
> Where the Zaire goes, limpid and long,
> River never seen by the ancients.

By this wide sea I distance myself at last
From the familiar Pole of the Great Bear,
Having already transgressed the hot limit
Where the middle of the earth is bounded.

Here I was, an English poet six degrees south of the Equator, in Africa but not of it, inheritor of Stanley's self-glorifying vision of the Dark Continent, of Joseph Conrad's ambiguous and anachronistic chronicle, and of almost a century of family history. I'm here, I kept telling myself, here at the myth's mouth.

I wished I could read the water like the fishermen. On its skin it carries stretchmarks, drawn sometimes by a thin mysteriously coherent line of mangled water hyacinth and débris from the swamps, sometimes as if by nothing more than a shift in refracted light. Across boundaries on this fluid atlas the water speeds or runs slow, eddies or goes into reverse at the shores of mainland or island, lifting *pirogues* effortlessly upstream. It is an aqueous machine whose liquid cogs obey unreadable laws. Adrift in the main channel, you can believe yourself motionless until you notice Banana Point's palms edging nearer and Angola's dark tree-line subtly shifting its shape above a long white beach. Light comes off the water as if off glass, silver, silk, lead. At every angle you look, and as the sun climbs, the river re-clothes and re-armours itself. It reflects men and islands like varnish on dark wood, or as the patina on a great and antique drum-skin shivers the hands that play it. The still centre is deep, up to 1,450 feet within the river-mouth, increasing, as the current cleaves the coastal shelf, to a drowned canyon, an inverted mountain-range of water building westwards to 4,600 feet.

If you look over the gunwale and peer downwards the water is opaque and, as André Gide observed, of a frightening thickness, however it sparkles off the blade of a paddle. We sped back towards Pirates Creek, an old slavers' thoroughfare between the islands of Dombo, now threatened with bulldozer and dredger to make way for a new deep-water port, and Bulabemba, infamous for its penitentiary. Much of the creek is just a fathom or two deep, and as wide as a respectable European river, but walled and barred by mangroves and worked by black-and-white fish eagles and prismatic dwarf kingfishers. The mangroves' air roots create cages at the water's edge from which shag-like African Darters make sorties, and the backdrop of high forest trees makes perches for haughty *nègre pêcheurs*.

We slowed and glided from the creek, as if between curtains, into a darker world of optical illusion where rays of sunlight, piercing the canopy of mangrove leaves, cross swords with long adventitious roots that arch and drop plumb from gnarled trunks and twisted branches. These pale rods grow ruddy towards the water, many straining to break the surface with ends cloven like forked tails or tongues. Until rattled by trespassers like us, they hang still among the lower roots' hoops and buttresses whose bleached curves seem to disappear into darkness painted on them by the risen river way above where they bury themselves in black swamp mud. Mangrove leaves are dark and waxy; the bark of the tall ungainly trunks is smooth, though the breathing roots are rough and finely pocked; the leathery fruits do not drop their seeds until the young root has emerged; they fall and thrust themselves into soft rich mud, or grow down to it from still-attached pods. Everything that drops is captured, along with river débris caught by the roots' basket traps, to create a luscious, stinking seed-bed, printed by the claws and beaks of birds and nuzzled by fish. Apart from the mangroves' sexual and vegetative spread nothing grows there but unseen organisms and stench and darkness. We pressed through a dream, where darkness and light are ambiguous, where near and far are confused, where everything is linked and dislocated, then doubled and distorted in the sheer onyx surface of the channel. As we shoved the hanging roots aside, they swung back like out-of-time pendulums and struck us with remarkable heaviness. Ripples meshed with buttresses and drove out a darter who scrambled from the water and flew the tunnel a little way, again and again until he lured us out into the glorious, savage brightness of Banana Creek.

We shared the light with two pairs of white egrets, little and great, and with a small boy at the island's edge gutting a glittering fish. We sprinted across open spaces to where smoke rose above the trees from a fishing settlement of mangrove rods and palm leaves; the boatman showed off his catch of *mindele* (whites), children jumped into poses and men rose from their haunches to demand money when they saw our cameras. After jokes in Kikongo at our expense, we revved up and roared off, but soon cut the engine and manhandled our way under mangrove roots. Open water lay spread beyond their cage one way, impenetrable growth and shadow the other, and, above, the high forest trees. In there we could see no living thing, though we could hear the chiming notes and wild screams of birds, the staccato banter of monkeys, the same unearthly gossip of the forest that greeted Diogo Cão, the same reticence, blank sky, dark luxuriance.

When he entered the river, spearhead of the fifteenth-century scramble for Africa, the white conquistador met head-on a Kongo kingdom in expansion. Five generations before, the founder-conqueror Ntinu Wene had crossed the river from the north, an exalted exile. He sickened, but earthed himself to the territory by submission to the ancestors' living representative, he "who was first at the nostrils of the universe", and to the healing lash of his water-laden buffalo tail. By marriage and migration, Ntinu Wene began to weld the clans. He was *Ngangula a Kongo*, Blacksmith of the Kongo, artificer of spear and hoe, war and culture. By 1482 the Bakongo sphere of influence had been expanding around Congo mouth for a century or so. Its provinces were never a unified state, but it was a "mighty kingdom" in Portuguese eyes, and Nzinga Nkuvu was its king.

The *mindele* (whites) who stepped out of the big water were not seen as *bantu* (men), but as *bakulu* (ancestors), or *vumbi* in the Bapende account of the impact on their forebears:

> Suddenly they saw a big ship on the sea. It had white sails which shone like knives. White men came out of the water, talking in a manner which nobody understood. Our ancestors were afraid, they said they were Vumbi; spirits come back to earth. They pushed them back to the sea with showers of arrows. But the Vumbi spit fire with a noise of thunder. Very many men were killed. Our ancestors fled away. The chiefs and seers said that formerly these Vumbi were the possessors of the land. . . . The big ship came back and white men reappeared. They asked for fowls and eggs; they gave cloth and pearls. The Whites came back again. They brought maize and manioc, knives and hoes, ground-nuts and tobacco. From that time until now, the Whites have brought us nothing but war and misery.

Diogo Cão came back with gifts in 1485. On his third epiphany, at the head of a fleet in 1487, he returned four hostages dressed as Portuguese noblemen; these *mindele miandombe*, "black whites", told of the wonders they had witnessed in Mpoto (the sea and, by extension, Europe). Priests came, with masons and carpenters. The first Kongo baptisms took place at Easter 1491. Nzinga Nkuvu became Dom João. The first church was built at Mbanza Kongo (São Salvador). The Virgin appeared in dreams as a symbol of *ngolo* (power). Men spoke in tongues. Polygamy was abolished. "Idols" were renounced; flames crackled under the first *nkisi*-bonfires. Here began the long struggle between the old and the new.

Relationships with ancestors and allied clans dissolved. The balance of power between the living, the dead and earth's procreative forces was disturbed. The roles of chiefs and *banganga* — healers, priests or "witchdoctors" — were disrupted. The ruler's sons, Mpanzu and Mvemba, embodied the conflict. Mpanzu and the witchdoctors denounced the new as sorcery, *ndoki*, root of evil in the country. But the old was defeated in 1506, and Afonso Mvemba Nzinga ruled the Kongo for forty years.

Painfully he learned what that stone pillar at the river-mouth meant, the hard lessons of patronage. He suspected the laws that trammelled his kingdom to suit Lisbon: "In Portugal," he asked, "what punishment is given to the man who puts his foot on the ground?" He protested about the import of alcohol and the export of slaves. Whites did not distinguish between free men, serfs and slaves, though they baptized them all and sometimes branded them with "IHS", Christ's monogram. In Lisbon dead slaves were thrown to the dogs, until King Manuel ordered a grave-pit to be dug. Mvemba's attempts to control the traffic failed, and he attacked the missionaries' immorality: "Today", he wrote, "Christ is crucified in the Kongo against his will."

His letters to Lisbon were full of plans and requests. Ships and weapons were always denied. Prospectors and smelters were sent, so that he feared for his prerogative, the copper forge. One Portuguese, who had spent fourteen years in Kongo, warned King João III that his fellows were "guided by envy, avarice and covetousness" and should be repatriated. Mvemba, the King-Apostle, survived a Portuguese assassination attempt on Easter Day 1540, but died three years later in the knowledge that patronage had corrupted his kingdom.

His successors both compromised and rebelled more crudely. Old ways were revived under the powerful influence of a prophet, Francisco Bullamatare — *bula matadi* means "breaker of rocks" — who desired to expunge the Church. But attacks from the Bateke to the north-east, the Portuguese in Angola and the Bayaka to the south-east brought destruction and massacre to Kongo. Survivors found refuge and degradation on the Isle of Horses in the mouth of the Zaïre River. Repentance and penance earned aid from King Sebastião of Portugal in 1571, and smelters to chase rumours of gold and silver. But it was not long before Sebastião perished, and the greatness of Portugal with him, at the hands of the Moors in the North African sands.

The mangrove shade at the fringes of the islands seemed to us to be primeval, to contain no history. We were deceived. Our leaking boat thudded across the creek. Small smoke rose blue from settlements and, among the trees on higher ground, big smoke billowed black from the oil-wells. Behind a veil of mangroves, mammoth earth-moving machines shifted ground of vivid orange soil, dwarfed only by gargantuan baobabs. The SOZIR refinery, like a secure zoo for writhing pipework, let down a limb to its concrete river terminal. A helicopter broke the horizon above Banana Point as it took off for the offshore oil-platform. We made an unexpected rendezvous with an inflatable boat full of red-berets, white French soldiers from the Central African Republic. Two very correct officers explained that they were scouring the river-mouth for signs of a French team lost shooting the Shongo-Inga-Kanza rapids. It had happened three weeks before. One body had been recovered near Boma, and one of their two rafts had been discovered beached and intact. Six men were still missing, one a Portuguese, son of the owner of the dinghy we sat in. Rumours about their fate were rife. Shootings by the army, cannibalism and, more believably, crocodiles were all part of the gossip. Our Cesna flight had taken us over the great Inga hydroelectric scheme which presides over zig-zag white water. The rapids looked angry and hungry enough from two thousand feet, and we understood the misgivings of the eighth and ninth members of the expedition who refused to go on. They were abandoned on a sand-bank, from which they took the last photographs of rafts and men being swallowed in a maelstrom of spume.

We kept our cameras out of sight as we approached Banana Point and its naval base. The ancient Woyo name for it, *Soso Ntshinga*, speaks of the fiery river's clash with ocean, but when Portuguese traders asked where the market was, they are supposed to have been told, *"Luende vana banana"* — "Starting at the little palm" — and *ba*, "palm", with the diminutive *nana*, passed back into the language as a proper name. Cartographers labelled it Ponta do Palmarinho, and on New Year's Day 1826 Captain Owen sent a lieutenant to reconnoitre Cape Palmeiro. From a distance, the sliver of land parting shimmering waters looks idyllic. The point peters out into slipways and little beaches below a few coconut palms and the rust-stained concrete of antiquated fortifications. Today's market is that of the squalid township which houses a good part of Zaïre's Navy, estimated at 1,500-strong. Among ruined houses there are sad relics of cannon and slaves' ankle-chains. American patrol-boats and Chinese torpedo-boats ride on the water. Rusting half-sunk hulks are memorials to Mobutu's ill-fated intervention in the Angolan civil war. Two smart vessels, registered in New Orleans and Los Angeles, which ferry cargo from large ocean-going ships to the present shallow port, offloaded goods by crane on to the quay. There, hollow-windowed and with a sagging ochre-tiled roof, the stone-built customs house harks back to the days when the Point's two-and-a-half miles of little palms were dotted with Portuguese, Dutch and English "factories", the Station of the Congo Free State and, towards its extremity, a graveyard and a powder magazine. The graveyard was the destination for many missionaries, merchants, agents and adventurers who, in the last years of the last century, survived the voyage from Europe and a few weeks, months or, if they were resilient, years of life in the Congo before succumbing to dysentery or black-water fever.

Joseph Conrad embarked on the French ship *Ville de Maceio* at Bordeaux in May 1890. He had enlisted as a river-boat captain with the Société Anonyme Belge pour le Commerce du Haut-Congo. From Freetown he wrote to his cousin:

> What makes me rather uneasy is the information that 60 per cent of our Company's employees return to Europe before they have completed even six months' service. Fever and dysentery! There are others who are sent home in a hurry at the end of a year, so that they shouldn't die in the Congo. God forbid! It would spoil the statistics which are excellent, you see!

In the manuscript of *Heart of Darkness* Marlow says, "Of all my life this passage is the part most unreal. My idleness of a passenger, my isolation amongst all these frenchmen." In the book, Conrad brilliantly recreates that sense of unreality and ascribes to Marlow a deeper, prophetic unease. After a little more than a month at sea, the *Ville de Maceio* called at Banana, before making upriver for Boma, "the seat of government".

In 1883 Roger Casement had been working as a clerk for the Elder Dempster Shipping Company in Liverpool. He confided to his sister Nina, "I must have an open air life, or I shall die," and took his chance as a purser. On the *SS Bonny*, a day out from the Congo river-mouth, he first felt the step in the sea where salt meets fresh water and turns from blue to turbid green to brown. He thrilled as the ship's engines laboured against the Congo's thrust. Ruddy cliffs, backed by yellowing hills, parted to show him, between Shark Point and Banana's string of palms, the sheer weight of water against which he pushed past mangrove-shrouded islands and shores of baobab and screw-pine

to Boma. He did not endear himself to the captain, but he fell in love
with Africa. In 1884, aged twenty, he joined Stanley's volunteers,
the Congo International Association. It was not until 1902 that he
"felt like turning tail at the mouth of the river".

My great-uncle Dan Crawford at nineteen embarked on the SS
Saõ Thomé and sailed from Lisbon in April 1889. In Gourock, on the
Clyde, he left his mother; in Bath he left the girl he loved; he
expected to see neither of them again. On 15th April he wrote in his
journal, "Sickness hovering around me all day." He coughed and
examined the blood on his handkerchief; his father, master of a
schooner in the coastal trade, had died of tuberculosis when the boy
was four. On 23rd April, the peak of Principe Island was overhung
with mist, beautiful in the tropical sun, but the town in its shadow
was in the toils of fever. "Ugh! dreaded malaria is there." On the
25th, a ship came alongside with news that a homeward-bound
missionary had just died of fever and been buried at sea. The
following day, "Just outside our cabin door . . . one sailor murdered
another. Six knife wounds declare the deliberateness of the foul
premeditated deed . . ." On the 30th, they sighted the continent of
Africa, and on "Wed., May 1st. At 10 o'c. we entered the Congo.
After a fine sail of an hour anchored off Banana . . . There is a pretty
little cemetery almost hidden among the palm trees, where are
buried many 'of whom the world was not worthy'."

H. M. Stanley says, "It is a place to be avoided by those apt to be
afflicted with presentiments." When the *Madura* entered the mouth
on 18th March 1887, the officers of his Emin Pasha Relief Expedition
had been demoralized by English traders' tales of the sad state of the
boats on the river; "I only marvelled why they had not been politely
requested to accompany their new acquaintances to the cemetery,"
Stanley comments caustically, "in order that they might have the
exquisite gratification of exhibiting the painted head-boards, which
record the deaths of many fine young men, as promising in appear-
ance as they."

Stanley's two earlier visits were notable:

On the 12th August, 1877, I arrived at Banana Point after crossing
Africa, and descending its greatest river. On 14th August, 1879, I arrived
before the mouth of this river to ascend it, with the novel mission of
sowing along its banks civilised settlements, to peacefully conquer and
subdue it, to remould it in harmony with modern ideas into National
States, within whose limits the European merchant shall go hand in hand
with the dark African trader, and justice and law and order shall prevail,

and murder and lawlessness and the cruel barter of slaves shall for ever cease.

Stanley had failed to interest the British Government in the Congo, but King Leopold II of the Belgians had bought the man and his ambition. In 1879 Stanley was met by the genial pilot Mr Youngblood who had lived on Banana Point for ten years and whose clothes "would have graced the boulevards of Nice". They prepared the expedition's flotilla of eight vessels, including the *Royal*, gift of King Leopold, a mahogany lifeboat built by White of Cowes and fitted out with plate glass and hangings of blue silk. And here at Banana, after much ignoble international horse-trading, the Englishman Sir Francis de Winton, successor to Gordon of Khartoum as Leopold's Agent-General, proclaimed the constitution of the Congo Free State in July 1885.

The peninsula, Woyo ground, sacred spit, was a threshold and a stumbling-block. Overlaid by factories, by offices of the State, by rudimentary defences, and now by a naval base, it holds so many ghosts, convocations of slaves on their way out, explorers on their way in. We penetrated its security barrier at the second attempt. In memory the people of Moanda, the sea-village, and Mamputu, the river village, convene at the sacred baobab near the neck of the peninsula. Libations fill a hollow at the tree's roots. Prayers are offered. A virgin boy and girl mix fresh and salt water there to conjure catches of estuarine fish such as grey mullet. Two men walk to the tip of the Point, the Mamputu man at the river-side and the Moanda man by the Atlantic. Each solicits the harvest by brandishing bundles of *mbonzo* leaves; neither may look behind him. The clans' chiefs stand back to back and each, moving to his own side, lies face-down on a mat. They represent shoals and, when the two clan-members return from the Point, they rise. The ritual ends.

Our dinghy slid in to the little beach at the neck of the spit. The boatman and his old companion lifted off the outboard motor and bailed out river-water. In the old man's eyes we were two more white creatures with cameras who paid to trespass on his inheritance. Hundreds of crabs emerged and retreated at the mouths of their holes in the sand. In what was to us a crazy choreography, they stood high on their six legs and performed indecipherable semaphore with one large claw and one small, before scuttling back into the dark. We took the sandy track that links flimsy fishing-settlements with the tarmac road to Banana village. Two men rushed us, shouting; not to arrest us but urgently to advise us not to photograph the Point. Soon we waded into the grass with small boys who warned us against snakes, and against naval personnel whose grass-roofed houses backed on to the old European cemetery. Here were graves of the '80s and '90s, slabs and crosses including, at the foot of a palm tree, that of the Baptist missionary Annie Comber, buried here in 1890 aged twenty-six, shortly after she entertained Conrad up-country. She was one of the Comber family who, as Sir Harry Johnston wrote, "may be said to have given their lives to the Congo", one of a multitude interred on this frail strand between the ocean and Africa's greatest artery.

The road ran on between mangroves and dwarf orange-berried palms on one side, and the long, long beach on the other: the beginning of Zaïre's twenty-five miles of coastline. With adzes and fire, men shaped a newly hollowed-out canoe of startlingly white wood. Others wrestled to launch one into the breakers. Groups heaved on ropes and chanted as they hauled in large nets; two men walked in the surf spinning out small ones. So we left the river-mouth, with its islands of blood and exile, its fishing villages reticent behind their living barricades of mangrove, its maze of dark creeks and subtle currents on which a team of white soldiers rode, hoping, hopelessly, to find the bodies of men killed in distant cataracts.

II

BLACK GOLD

There are also certaine other Creatures, which being as big as *Rams*, have wings like *Dragons*, with long tailes and long chappes, and diverse rowes of teeth, & feede upon raw flesh . . . The *Pagan Negroes*, do use to worshippe them as *Goddes*, and at this day you may see divers of them that are kept for a marvaile. . . .

PIGAFETTA & LOPES *A Reporte of the Kingdome of Congo*

We carry within us the wonders we seek without us: There is all Africa and her prodigies in us.

SIR THOMAS BROWNE *Religio Medici*

What does Africa . . . stand for? Is not our own interior white on the chart? black though it may prove, like the coast, when discovered.

HENRY DAVID THOREAU *Walden*

The world is a strange place. Five minutes from home it's strange. Moanda is no exception. Home there was a cell in the house of the Scheutist Fathers on the cliff. We went to sleep, in narrow cots under nets, to the sound of the Atlantic's liquid breathing and the fidgeting of cicadas. Strange and familiar constellations swivelled overhead. Orange torches of offshore oil-rigs flamed somewhere near the horizon. Moanda's lighthouse, on a modest promontory, was dark. Inland, oil-flares' glow pulsated pink above the continent so that the very darkness staggered to snatches of intoxicating drum-music blown from the Cité on an offshore breeze. The night was relatively cool.

The cock in the cloister announced dawn and, with a crow like a cracked guffaw, punctuated the choral sacrifice of the mass. Two companies of soldiers, running in close order along the cliff road, raised dust and a vigorous antiphonal chant in praise of the Republic. The cock settled down to the day's sexual skirmishes, scattered squawking hens and cheeping chicks among brittle leaves accumulated around roots of mango and bougainvillaea or the flat tyres of an Audi rusting in the corner. The sickly smell of incense gave way to the acrid smoke of burning rubbish which wafted around an uninhabited dove-cote. The air-buffeting throb of a helicopter gusted upwards, and I glimpsed glinting rotor-blades, as it hugged the cliff and scoured the shore for bodies beached with the night's flotsam. The sea glittered and, far out, I counted eleven dug-outs. The breakers' foam ran up pale sand into deep shadow cast by dark red cliffs. A fisherman unravelled ropes of raffia and disembowelled sacks of nylon nets and vegetable floats, leaving a fresh maze of footprints in the sand between the tackle's neat hieroglyphics and his upturned, broad-brimmed straw hat.

I thrust an ancient galvanized bucket into one of the oil-drums that clustered before the dark door of the kitchen and carried it back brimming with water for washing and flushing latrines. The mass was ended. Noëlle slipped into a dress. We gathered, black and white brothers and sisters, around the long table in the refectory. At night, with dogs pressing heavy heads against our thighs for bones, and bats flying in the dimness above us, it was a medieval hall. Now it was a ship's saloon; on a high foundation, it projected from the house with a bay of windows looking seawards and opening each side into arcades like decks. After grace, Père Cyrille in a white soutane presided over a breakfast of black coffee, bread, margarine, jam and bananas, and the lively invention, in Zaïrian, Belgian and Italian French, of new reasons for refusing the call to Christ's wedding-feast: "I'm not going, there'll be no beer or meat, only manioc and water, perhaps bread and wine if we're lucky" or, better, "I've got more important things to do than go enjoying myself".

By the time we went out, the stench of vicious pipe tobacco emanated from Père Cyrille's door, where supplicants queued as they have, I suppose, since the Belgian Scheutistes established themselves here in 1889, the year that Dan Crawford put in at Banana. Just beyond the Pères' ordered shrubs, tall cacti and fan-shaped travellers' palms, the sun caught something high in a raffia-palm. Two bottles, that once held rum and gin, were socketed neatly into the bases of young flower-shoots: European-inspired spirits, fruits of exploration and slavery, superseded by traditional *malafu*, palm wine. I thought of Captain James Kingston Tuckey's bitterly ironic comment on liquor and weapons, the currency of the slave-trade in 1816: "Brandy, muskets and gunpowder, all promoters of civilisation and encouragers of population". And I sympathized with him when he recorded the incredulity of Kongo chiefs at his having come so far "only to make walk or make book". In contrast to most whites, Tuckey had adopted a scientific approach. He admonished his colleagues:

> As one of the objects of the expedition is to view and describe manners, it will be highly improper to interrupt, in any manner, the ceremonies of the native, however they may shock humanity or create disgust; and it is equally necessary, in the pursuits of the different Naturalists, to avoid offending the superstitions of the natives in any of their venerated objects.

When the English captain's ship *Congo* anchored at Shark Point, one of the Bakongo who came aboard was a "priest" who could write his name and that of St Anthony, and who justified the keeping of five wives by appealing to St Peter. Up at Boma, Tuckey found that the king's sons spoke some English. Though they saw many crucifixes and relics — Christian *nkisi*, the expedition's Norwegian chief botanist, Christian Smith, concluded that "a few crosses on the necks of the negroes, some Portuguese prayers, and a few lessons taught by heart, are the only fruits that remain of the labours of three hundred years". He held that missionaries should have worked to civilize, rather than Christianize, the Kongo Kingdom. Tuckey advocated colonization. Fitzmaurice, Master Surveyor of the Expedition, and a colleague bribed an upriver chief with brandy to allow them to shoot at his war *nkisi* — an act considered fatal. "*Mindele Nzambi Mpungu*", the people said, "White men are gods".

The watchman swings tall steel gates open and we enter the walled compound of a large house, an oil-contractors' base. Its once-gracious garden is crammed with Portakabins. Coconut-palms lean alarmingly over the small swimming-pool. Chameleons climb their gradient. I recall the joke about the chameleon on tartan. I feel like it. Alan, a joker from north-east England, lets a pet goat climb him for a cigarette. "He's fussy mind, he doesn't fancy tipped." Sure enough, the goat spits out the filter and masticates the rest. A golden tabby-cat looks on from beneath the table-tennis table as Victor, the Portuguese business manager, tempts and teases two chimpanzees out of their cage with bananas. They walk on their hind legs and cringe and beg, to the apparent disdain of the agile blue monkeys in the next-door cage, until Victor drives them back inside with a jet of water from the garden hose.

Under a large *paillotte*, Nick, an engineer from Somerset, designs the cushions for a full-size concrete snooker-table. The cloth and the rubber, like everything else here, has been shipped out from Bristol. Hearing that we're from the West Country, he dives into a cool-box for cider, and soon the embryo table is a bar. Somewhere outside, the orange sun drops into the sea; floodlights spring up in the garden; night-sounds fight a losing battle with the thudding generator; in any case, a hi-fi system soon drowns the generator with British pop. A servant is running to keep up with vociferous demands for beer and lager, whisky and gin, ice and lemon. The accents are Welsh, Northumbrian, Mancunian, Somerset and Portuguese.

Hysterical shouts cut through the lot of them; there is an internecine struggle in progress amongst the Taiwanese in the kitchen and one of the cooks has taken up a sharp knife to fillet his fellow. Some occidental strong-arm stuff cools things and the offender is given the night, and possibly the rest of his life, off. Cloth-covered tables are laid beside the swimming-pool; the barbecue is fanned to red heat for a gourmand's feast of steak, sausages, hamburgers, salads, chips, fruit salads, fresh fruit and red and white wine: a shock to the system after frugal food and local beer. The African Grey parrot in its cage flirts a red tail and cackles incomprehensibly to itself. The talk is of wild-life around the well-sites: parrots, monkeys and monitor lizards, banded water-snakes in pipeline trenches, never-ending mambas crossing outlying roads. Noëlle reminds the men of home, draws them out, inhibits them. Memories of wild life, night-life, have in any case been blotted out at famous bars, though some girls' virtues are vividly celebrated in my ear. Carlos, quiet and sensitive despite his nick-name Disco Dago, discovers our love of Portugal and fetches a thick packet of photographs of home near Oporto, and his young wife. He gazes deeply into them, perfectly expressing *saudade*, that peculiarly Portuguese species of yearning nostalgia.

Camouflaged French Jeeps are parked in the country-club surroundings of the Mangrove Hotel. The "Foreign Legion" is in good voice. Madam "Mangrove", with pale red hair and a vibrant orange dress, shows off the improvised, and well-worn, grandeur of her establishment. She conducts us to a bar where martial and sentimental songs are muted: a loud-mouthed Dutchman is well ensconced there, taking the piss out of the Zaïrian barman whom he calls "Stand-by". Alan winks consolingly, but tips the bottle the man is pouring all the same. The Dutchman winds himself up to tell ugly racist jokes in English. Our disgust, and the drink, only goad him into more extravagant attempts to shock. "The less intelligent the white man," says André Gide, "the more the black man seems to him to be stupid." I seldom want to push someone's teeth down their throat. I do now. My anger distracts me terribly from the fractured French conversation I am having with a tiny black official; he is smart and crisp and tells me how I can buy very cheap diamonds; his eyes shine as he urges me to keep a rendezvous on the beach tomorrow morning.

The women are distracting too; five preening prostitutes who monopolize the easy chairs. Two of them are beautiful, two of them look kind, and one is so encrusted with make-up it's hard to tell. Not that any of them have stinted on eye-liner, blusher and crimson lipstick. They glitter with jewellery and lamé, though one wears a wax-print outfit and only two have their hair straightened. The one in silver and white, with a richly-plaited coiffure, adjusts her blouse and her split skirt to exhibit as much night-flesh as possible. The Dutchman declares that the ladies have gone up-market with the oil-boom. "When I first came here," he says, staring at Noëlle who has long since moved out of his reach, "you could buy a woman for two fags and a Fanta". For some guys, some nights, it's hard to have constructive feelings. Like pity. As we leave, I fervently hope that if he wakes up tomorrow morning, he wakes up very, very sad indeed.

The lights are dimmer if more mobile in Le Trident. The ladies of the night follow us in. The disco is loud, but the crowd is papering the walls of dark alcoves or using the crescent-shaped bar as a pedestal for their busts. A Portuguese with luminously blood-shot eyes insists on standing costly drinks we could do without. Carlos asks Noëlle to dance and introduces his companion, Manuela, as his wife's friend. Her father squats watchfully at a table, a frog on a stone, ready to reel her in like a fly with the length of his tongue. You have to shout, the music's heartbeat is suffering palpitations, the lights do not illuminate, and I fear that we must match the frieze of tired, emotional black and white faces that protrudes above the bar's horizon. Alan, good angel, drives us back to the Pères' house. So that's how days go, for some, in Moanda. Our cell, and cold water from a bucket are delicious. It is good to be naked in a cot, until you must escape at speed from beneath a mosquito net. Asceticism rules OK, but not before I've vomited eloquently into the basin. Next thing, I wake feeling wonderful.

White gods? Succeeding generations of people near the coast have been awed and disillusioned by them. Europe's divine influence was at a low ebb by Tuckey's time and the Kongo Kingdom itself was not much more than a memory. It had turned from Portugal to Rome; Duarte Lopes was sent there as ambassador in 1583. Lopes provided the first-hand matter for Filippo Pigafetta's book *Relazione del Reame di Congo* . . ., published in Rome in 1591 and translated, within seven years, into Dutch, English and Latin. The Portuguese of Luanda allied with the Bayaka to assault the Kongo, winning the victory at Bumbi in 1622. Captives were exported to Brazil or eaten; the Bayaka had six months' stock of smoked human flesh. To escape reprisals, Portuguese families abandoned Kongo for Angola. A black prophet, baptized Francisco Casolla, preached against the Catholic faith in the tradition of Francisco Bullamatare, but more, performed healings and claimed to be the son of God. The missionary Pero Tavares, infamous for his *nkisi* bonfires, set out to catch "this anti-Christ" during Lent 1632; the messianic "monster" was concealed by the people.

Rome insisted that Lisbon accept a Capuchin missionary monopoly when the *padroado* was restored to Portugal in 1650. The Capuchins were less corrupt than many earlier missionaries; they could be trusted to leave women alone, to eschew commerce and, in particular, the trade in slaves. Their zeal was extreme. The Flemish Georges de Geel rounded up witchdoctors and had them beaten. In November 1652, as he consigned a temple and its fetishes to the flames, a witchdoctor, or *nganga*, cast the first of many stones from whose wounds he died the following month. Rome celebrated him as the first martyr in the Congo.

In two decades Girolamo de Montesarchio burned many temples, thousands of *nkisi* and claimed 100,000 baptisms. King Congobela, and other notables wishing to have progeny of a priest of the Pope, offered him their daughters. The legendary "king" Makoko of the Bateke invited him, fruitlessly, to his court near today's Brazzaville. Girolamo suffered with the plague that ravaged Kongo and killed half the population in 1655-6. He saw devastation wrought upon the weakened Kongo by the Portuguese and the Bayaka, that old unholy alliance, at Ambuila in October 1665. Following the battle the first black priest, Manuel Roboredo, was eaten; the flesh of such a great monk — Georges de Geel's language teacher, royal chaplain — was powerful holy stuff. He it is who should be seen as the first Kongo martyr.

Moanda was a holiday-paradise for colonials. We took the dirt road from the Pères' house down to the beach. The ocean's white hem rearranged its folds continuously along silver-gilt sand at the foot of a long arc of ruddy cliffs topped with dense green. Two black lads, in invalid tricycles with guttural engines, raced past grinning and waving. One hotel's main attraction was a huge, round, rusting metal skeleton for a *paillotte* in which, some time, someone may dance the hot night away. The barrier here, unlike so many road-blocks in Zaïre, was permanently open, manned by a knowing girl with a stall of bananas and cigarettes. With pity and resignation, she watched cocky and coquettish Portuguese kids approach in fickle formation across the sandy car-park from the restaurant. One Land Rover, one Landcruiser, and one couple eating a modest meal that cost months' worth of local wages. A third vehicle brought an oil-man, with towels and bottles and a shy *deuxième bureau* — "second office" or mistress — whom he introduces. He was glad to have snatched a day for love out of a punishing schedule; she was bright-eyed because he'd promised to buy her lingerie and school-books. This, she said, would make her family very happy.

At a gap in the cliff the tide plunged through a channel in the sand, crumbling into the water as it widened, undermined too by the undertow rushing back from the lagoon that lay behind the beach. Thigh-deep thrusting water made a treacherous crossing; we soon learnt to pick our way across the shallows of an inner sandbank. The breach was overseen by a derelict villa on the cliff; other houses looked down on quiet water and mangrove swamps into which its bright surface disappeared. One boy spun a net near the swamps and another looked after a small white child in the shallows. The child's mother, sunbathing on the sand, turned out to be a lively Canadian missionary; she offered to make radio contact with Boma, warn them of our arrival in a few days if we can get transport. Her companions were English oil-men's wives whose whole conversation was a kind of exasperated gossip, symptom of expatriate *ennui*. Groups of Zaïrians swam or played catch, and wet kids rolled in the sand, turning themselves into instant whites. A little way off lay the beautiful oiled body of a blonde dancer clad in white bikini fragments linked with delicate gilt chains, guarded by an Alsatian *couchant*.

Towards the lighthouse, Noëlle dozed beneath an orange sandstone cliff founded on bands of mustard, cream, red. I kept my eyes open. I used to think that serenity and restlessness were words for laziness and vigour. Not so, and anyway I had to learn to wait. Pied crows roosted on the cliff; black-and-flame-coloured lizards squatted there as they do on mud walls, then darted, froze as if caught in the act, jutted heads out, and swivelled eyes as fish-eagles took the cliff's updraft before coasting over the breakers. I coasted, waited. It was glorious to half-sleep on the continent's margin, ears full of ocean's voice. It asserted itself without sweat or argument, just as Tshinday Lukumbi wa M'Bombo has it, in *La Mer de Moanda*:

> The sea, it is the sea.
> To newcomers without ideas,
> To those leaving frustrated,
> To the repentant dying,
> The sea, the abominable sea speaks.
> This language without syllables or letters, is the sea . . .

The Dutchman Olfert Dapper understood those arrivals, departures and deaths. He published his account of Africa in 1668. It presents a Kongo kingdom where conflict was endemic: war, which recurred in 1672, civil wars, and the long conflict between the old and the new. The witchdoctors held that the white way was death, while missionaries saw them and their fetishes as the devil's tools. Dapper knew that *nkisi* were not idols, and that, in the Bakongo universe, witchdoctors stood for good against evil sorcerers or *bandoki*. The props of white man's magic — *mindele ndoki* — were easily appropriated for traditional use, the channelling of *ngolo* or power. A monk's corpse might be exhumed so that teeth and the point of his hood could be removed. Were these fetishes or relics? When Merolla da Sorrente went to Noki, near Matadi, in 1688 and baptized 126 people in two days, did he know what meaning the cross held long before missionaries came? What new, or old, glosses would his Christ figures, crucifixes and figures of St Anthony — *klistu, nkangi kiditu* and *toni malu* — acquire? Did not Makoko himself request one half of Merolla's beard?

Nzambi Mpungu was the supreme power who alone was worthy. Merolla and his brothers were devoted to God the Father, and to the one mediator between God and Man, the man Christ Jesus. Could they convey the love that this God implied by beheading witchdoctors, by burning *nkisi*, by beating the man who inherited the wives of his relatives, by excommunicating the slave who found himself on a Protestant plantation, by adopting the oppressive mechanisms of a temporal power? Not only high-minded Capuchins were tempted by worldly ways. The monks found themselves at odds with the hypocrisy of secular priests who kept women, drank, traded in liquor and slaves, sold the Sacraments and sometimes, it was said, participated in pagan rites and ate men's flesh.

A century and a half before, Mvemba Nzinga had mourned Christ crucified in Kongo. Where was God's Kingdom? Where, after plague and wars and factions, was the one Kingdom of the Kongo? What of the deserted sacred city, Mbanza Kongo? What could stand for a spiritual home, or approach most nearly paradise on earth? It was far away across the ocean. Of ten thousand slaves exported from Kongo to Brazil each year, some escaped to a seventeenth-century independent state in the north-eastern corner of the country. It was called Palmares, a small African kingdom-in-exile which King Ganga Sumba ruled from a capital called Makoko. It was black nostalgia incarnate, and freedom of a sort.

It was not long before Kikongo chatter added frothy descant to the sea's surge. Three girls paddled and began a naïve, self-conscious strip-tease; first one and then another removed a garment; back in the water each decided that more should be added to the wet pile, in and out until the eldest danced a shapely dance to the waves in a white bra and green pants; the second wriggled in the surf with plump breasts held high, an umbilical hernia — a deformity valued as an erotic refinement — and pink drawers clinging darkly to proud buttocks; while the third, a budding twig of a girl in white pants, leapt at each new breaker. We joined them in the warm brown sea and swam for a long time.

A cool breeze blew onshore and we dressed to walk to the promontory. Water-hyacinth from the river and driftwood littered the beach. Crabs, so well camouflaged as to seem transparent and ghostly, sprinted sidelong for their holes at the tremor of our footsteps. The larger ones' dark antennae wavered, disembodied threats. The red wreck of a ship's boat, with the name *Piraeus* on ripped plates, lay beside bits of a raffia-palm: water-worn trunk springing its layers like an onion; bare mid-ribs of fronds straight and smooth as polished spars. Where the beach was cut off by the headland, rough stakes made look-out posts for a pied kingfisher. Up above, a brick tower with white stone quoins was topped by a delicate glassless lantern. We clambered over rough boulders of ironstone and conglomerate to the outermost rocks where the Atlantic rushed, shattered, rumbled as it withdrew. Behind us the beach was shrinking.

We climbed a zig-zag staircase cut into the cliff-face and found ourselves a short walk from the Pères' house. The gin and rum bottles had filled a little. Copper and green sunbirds flickered among fan-like fronds above the swollen bole of a borassus palm. Two pied crows possessed a eucalyptus tree. A flock of southern cordon-bleus picked among the dusty grass, like sparrows with faces, breasts and tail-feathers the colour of sky. Jean-Marie, the young abbé with the laughing little-boy face and the mincing walk, had catapulted enough birds that morning to feed the kittens he found, hungry and motherless, in the dunes towards Banana. He was a devoted foster-parent and, after Noëlle urged their need of light and air, he let them out of their cardboard box and supervised play in the arcade outside his cell. Ginger coats and blue eyes shone, and he showed us iridescent sunbird feathers as evidence of his care. Noëlle, lover of cats and birds, winced and smiled. Before returning to his studies in Kinshasa, he planned to present a well-reared pair of cats to the Soeurs de la Charité de Gand whose house stood beyond the church. He laughed to think of the fate of the Sisters' rats.

The bell chimed for lunch: green soup, fish, beans, sweet potato, rice and expressions of Bakongo brotherhood provoked by an Angolan traveller who shared our table, nostalgia for the old kingdom now split between Zaïre, Congo, Angola and Cabinda. The Italians celebrated tribal differences: the exuberant Sicilian frère Luigi couldn't convince his quiet Milanese brother of the virtue of sprinkling salt on your lemon before sucking it dry. Northerners' vigour was called into question; dark remarks were dropped about Luigi's dark glasses and his links with the Mafia. Two mulatto girls, otherwise implacably silent, giggled at the mock battle, and the squat Belgian who accompanied them launched into a discourse on travel in the old days. Then, if you worked for a company or for the government, you could cross the Belgian Congo without a sou, simply signing chits for boats, trains and hotels, so long as the monthly bills were paid . . . but if you were suspected of any indiscretion you were subjected to blatant surveillance by the secret police; they'd transfer you to Boma and the custody of the captain on the first boat for Europe.

Luigi pushed the lemon skin to the side of his plate and recruited Jean-Marie to perform post-prandial surgery. He sat in a low chair with his feet on a small table, while Jean-Marie's long-practised hand deftly scooped jiggers from between his toes with a needle. The jigger, the female of the burrowing sand-flea imported from the Americas, enters the foot with no more than a slight pricking sensation; it feeds and swells with eggs until the place itches badly. Untreated, it causes an ulcer, from which ripe eggs are extruded, and can turn gangrenous. Luigi gripped the chair and scowled and grinned, then winced gratefully as the craters were doused with alcohol. On mercifully jigger-free feet we set out for the Cité.

In Belgian times each town had its white residential area, its commercial area, and its Cité, or "native quarter". There were still immaculate Belgian houses, Portuguese villas, and high-walled compounds like Gulf Oil's, where generators throbbed all day and air-conditioning insulated the inhabitants from Africa. But only the rich could afford paint. Many villas, like early ones standing on stilts at the cliff-top, were run down; a number had stalls set into their fences where you bought sweets, fruit and cigarettes through a hole in wire-netting. The dust roads were smoothed by the oil companies' earth-movers, though in the rains everything turned to mire. The main street — named, like main streets everywhere, 30 Juin, the date of Independence in 1960 — was a dual-carriageway of sand parted by rough grass, flanked by Le Trident Disco Restaurant, the Mangrove Hotel and business offices. One extortionate European shop was attached to a restaurant at Cabana beach, and most people's business was done in the Cité's market a long way from uptown Moanda.

Men loitered to talk in an open space that might have accommo-dated several soccer pitches. Old women in their forties crossed it with loads on their heads: enamel basins stacked high with bread, *régimes* of bananas, or piles of manioc leaves like large green feathery hats. Boys played wild and skilful bar-football on two weathered tables set beside the sandy highway; players' effigies spun, the balls ricocheted, and goals were celebrated with a kind of war-dance. Across the road, Kinshasa pop music blared from a row of lock-ups. Entering the market was like diving into a maze; narrow alleys of thickly packed, densely stocked stalls where two people could hardly pass in shadows cast by corrugated-iron roofs with wickedly ragged edges designed to gouge my eyes out: a stooping progress through a world of smells, eyes and ears drawn this way and that by proffered goods and rival cries, "*M'sieur . . . venez, venez voir . . . bon marché . . . voilà M'sieur . . . c'est un bon prix! . . . achetez, achetez, achetez!*" Some women kept their counsel but stared as if daring me to affront their humanity or — blatantly smiling, looking, adjusting blouses — their femininity by not buying their wares. Cloths, gorgeous glowing wax-prints and cheaper cottons, jewellery, bright accessories, men labouring at sewing-machines, whole stalls of soap like long cheeses, onions, tomatoes, garlic, ginger, heaps of plastic sandals, hoards of silver sprats, spiced fish and, a special feature, caches of nails, screws, bolts, bicycle and car spares, tools and welding gear, all "imported" from Angola and displayed in profusion. We bought a hand of bananas for five zaïres, about seven pence or ten cents, and ducked out into the light of the street once more. I wondered who could afford those spares and elaborate tools, and why, with so few vehicles and machines in evidence.

In the heart of the Cité, a man and his son made tables, round-topped ones, with three interlocking legs carved from one block of wood. The father finished the linked eyes at the centre of one sinuous set while his son hacked with a machete at a log from which another was roughly emerging. The handsome ladies and inquisitive children of Lelo's household watched us watching. Lelo was half-Portuguese and worked as general factotum for oil contractors in a world of high technology and gratuitous luxury. At each shift's end he returned to mud brick, concrete block and tin-roof architecture, the warp of dust roads and weft of alleys, to a world where necessity and art are hardly distinguishable, where pride in one's person and work is basic and all-embracing.

The ancestor Banota, whose reply to the Portuguese gave us the name Banana, stood tall in concrete opposite the offices of the Collectivité de la Mer. So that the new might comprehend the old, and the old authenticate the new, his statue carried the emblem of state, the flaming torch of the Mouvement Populaire de la Révolution. The MPR is Zaïre's one permitted political party whose enemies risk exile or internment in, among other places, the terrible penitentiary on the island of Bulabemba. Lelo drove us, in a slithering, jiving Land Rover, past *poissonneries* and out towards the oil-torches that symbolize another kind of power. The sky looked heavy, but Lelo was adamant that the rains would not come. The drizzle, that smudged dust on the windscreen and compelled him to use the wipers, simply did not exist.

He showed us the Zaïrian/Italian refinery, SOZIR, a bizarre example of international collaboration, designed to refine oil of a grade which did not come out of the ground here. Crude from the seventy-odd onshore wells of ZAIREP was exported, and crude compatible with the plant imported, mostly from Brazil. It was a simple equation which transformed oil wealth into deficit. Nearby, at Kifuku, a small orange desert dropped from ridge to gangling mangroves by the river. Yellow bulldozers caressed its pure surface and pressed outwards at voracious vegetation. No one could, or would, tell us what the site was for. A procession of fishermen, carrying machetes, pliant mangrove rods and spear-like paddles on their shoulders, climbed a path from the creek and passed under elephantine arches formed by baobabs. They say that the devil, or God grown careless in the toils of creation, planted these trees with their roots in the air. Fruits, olive-green velvet-covered baubles, hung from vegetable architecture. Where they'd plummeted they protruded from the sand, surprisingly large, like unexploded bombs.

The site at Kinkasi was furnished with offices, pipework and whirring gas compressors; turbines performed stroboscopic tricks. The mouth of a man-made volcano slobbered with thick translucent flame; its slender points broke away and evaporated high up; its heat dried the drizzle from the air and blasted the skin, a concession to nature's anarchic power, otherwise unleashed so tamely from the underworld. We drove north towards the Angolan enclave of Cabinda. Inland were the Crystal Mountains; seawards, savanna and swamp lay dormant beneath a net of pipelines drawn ever more tightly. A hunter, carrying a locally-made flintlock gun and a cloth-wrapped corpse, was enveloped in our dust-cloud despite the dampness. It was not rain, you see.

At Liawenda too, near the border, floodlights supervised banks of silver pipework with red valves like fairground organs, and flame heating a grey sky. The lines of this perspective converged upon Mibale by the sea; there, the plumbing culminated in storage tanks for the offshore tanker terminal. A pile of unused lengths of pipe led the eye out to the Gulf Oil platform, with its five-storey hotel, dominating the horizon. Its flare, seen from Moanda as a night-time beacon, was a wan flame flickering behind the gauze of the day's weather. We sped down a rutted track between lush marsh and papyrus to Nsiamfumu, "place of the chief". In the old village of rod walls and grass roofs, women eyed us with resentful curiosity before resuming pounding. We stood before the image of *nlunda bantu*, the guardian of the people. Her thatched shelter had collapsed but, after the imperious male effort of the oil industry, she is serene as a madonna on a stepped concrete plinth dated 2–8–81. Bakongo stone sculpture, a tradition continued in cement since the 1920s, has always exploited asymetry, and, though she stares straight back at us, her head and trunk lean to the right. Her naked breasts are restrained by a band. Her right hand holds a hoe, and points at the clan child seated on her left shoulder like a medieval Christ in Majesty. The chief's staff in her left hand is carved with ideograms whose lineage can be traced back to the seventeenth century in the Kongo cave and necropolis at Lovo. Remnants of white and red-ochre paint cling to the figures, to the incised tree on the plinth, to fronds on a yellow ground. Two attendant white leopards flank the sculpture. Their spotted coats imply mediation between light and darkness, village and forest, the world of *bantu* and of *bakulu*, order and disorder. Their eyes of yellow glass are watchful. Before them, bowls await libations. The matriarch nurtures the spirit of her clan.

Such a guardian was Kimpa Vita, born in the 1680s into a fragmented and despairing kingdom. She was baptized Dona Beatriz and dreamt that two white children with rosaries played with her, and chose her. Later, as an aristocrat of the Marinda secret society, St Anthony appeared to her and possessed her. She burnt all *nkisi* including crucifixes. She was a prophet of negritude, and wore a crown woven from *musenda* bark, the fig-tree from which all blacks are descended, just as whites derive from *fama*, a clayey rock. She preached that Jesus was born in Mbanza Kongo and baptized in Mbanza Sundi. She was St Anthony, her husband Barro was St John, and her child was born of the Holy Spirit.

She died each Friday and was resurrected each Sunday, eating with God meanwhile and pleading the Kongo cause. Mbanza Kongo was to be the New Jerusalem. Gold and silver lay at the roots of its trees. Kimpa Vita called on the Kibangu king to come into his inheritance. He came down the mountain but no further; it was left to her and her followers, *les petits antoniens*, to revivify the city and country, commerce and agriculture. "In this manner," wrote Bernardo da Gallo, "the false saint became the restorer, ruler, and lord of the Kongo". She imbued with a quite new power the mystical/political/messianic tradition of Francisco Bullamatare and Francisco Casolla. She cured sickness and sterility in women, reinstated polygamy, and preached that Pope and Church were travesties of a black gospel. Fearing that she might favour his rival for the throne, the king collaborated with the Capuchins; it was a black council in a black court that committed Kimpa Vita and Barro to the flames. A tall pyre was built for St Anthony and St John and, as the torch engulfed their flesh, Kimpa Vita died like Joan of Arc with the name of Jesus on her lips. Next

morning the remains were re-burned to finest ashes, but not before
her followers had extracted relics of bone. On 2nd July 1706, the
vision of the Kongo Kingdom of God, of transcendent negritude,
flared and died. The guardian of its spirit would not rise again for
some time. The dream, and the reality, of Mbanza Kongo faded once
more.

Noble trees lined the track to the old resort of Vista. A girl rose from
the papyrus-fringed bathing-place by the bridge, water spilling off
proud black nipples. The village was built above the cliff on swelling
sand-banks among shrubs and palms, with huts and houses of rod and
reed, mud and grass or brick and corrugated iron, some painted blue
and yellow like a child's crayoned visions of home. There was a square
of log benches where men palavered over palm-wine in tree-shade: a
reflection of the regal court and of the sober court of judgment where a
matter, or *mambu*, was debated in proverbs, songs, questions and
answers, in order to cure, not just an individual's problem or a
problem individual, but the whole community. I saw the age-old
gestures of confrontation, hauteur and enclosure, of the blocking of
evil, reconciliation and submission that the carvers of stone *mintadi*, or
guardians, captured so fluently for the graveyards of the ancestors.
The gesture and the proverb are woven into the iconography of this
people: basket-weaving, house decoration, wood and stone sculpture,
and the figured pot-lids of the Bawoyo with which a woman might
convey a proverbial admonition to her man, are all eloquent with this
language of strenuous decorum. It was a decorum enlivened here with
alcohol, but in *mambu* of moment it is *mpeeve*, the wind from the dead
which fans the elder or judge into an ecstatic blaze of dance, of
brandished regalia, of sudden mordant verdict. This palaver was
conducted within a stone's throw of an octagonal assembly room, of
derelict colonial villas and of concrete shells, big houses being built for
the Zaïrian *nouveaux riches*.

How can richness of tradition and the appetites of materialism be
reconciled? Many Europeans could not see the richness. How could
palaver, which was idleness, continue endlessly? There was work to
be done and money to be made, though not by the same people. The
work ethic had its own rewards. "It seemed to me that with their
animal-like lives the natives should have the health of beasts," wrote
Hermann Norden as late as the 1920s:

But animals exercise and fight each other. Since intertribal warfare has been stopped the activities of the natives have stopped. . . . These people need nothing. We must create wants in them. The building of decent houses for the chiefs is a good plan; others will desire similar ones, and work to get them.

We drink gin and fruit juices in Habitat-style comfort with a Nigerian oil-man I shall call Albert. He talks of the clan's authority, the extended family's support and total hospitality. On the terrace Alphonse, a suave and supercilious Zaïrian servant, plants *hors-d'oeuvre* of egg and bean salad on the table. Albert admits the claustrophobia of tradition. Alphonse flies pork chops, chips and peas in over our right shoulders. Albert is detribalized, finds it difficult when local workers take him to their bosoms, finds himself quibbling over hygiene, the legacy of seven years in the USA. Alphonse dispenses banana fritters on to sparkling china. If an individual — an inadmissible creature — succeeds, he must share his success; a young man with a "good job" bears an insupportable burden. One who insists on his individuality may as well be dead; jealous relatives may employ poison to that end. Alphonse indicates coffee served inside. Thoughtful, gentle Albert compares Nigerian aggressiveness with Zaïrian friendliness. "Not that you get much of a welcome at N'djili airport. You whites may think you have a hard time." We thought that. "They let you go ahead. Foreign blacks are herded into another room, papers confiscated. We're pumped for money. Mostly, they pay. I said I'd take the next 'plane back to Lagos. They let me through in the end." Racialism and tribalism, both, are ravening beasts. When we leave, and get beyond the range of the generator, an unseen bird is dicing the dusk with a call like the sharpening of knives.

We had almost finished packing our rucksacks for the journey to Boma. Earlier, a tedious walk in the dark to a missed rendezvous and an improvised meal in our cell made for a bleak leave-taking. Noëlle was weary with picking weavils out of emergency supplies, I was tense about tomorrow, small-talk was burdensome. We missed those who loved us. Even in Africa the heart seemed incurable. It was late. Forebodings overtook us. Then a sharp knock on the door. It was Luigi with, at his back, a diffident Irishman come to see the travellers. We warmed to each other at once. Patrick was a skilled engineer who would rather be a writer. Well, Conrad had been a sailor. Patrick travelled with a battered typewriter and had once met Graham Greene at Heathrow.

Suddenly we laugh a lot, talking of Irish writers we know and of the folk here. "They're a bit sharp at business, but they're good people right enough." Patrick speaks of the oil industry as a conspiracy against them, of how the local injection of wealth exploits them and creates prostitutes whom he eschews. He has a burden to share. His skilled men make very good money. After all, some can earn in a week what he earns in an hour. He gives them cash from his own pocket and they call him a good man. "Sure, I only do it to make myself feel better. A bit less worse, anyway. The skill I have in my hands, after many years, doesn't seem to belong to me. When I've done a day's hard, mending a pump at Mibale for the whole oil-field, it would have pleased me in the old days, but now I think maybe I haven't done such a good day's work for the people after all." We had heard soldiers singing their way along the cliff; he was flagged down by them. It is wise and unwise to stop. Patrick stopped. He was ordered to take two squaddies, near to death with fatigue on an exercise in the bush, back to camp. "It was a terrible, terrible squalid place, with a Belgian officer in charge." He feels implicated. He confesses to paranoia about surveillance on his hotel room. He is trapped, vulnerable. "Two years or so ago, the rig went up. Eighteen Frenchmen were incinerated with about thirty Zaïrians. It never made the newspapers at all." He sighs. There is one more question we can't answer: why didn't we meet earlier? We drink up and embrace the man.

We finished packing, tried to sleep. As mosquitoes buzzed my net, wanting blood in exchange for the gift of a parasite, I brooded on one picture Patrick had painted. The rig out there, the beacon squatting over the waves, that pierced down and sucked up black gold, also discharged rich effluent and attracted all the life of the ocean. Out there, on dark water under a tower of light, fishermen in dug-outs battled with currents and shoals. As moths at flame singe their wings, they ripped nets to tatters on the molluscs that encrust the rig's great legs. For the sake of some sort of living they risk, and suffer, wrecking and death. To be sure, the world is a strange, sad place.

III

THE SEAT OF GOVERNMENT

Boma (Mboma) has a history, a cruel blood-curdling history, fraught with horror, and woe, and suffering. Inhumanity of man to man has been exemplified here for over two centuries by the pitiless persecution of black men, by sordid whites.

H. M. STANLEY *The Congo and the Founding of its Free State*

We went up . . . and anchored off the seat of government. I had heard enough in Europe about its advanced state of civilisation; the papers, nay the very paper vendors in the sepulchral city were boasting about the steam tramway and the hotel . . . the tramway ran only twice a day, at mealtimes. It brought I believe the whole government with the exception of the governor general down from the hill to be fed by contract . . . An air of weary bewilderment at finding themselves where they were sat upon all the faces. . . .

JOSEPH CONRAD *Heart of Darkness* manuscript

For some reason we could not fathom it was impossible just then to take a boat from Banana to Boma. Noëlle was relieved. Luckily César, a young Zaïrian abbé, was catching the bus. A craggy-faced Belgian priest gave the three of us an early-morning lift to the Cité in a truck loaded with women and wood. He dropped us at the Auto-Express bus-stop, a palm-roofed shelter beside a bar and a stinking hole-in-the-ground *wai-sai* (W.C.). The crowd under the shelter swelled: men and women with boxes, knotted cloths, sacks of coconuts, *régimes* of plantains, chickens with tied legs, and babies bound on to mothers' backs, all waiting quietly for the bus. When it arrived, a red ex-army truck with high small windows barred on the inside, César credited us with its promptness. He approached the driver to reserve us seats in the cab. That way, he said, we'd see the country.

Noëlle was in the *wai-sai* when two teenagers in T-shirts appeared at my elbow and ordered me to open the rucksacks. I demurred. They claimed to be the anti-fraud squad. I might be smuggling diamonds. I wasn't, I said. They glared, barked *Ouvrez!* Then César, immaculate in tweed trousers and black clerical shirt, intervened, invoking Church and the good name of Père Cyrille to vouch for our good character. If I'd been a Catholic I'd have told my rosary. Noëlle took in the scenario and together we imagined carefully-packed gear for four months' travelling — cameras, film, and bundles of money secreted amongst clothes and towels — strewn on the gritty sand, and wondered how much we'd end up with; the palaver moved to the bar and another official; back and forth until the lads sulkily retreated and César reassured us out of the side of his mouth. After the lorry's interior had been swept, baggage was stored under the wooden seats. We sat in the cab and watched the anti-fraud squad spread the contents of a woman's cases — cloths, blouses and underwear — over the ground with no apparent result. She raged impotently as they slouched off, grinning. Within the hour everybody was loaded. We guarded César's briefcase, squashed beside the driver and a woman going to see her sick mother.

We roared out of the busy Cité, on the infamous *poto-poto* road, seventy-five miles of sand and rock that leads to the old seat of government. We climbed away from the oil-wells and flames, the glistening rivermouth and its islands, and met a road-block. Bamboos on three forked twigs spanned the road. Two of the soldiers reclining on the bank roused themselves and their rifles; one asked me for cigarettes which I had not got, though the driver obliged him with cynical goodwill, hoping for a quick getaway. We cooked in the heat. Cursing, the driver switched off. All over Zaïre it is standard practice for the military to stop buses like ours, or *fula-fulas*, and relieve passengers of five or ten zaïres each; a sensible habit for an army whose wages pass through numerous sets of sticky fingers. The story was that they were checking out all the men in an attempt to catch a thief. After twenty minutes the driver began shouting.

The order was given, and a third soldier strolled across and languidly lifted the bamboo barrier. At least the hot air moved as we crossed hilly country through villages of plank-walled houses, past roadside boneyards with spiky crosses. After the long climbs and slow descents of the Crystal Mountains, the road flattened and we passed a hunter carrying his flintlock and an antelope. Carcases and snake-skins dangled by the road in some villages, but we did not stop until we got to Kanzi; among market stalls I had brief respite from the door-handle that dug into my hip and jarred with every rock and rut. Then off again, past the Catholic mission and its shrine set into a massive rock, through a village hung with cream and purple straw hats and baskets, and a sinister landscape of palms whose trunks were bottle-brushes of black serrated petioles. I concentrated on details to distract me from discomfort; Noëlle practised the African art of blankness that numbs the senses against the pains of travel and waiting. More mountains loomed, dark and craggy with squarish, tablet-like rocks, a scene of sombre and exciting monumentality pierced by our serpentine road. The driver seemed to know every sand-slide, rock-shelf and pot-hole in it; we clambered up and slithered round hair-pin bends, anticipating the occasional crowded lorry or car, side-stepping pigs and goats with horn blaring, careering down and rumbling over the timbers of bridges spanning stream-beds at the bottom of deep valleys. Villages of mud and grass houses were piled steeply uphill from oil-palms and bananas and framed with the dry-season ochres of hardwood foliage. Suddenly sculptural summits and plush deeps were succeeded by papyrus and rich green marsh stretching away to the greater expanse of the Zaïre and the islands of Mateba.

On the north bank the Lightning Stone *Matadi Nzazi*, or Finger of God, stood on a dome-shaped hill, complemented on the Angolan side by Fetiche Rock, a huge natural *nkisi* engraved with figures and signs. Westwards the river swelled to a width of thirteen miles and, way out of sight, narrowed again towards Ponta da Lenha, thirty miles or so downriver, half-way to Banana. Captain Tuckey's party sailed up here in July 1816 and Lieutenant Hawkey learned the meanings of Fetiche Rock's figures from a learned *nganga* of Noki. Tradition tells of white man's ships bewitched and spun in whirl-pools by the power of *Seembi*, spirit of the Rock. At Boma, Tuckey reunited a Congo slave he had brought from England with his father. Christian Smith wrote that the father's "excessive joy, the ardour with which he hugged his son in his arms, proved that even among this people nature is awake to tender emotions". The expedition overcame enormous obstacles to get upriver beyond Isangila. Sick-ness and the stubbornness of bearers stopped them. Tuckey, Smith and Hawkey climbed to the summit of a hill on the south bank "where we perceived the river winding again to the S.E. but our view did not extend above three miles of the reach". Of fifty-six men, eighteen died, including Tuckey and Smith. Three lie in the burial-place of the Boma chiefs. The last words in Tuckey's journal, 9th September, are, "Flocks of flamingos going to the south denote the approach of the rains".

A Hungarian, Ladislaus Magyar, found fifty-odd slavers' houses at Boma in May 1848, and multiplied Tuckey's estimate, of two thousand slaves per annum exported from Congo, ten-fold. He sailed on past Tuckey's "Booka Embomma", Stanley's Princes' Island, at the mouth of the narrow stretch of river leading to the cataracts; he reached the first of these on 1st June. Magyar's journal ceases there, long before "Tuckey's Farthest". Richard Burton's *Two Trips to Gorilla Land and the Cataracts of the Congo* recalls travels of 1863 when "all traces of Christianity had disappeared", though Catholic fetishes were preserved. Burton condemned missionary despots and bestial slavers; we needed the labour of the "lower races" in tropical regions, he said, but by voluntary emigration. Adolf Bastian, a German explorer who came upriver in 1873, was a more reliable observer; he saw how local cults had absorbed Christian practice, but blamed missions rather than slavers for the "half-civilised bandits" who held travellers for ransom at Banana. However, he had no reason to change his observation of 1857: "Among the negroes one thought was established; that the olive oil imported to the Congo was made from slaves who had been transported to America."

Bastian did not use Burton's phrase, "lower races", but he re-counted creation myths which revealed how the Congolese saw themselves. In one, all humans were created white by *Nzambi* in *Mpoto* — Portugal or Europe. A couple, deeply in love, entered a forbidden room; there they knocked over a barrel of pitch paint and were blackened in punishment for trespass; in terror they fled from *Mpoto* to the Congo River. In another, the country was inhabited by apes who reviled *Nzambi*, so he created two pairs of humans, Nomandamba and Mundele and their wives; on the morning of the first day, Mundele woke early and ran to the well to wash and whiten himself; but Nomandamba, washing late in the dirty water, became black. The Congolese self-image was seriously tainted. Bastian found no one left who could decipher Fetiche Rock's inscriptions. Four years later, the first white man entered the old Kongo Kingdom from upriver, and the rest of the century would see confrontation with *mindele* on a quite new scale.

When Stanley arrived at Boma in August 1877, he was shocked by the traders' colour: "As I looked into their faces, I blushed to find that I was wondering at their paleness. . . . The pale colour, after so long gazing on rich black and richer bronze, had something of an unaccountable ghastliness." And he looked on the river with new eyes:

> Ah! the hateful, murderous river, now so broad and proud and majestic-ally calm, as though it had not bereft me of a friend, and of many faithful souls, and as though we had never heard it rage and whiten with fury, and mock the thunder. What a hypocritical river! But just below the landing-stage a steamer was ascending — the *Kabinda*, John Petherbridge, master. How civilisation was advancing on me!

As we neared Boma, a century later, cranes punctuated the skyline of an apparently derelict naval dock-yard and field-guns and hulks of military vehicles marked the Fortress of Shinkakasa, every brick of which was shipped from Europe. Here, in April 1900, Sergeant Motuwe distributed arms to his Bahuyu brothers in the Force Publique. In protest against maltreatment and the compulsory extension of their seven-year contracts, the soldiers from the east turned cannon on the port of Boma and bombarded a vessel there. The whites were taken unawares and the Governor General struggled to put it down. Mutineers escaped into the Mayombe forest and northwards along the river to the Swedish mission of Kinkenge. There Wilhelm Walldén fed them and treated the wounded. Secretly he sent couriers to procure guides for their escape, but also to alert the military at Luozi. The protracted massacre that followed relied upon the missionary as double-agent. Afterwards, all white State func-tionaries were armed, and obliged to attend shooting practice on Sundays.

Our lorry hit tarmac and Boma appeared on hills to our left. Ahead on a plateau we could see the massive brick cathedral of 1949 and, like a shining trinket, the porch and bell-tower of the prefabricated metal cathedral that was barely finished when Conrad first set foot here. We arrived in black Boma, and our bus stopped by the painted statue of a palm-nut cutter. Should we get off? We didn't know, and neither did the driver. Two stops later, in the Cité, César alighted and so did we. Where was the Canadian mission guest-house that had, we hoped, received our radio message from Moanda? He didn't know, but he was thrilled with the speed of the trip. He put the lack of hold-ups down to us, to white man's luck, a thesis confirmed almost at once, for he spotted the chauffeur from the Catholic seminary. Soon we were tearing back down the dirt road, between shops and stalls, with lads in the back of a pick-up. We slewed to a halt and César blessed us again when he caught sight of friends, for whom he had important letters, at a tyre repair workshop nestling under a hill beside a grotto of the Virgin. Exhaust and dust gusted from passing lorries and taxis and the sound of hammering filled the air. I hung on as we climbed the steep hill towards the large white Protestant church on the top. The watchman opened the mission's gates on to a driveway of nut-shells. We were greeted by two aggressive dogs, a Canadian lady, and the news that when our radio message got through the guest-house had been full, but that now it was closed for a week. She looked us over and took pity on us. Thankfully, regretfully, we took our leave of César. We had a house on a hill to ourselves.

We woke to the sound of sirens. We ate a breakfast of pineapple and eggs, toast and mango jam, serenaded by the breathy whistling of an invisible bird in the steep garden below. We looked down upon skeletal frangipani trees, bare but for fragrant waxy pink and white-gold blossoms on flattened branches. Mousebirds trailed their tail feathers and sunbirds glinted amongst the feathery foliage of a Thevetia tree full of yellow trumpet-shaped flowers and squarish green fruits. Flame fermented on one of the Angolan islands and sent up a pall of smoke which thinned and hung like mist above the river and the long line of cranes. The gently decaying commercial sector was shaded by palms and flame-trees; on a low hill to the west the new naked Banque Commerciale Zaïroise faced the cathedral and government offices on their plateau to the east. Southern cordon-bleus pecked around the nut-shell drive and, near the guest-house, a Heidelberg press of the 1890s and a modern offset-litho machine were churning in the print-shop. On top of the hill the church stood, spacious and cool, with a great bell poised on legs to toll its message to further hills thickly covered with rust-red roofs, mud-brick houses and shops, trees and market-places, clambering and diving dirt roads, amphitheatres artlessly cradling all the sounds of the cité. Beyond, the mountains rippled away towards Cabinda.

We walked down past new houses, foundations and vacant platforms of ochre sand steeply stacked one above the other, to the sculptor Makakala's statue of the palm-nut cutter where we should have got off the bus. Across the road stood a ship's wheel crossed with a long-bladed knife or *coup-coup* and a hoe, a monument to work —

Salongo I Mai 1973 — in the national colours of yellow, red and green.
Both sculptures were embalmed in red dust from traffic which rumbled
across the bailey bridge over the Kalamu river, or Crocodile Creek. We
stood on its shaking boards and watched people bathing in the grass-
filled stream below the narrow-gauge railway which runs ninety miles
north to Tshela. Sellers of onions dominated the stalls arrayed in front
of a colonnaded colonial confection, and soldiers kept an eye on the
commerce of the street. We crossed it, stepping over an open drain that
was being noisomely cleared, and climbed towards the cathedral and its
relict prototype.

The first, with its multi-lanceted façade, tapering central tower, and
heavily moulded Romanesque portal, squats monumentally up there.
It possesses African soul. The second, fragment of King Leopold's gift,
sits lightly on the edge of the plateau, a white tin chapel of elegantly
moulded panels, a seven-sided tower surmounted by a conical red spire
and a gilded weathercock. It might blow away. Up flights of stone steps
flanked by wind-blown flamboyant trees with rattling pods we ascend,
between ill-matched sisters symbolic of the consonance and dissonance
of Boma's history, to the road above and the Hôtel de Ville.

We ask for the Chef du Protocol and are led through the building and
up outside stairs from the verandah to the balcony. The Chef du
Protocol is sick, but after a short wait we are ushered into the office of his
deputy who examines our papers and ceremoniously passes us on to
Citoyen Lomboto-Botelokole Ilelo, Chef du Service Urbain de la
Culture et des Arts. He too examines our papers. "I am new to the post
and to the region," he says, "and will find it hard to answer all your
questions; nevertheless I will show you what I can."

Soon we are across the road at the old Governor-General's residence,
now that of the Commissaire Urbain. It was three years old when
Conrad came to Boma in June 1890. Like the first cathedral it is a
prefabricated metal structure; its core seems solid as a steamer's
bulkheads, but its surface is airy; a broad staircase rises to a bandstand-
like balcony; stilts and pillars, balustrades and lines of small windows
are interspersed with tiers of roofs and crowned by a small tower like the
knob on a birdcage. A man gathers leaves from the driveway that
sweeps through a garden of trees including a giant gaunt baobab. At 6
am, 11.45 am and 6.30 pm the steam trams, that excited Brussels'
newspaper vendors and at first so astonished the blacks of Boma that
they ran after them laughing and clapping, used to make the descent
down the present Avenue Nanga to the hotel that Conrad describes in
the manuscript of *Heart of Darkness*:

I beheld that wonder . . . It stood alone, a grey high cube of iron with two tiers of galleries outside, towering above one of those ruinous-looking foreshores you come upon at home in out-of-the-way places where refuse is thrown out.

It stood, in fact, beside the post-office which still survives like a picturesque antique among the port buildings, with its baroque letter-box and tiny array of decorative *boîtes postales* beside exuberant electric mauve displays of jacaranda trees. In his manuscript Conrad has little time for brand-new trappings of civilization, nor for the pretensions of its officials:

> in their demeanour they pretended to take themselves seriously just as the greasy and dingy place that was like one of those infamous eating shops you find near the slums of cities, where everything is suspicious, the linen, the crockery, the food, the owner, the patrons, pretended to be a sign of progress; as the enormous baobab on the barren top of the hill amongst the government buildings, soldiers' huts, wooden shanties, corrugated iron hovels, soared, spread out a maze of denuded boughs as though it had been a shade giving tree, as ghastly as a skeleton that posturing in showy attitudes would pretend to be man.

The book itself has no time at all for details culled from the Boma Conrad knew. He cut them out. Purposefully he plants Marlow in an anachronistic setting; everything is less developed than it really was. To this end *Heart of Darkness* shrinks the seat of government to a "miserable little wharf".

Boma was more than that when Stanley first arrived from the east thirteen years earlier. On 3rd June 1877, he had lost the last of his white companions, Frank Pocock, in the Masassa Falls — "A BLACK WOEFUL DAY!" heads his long diary entry. By late July he had passed "Tuckey's Farthest", and on the 30th arrived at Isangila. Livingstone's river was one with Tuckey's Congo, and, having proved that, Stanley decided to abandon it and strike overland for Boma. At sunset on the 31st his boat the *Lady Alice*, after 7,000 miles, was carried to the summit of some rocks and "consigned to her resting place above the Isangila Cataract, to bleach and to rot to dust!" Stanley's caravan of souls was in similar danger: local people were hostile and demanded rum from an explorer reduced to scavenging for manioc, bananas, ground-nuts and water. From Nsanda, he wrote on 4th August:

> *To any Gentleman who speaks English at Embomma.*
> Dear Sir,
>   I have arrived at this place from Zanzibar with 115 souls, men, women

and children. We are now in a state of imminent starvation. We can buy nothing from the natives, for they laugh at our kinds of cloth, beads, and wire . . . as you are a Christian and a gentleman, I beg you not to disregard my request. . . . The supplies must arrive within two days, or I may have a fearful time of it among the dying. . . . For myself, if you have such little luxuries as tea, coffee, sugar, and biscuits by you, such as one man can easily carry, I beg you on my own behalf that you will send a small supply, and add to the great debt of gratitude due to you upon the timely arrival of the supplies for my people. Until that time I beg you to believe me,

Yours sincerely,
H. M. Stanley,
Commanding Anglo-American Expedition
for Exploration of Africa.

P.S. You may not know me by name; I therefore add, I am the person that discovered Livingstone in 1871. — H.M.S.

This he sent ahead by four of his men and two local guides. The guides deserted, but the party followed the river and Stanley was soon supplied, not just with the cloth and rice he had requested, but with sweet potatoes, fish, tobacco, rum and:

Pale ale! Sherry! Port wine! Champagne! Several loaves of bread, wheaten bread, sufficient for a week. Two pots of butter. A packet of tea! Coffee! White loaf-sugar! Sardines and salmon! Plum-pudding! Currant, gooseberry, and raspberry jam! The gracious God be praised for ever!

Then 999 days after he left Zanzibar, Stanley reluctantly allowed himself to be carried into Boma in a hammock to a great welcome from the traders there. There were then some eighteen whites and some six factories, Portuguese, Dutch, French and English. One of the whites was John Scott, a St Helena half-caste slaver with a Spanish wife, who in this same year made himself infamous by chaining together forty troublesome slaves at his downriver factory, loading them into a boat and tipping them overboard at mid-channel. The corpses snagged on a sandbank and were discovered by the British Consul, Captain Hopkins, who was ascending the river on a tour of inspection; the fetters revealed the impress of their owner. But John Scott was well used to running into the bush to escape British men-of-war. In 1878, he touched up his reputation by helping the Baptist pioneers George Grenfell and Thomas Comber upriver to Musuko, and so across country to San Salvador where they carved their names beside Grandy's in the grey bark of a noble baobab.

Stanley does not describe the old slave-market, now partly built over by the Hôtel de Boma, but he does tell us that whites' residences lined the river-front, some with gardens of fruit-trees, vegetables and vines, and that the factories, built with wooden boards and corrugated zinc roofs, had compounds in which cotton, glass-ware, ironmongery, crockery, gin, rum, guns and gunpowder were bartered for palm-oil, ground-nuts and ivory. Today, just beyond the imposing façade of AMIZA (Agence Maritime Internationale du Zaïre) disused rails run off the Avenue du Zaïre, the old Quai du Commerce, into the PLZ factory (Lever Brothers) where blackened tanks and rusted pipework writhe within the compound's walls. Confined between this and the port's medical centre is the great tree known as Stanley's Baobab. Preserved as a symbol of authenticity it would be no surprise, for Bastian tells us that the kings of Boma conducted palavers in the shade of an ancient tree which acquired sanctity thereby. But it survives as monument to the great white pioneer. Am I obliged to approach reverently from Avenue Mobutu up the narrow entry that leads to a white wall painted with the legend "*Ici campait HM Stanley avec sa troupe du 8–7–1877 au 11–7–1877*" and overhung by the massive splayed limbs of the baobab? It is as if HM stands for "His Majesty". Here, regal Stanley arrives a day earlier than he did. The serpentine roots that welcomed him now run between table-legs in a café cramped between walls painted with Boma scenes, whose melancholy proprietress might have brightened serving him a beer.

The tree's pachydermatous hide is thickly engraved with century-old graffiti. BURT may be the remains of Burton's 1863 signature. GRANDY is faint beside the date 1874. How did the Boma chiefs read the white man's runes? They objected zealously when branches that threatened a factory roof were lopped off; a battle was narrowly avoided. Here is PANDORA, an English cutter deployed against Solongo pirates who had seized a Dutch long-boat laden with gunpowder; the punitive expedition burnt their village, sunk dug-outs and fired their maize crop in December 1868. Later reprisals were carried out by Commodore HEWET, with the steamer FOAM, gun-boats H.M.S. ARI (el) and MERLIN, the corvette H.M.S. ACTIVE and others. One carving is elegant indeed: TAMEGA 77, the name of the Portuguese gunship that took Stanley from Kabinda to Luanda in the year of the inscription. Ten years on, J. ANDRIES wrote his name in the grey bark; he was one of five mechanics engaged to bring the steamer *Roi des Belges* out from Antwerp, to unload its components at Boma and transport them overland to Kinshasa, where a slip was built for the boat's launch into the Pool in July 1888. Thus, on Stanley's baobab, Andries added a footnote to our story, for the *Roi des Belges* was the "two-penny-halfpenny river steamboat with a penny whistle attached" in which Conrad ascended to Stanley Falls, the "tin-pot steamer" which took Marlow into the heart of darkness.

Citoyen Lomboto showed us Stanley's initials in the tree's hide. Hard by PLZ's wall was a low doorway into the bole; I stooped and entered. It was dark at first, spacious and dry. Light pierced high skylights, where boughs had been lopped from the trunk, and slowly revealed the swirling texture of wooden walls, and the natural arch that buttressed the interior of the living monument. Some twelve feet up was a rudimentary framework of sticks which Citoyen Lomboto explained was Stanley's bed, while his troup slept on the ground. I didn't ask how many of the 115 found shelter here, nor mention that the initials H. M. S. stand for Her Majesty's Ship. Not for Henry Morton Stanley, the name the explorer took from his American benefactor to replace that of his father, John Rowlands, in which his mother Elizabeth Parry registered his illegitimate birth at Denbigh, North Wales. At the end of his 999-day trek he neither carved his initials nor slept in the Baobab of Kings, or Pioneers' Tree. He stayed comfortably, for once, in the two-storeyed residence on piles belonging to the factory of Hatton & Cookson. He enjoyed two nights there and three little banquets when "I do believe everybody toasted me, for which I felt very much obliged".

Roger Casement's uncle, the Protestant Edward Bannister, was the West African agent for Hatton & Cookson and knew Boma well. Casement's imagination was tempted by his uncle's tales; he dressed up in make-believe African costumes to entertain his cousins, followed this man of action and father-figure to Boma and, later, into the consular service at Loanda. But throughout his apparently rootless career, the mother who had him and his brothers secretly baptized into the Catholic faith in 1868, his Liverpool aunt-mother Grace Bannister, and Mother Ireland herself exercised their spell. Religious, political and sexual ambivalence was at his core. He was a physical adventurer, loyal Unionist, charming snob, friend of the African and South American oppressed; he was the author of poetry, of the Congo Report and the Black Diaries; he was a British diplomat, Sir Roger Casement, Commander of the Order of St Michael and St George; an Irish Nationalist who tried to enlist German help during the First World War and who, after converting to Rome, was executed for treason at Pentonville in 1916.

He first arrived at his uncle's Boma base in 1883, and passed through the seat of government many times in the course of his work for Stanley's volunteers, the Sanford Expedition, the Free State and the British Consular Service, but he left no account of the place and only fragmentary glimpses of his African experiences in private letters, official correspondence and, latterly, diaries; though the diary for 1903 had its first twenty-two pages ripped out to furnish evidence of a lively homosexual appetite. It is hard to find Roger Casement in Boma. Rather too optimistically, we return to the Hôtel de Ville to ask after him. A second, more bureaucratic official embarrasses us by throwing a Zaïrian woman out of his office in order to give us audience. He spends an inordinate amount of time copying every last detail from our passports, and then responds to our queries as if to inexplicable riddles whose penetration requires much ponderous weighing and measuring of tomes; he is thin in his *abacost*, the "authentic" Zaïrian short-sleeved suit worn with no tie; he is fine-featured and blank; to him, further explanation is an insupportable interruption; supplementary questions are burdens too heavy to be borne; he leaves us alone for a long while in his quest for knowledge, returns dutifully, politely, pompously, with nothing; then, after our escape, summons us back off the street for a tantalizing fragment of intelligence. The British First Secretary in Kinshasa had told us that Casement's car is preserved here. This man says go to the ELBEMA factory. We will, we will. Many thanks. I don't think he had a car.

I sit with a citoyen on his verandah half-way up Avenue du 24 Novembre, the date Mobutu became President in 1965. It used to be Avenue du 1 Juillet, the day the Free State was declared in 1885. The roof is supported by alarmingly eaten-through wooden posts set into concrete pillars. The verandah steps give on to an ex-colonial vista, quite unlike the Cité: an estate of similar houses running downhill to the river, a view of the Coca-Cola factory and of Mont du Saint-Esprit on which the first Catholic mission was founded. Uphill, behind us, the Belgians built smart two-storeyed houses and laid a road of nutshells on the Kinlele Plateau of the Boma chiefs, though, in the 1920s, Douglas Fraser wrote that Boma's "wharf, public buildings and bungalows speak of a lack of perspective and paint". We drink beer and I talk of Casement while eleven children scuttle like inquisitive ghosts in the dilapidated darkness at our backs.

By 1900, Casement had persuaded the Foreign Office to allow him to relinquish responsibility for Portuguese West Africa and establish his consulate in Congo. It was planned for Kinchasa, to be near the

French Congo, but eventually built in Boma. He had two audiences with Leopold II in Brussels in October 1900, but was not deceived. In the spring, he toured Stanley Pool and concluded that the State "has become by a stroke of the pen the sole property of the governing body of that State; or, it should be said, in truth, the private property of one individual, the King of the Belgians". From Boma he wrote that the governor should be subject to a European government, "not the unquestioned rule of an autocrat whose chief preoccupation is that autocracy should be profitable". In August he confided to his cousin, Gertrude Bannister: "I shall be awfully glad to get away from the Congo — it is a Horrid Hole."

My beer is finished and the children are summoned on to the verandah to have their photograph taken. I wish I could snap Casement's consulate like this, but in 1902 the authorities were still frustrating his efforts to secure a site. He was living most uncomfortably in a two-roomed hut with his bulldog John, tending his fever, and putting off a tour into the interior until building work was begun. He travelled to Ireland and England instead. Before embarking for the return passage at Liverpool, he went to the Bannisters', and the Sailors' Home which provoked a typical entry: "H. Abrahams from Demerara, 'Arthur' 11/6 . . . Medium — but mu ami monene, monene, beh! beh!" The voyage reads like a recital of well-known ports of call, old acquaintances and partners. At Las Palmas he picks up his dog John and more lovers despite feeling very seedy with "near dysentery . . . lots of blood passing". On the *Anversville* he's still "bleeding badly aft", but sleeps and reads and recovers until just off Banana: "X X X 'Accra' enormous in. Beautiful morning. Congo water . . . Monrovian [details inked out] Down & oh! oh! quick — about 18."

Back in Boma in May 1903, he treats John for his canine ailments with castor oil and quinine enemas. He finds the Vice Governor-General, Fuchs, "*very* amiable — too much so" and looks over the site for his consulate. Grass is cleared from the plot and the masons he has engaged begin work on the building. Not that he will ever inhabit it. His momentous journey into the interior, a time-bomb under the Free State, is still to come, and soon afterwards, his farewell to Africa.

A beautiful, poorly dressed woman approached the verandah, cooing. The red plastic crate on her head contained tarry lumps of dried elephant meat and fresh silver-pink *monganza* fish. We left the citoyen and his family bargaining, and followed up our slender lead. We couldn't find Casement's Consulate because he never really had

one, but we might find his car. Sandy streets led to ELBEMA, a great
tank like a gasholder and sheds where palm-nuts from the Mayombe
region are transformed into oil and oil-cake. A manager there sent us
out of town, along a track by the river past three laid-up vessels and
the rusty prow of a sunken steamer. We were told, and didn't argue,
that it was the first ship to come to Zaïre. Two boys at a stall begged us
for *argent*; on the way back they asked for *mbongo*: money in any
language. A third carried two bloody-headed monkeys, tails tied
round their necks for handles.

It was a hot walk. Men sweated, digging a trench by the track. The
grass and manioc gardens of the bank gave way to trees and a riverside café. A plump citoyenne, swathed in fiery cloths and adorned
with gold jewellery, pounded chillies and tomatoes in a wooden
mortar. We drank beer and Fanta, and met the President of the
Fishermen of Boma, his shimmering catch and a man making nets. A
pontoon, with wrought-iron railings and lamp-stands, had been a
floating dance-floor, but foundered in shallow water. Across this
wreck we looked at the island, now Angolan, where plumes of smoke
rose from flat land and a hill climbed high above mighty trees, a
summit from which soldiers kept watch on Zaïre. A patrol boat,
watching them, leant at the current and made upriver for Matadi, guns
bristling. Dug-outs tethered beside the dance-floor were transports
for black-market trading of Zaïrian beer for meat killed by Angolan
troops.

Behind gates and walls topped with iron railings the ELBEMA
director's house stands upon white fluted pillars in a garden dissected
by concrete paths high above the café and the river. We climb stairs to
the verandah where pigeons perch in a cage, puffed up with silence.
The house lacks paint but is cool and well furnished with green plush
and polished wood. The servant and the director's wife are not
surprised that white folk want to see the British Consul's car. "Mr
Fisher lived here; people come from Kinshasa to look. Yes, do take
photographs." At ground level, between Greek pillars, two roofless
and rusted cars with sweeping running-boards stand on wood-blocks
and deformed tyres. One bonnet is missing and neither have maker's
marks to help me. Avis, Bentley, Riley, Lanchester? I know that
neither of them was minted until long after 1903. I photograph them
anyway. It was news to me that Casement had a car. It still is.

As we walk the long road back to town for the fourth time, I think it
would be good to have wheels. The only Boma taxi we took ripped us
off. The Zaïrian with us shouted "*Voleur!*" at the receding cloud of red

dust and unconvincingly threatened to report the driver. I imagine myself a 'Twenties Consul being chauffeur-driven along the port in one of those cars, brand-new. At the Mabuilu hotel, alongside gourmandising black businessmen, we console ourselves with *capitaine* fish in an excellent spicy sauce, with rice and *saka-saka*, manioc leaves cooked in palm-oil, followed by a fruit salad of banana, pineapple and paw-paw. Outside the window, wren-like birds flit fitfully between shrubs, heavy black insects infest a flowering tree with their buzzing, red sunbirds shimmer, a shapely baobab puts out fresh leaves, and long curved beaks sip, sip at nectar between the bases of scarlet hibiscus petals.

Under tall grey cranes, gargantuan trunks from the Mayombe forest lie in heaps on the barren wharf, on long lorries and on timber boats riding the river. In the old and dusty *Bibliothèque* nearby, pulped and printed European wood is stacked horizontally on shelves. The books are covered in brown paper, hand-written titles fading on the spines. A young official enthuses about reclassifying this cache of displaced culture and opening it to the public. Nobody will tell us why it is so hard to find contemporary Zaïrian books anywhere. I lay my hand on André Gide's *Voyage au Congo* of 1927, dedicated *à la mémoire de Joseph Conrad* with, on the first page, the voices of administrators and merchants, who accompanied Gide on his voyage out, asking:

> — What are you going to look for down there?
> — I'm waiting to get there to find out.
> I threw myself into this journey like Curtius into the gulf. It already seems to me that it wasn't exactly that I wanted to do it . . . as that it imposed itself on me by a sort of ineluctable fate — like all the important events of my life. . . . I was not yet twenty when I promised myself to do it; that was thirty-six years ago.

I know the feeling. Conrad knew the feeling. Conrad found out things in the Congo which he did not want to know. Marlow says, "It had ceased to be a blank space of delightful mystery — a white patch for a boy to dream gloriously over. It had become a place of darkness." From Boma's wharf Marlow took his passage upriver to the Company Station on a small sea-going steamer captained by a Swede. Conrad left Boma in June 1890, almost certainly on Axel Tjulin's boat. Scandinavians figured largely in the traffic on the lower river, and Harry Edmund Martinson's *On the Congo* conveys the feeling of the passage:

Our ship, the Sea Smithy, swerved out of the tradewinds
and began to creep up the Congo River.
Vines trailed along the deck like ropes.
We met the famous iron barges of the Congo,
whose hot steeldecks swarmed with negroes from the tributaries.

They put their hands to their mouths
and shouted, "Go to hell" in a Bantu language.
We slid marvelling and depressed through the tunnels of vegetation
and cook in his galley thought:
"now I am peeling potatoes in the middle of the Congo". . . .

Boma wears its history very lightly. It plays anachronistic tricks. It is a
living thing, spreading over hills and plateaux. White men have left
their marks in its hide, ambiguous myths carved around a door into
the aromatic, welcoming, sheltering, horrifying dark. They replaced
blankness on the map with a Dark Continent; a sin of the imagination
that is unforgivable and understandable. They came to cure sick
hearts, and found the heart of darkness. In an age of optimistic rational
imperialism, they held up this barely mapped territory as a mirror to
the dark side of their souls. Some, like Dan Crawford, went deep and
luminously thought black. Upriver, we shall meet Africa more fully,
and Conrad and Casement whose shadows I have poised on Congo's
brink: Boma, chief Mboma a Ndongo's place, slaver's port, seat of
government, miserable wharf.

And I must meet myself. In the office next door to the *Bibliothèque* I
found a fine and grotesque image of blackened wood, not shorn, like
so many museum-pieces, of its parcels of fetish matter. Packages of
nail-parings, hair and grave-soil, and bundles of leaves and roots,
festooned it. The officials allowed me to take it out into the sun. Was it
my presumption, or the *nkisi*'s power made them so nervous, so
visibly disturbed? They wouldn't say what agitated them. My lens
looked coldly at the chiefly hat, the boss eyes, squat nose, open mouth
with jutting lower teeth, upraised arm with aggressive spear-blade,
and at the navel, where an embedded mirror hid magical materials
within. Look at my core, it said, Look, look. What do you see?

At the port's west end was a yellow-washed railway station with
white balconies and powder-blue arches. In the open space before it,
stalls of fruit glowed under jacaranda and flamboyant trees, bright
setting for a stern pyramid commemorating seventy years,
1886–1956, of temporal power, the feared Force Publique, on the site
of the first garrison. We walked Avenue Lumumba's uncertain
pavements past engineering shops and garages, past banana stalls,

men at sewing-machines, a cobbler at his last, past bars and dim *quincailleries*, exotically basic general stores and sparsely-stocked electrical shops. Across the bridge, near the palm-nut cutter's monument, an oompah-band struck up for a trade-fair well lubricated by beer. The grandee who was to open it failed to appear. Loudspeakers broadcasting Kinshasa music usurped the band, darkness fell and coloured lights went up. We had enough appetite and language for it, but lacked the energy to join in. We understood the "air of weary bewilderment" Conrad described on the faces of white officials. Throngs gyrated from stand to stand until the power failed. There was darkness and silence. Up the hill, we greeted the watchmen below our window. They squatted, chatting beside a roaring wood-fire, the scent of coffee filling the night. Next morning early, there was not a charred stick or a smear of ash on the concrete path where they had sat. It was a new day, and we clambered up into a timber lorry which would take us to the forest and Matadi.

IV

CITY OF ROCKS

The only *raison d'être* for this town is its position at the end of the navigable section of the river and at the head of the railway line. Built in haste amid the rocks, in conditions as unhygienic as possible, it leaves the most detestable impression with all French people who are obliged to stay there, in spite of the civility of the officials of the Belgian railway.

A. CHEVALIER *L'Afrique Centrale Française*

> what's it worth to you your
> glances your laughter your unfinished sobs
> oh you who carry death like an ornament
> and to which conqueror will you offer your neck at last
> for the *coup de grâce*
>
> Your feet without toes
> leave grains of blood on the sand
> and the horizon always before you
> recedes
> Where are the gods towards whom you march
> KISHWE MAYA *L'Errant*

Sweating diesel, the green lorry rode the tarmac out past the air-strip and the Coca-Cola factory, through the Cité and its swarming market, towards the mountains. Here was Makakala's statue of a woman, a baby bound to her breast and a towering load of wood in a basket on her back, leading a child by the hand. Here, a stone ancestor-figure squatted like a slim Buddha. And here, a boy leant as far as he dared into the road, to offer a long fat rat swinging by its tail. Substantial huts and houses were set within ordered parcels of swept earth hedged with shrubs. Small hills swelled up in series, upholstered with moorish vegetation, cleft by streams. In more wooded country, we passed Makakala's sculptures in the flesh — women with children and ponderous baskets of wood, palm-nut cutters with *coup-coups*, calabashes and liana hoops — and hunters with locally made guns. Palm and banana groves became lusher. An antelope dangled from a branch, stacks of charcoal stood by the road and a tree's boughs were hung with golden baskets. Houses were of yellow and orange fired brick, though, as trees became taller and thicker, and the earth redder, more and more were built of lapped planks. At a rare roundabout in the high sprawling town of Kinzao-Vuete, we turned off the tarmac and bucked across tall-grass heathland before plunging into denser forest. Our driver's few words of French and our few words of Kikongo reduced conversation to the vivid communion of gestures and exclamations.

In any case, he laboured, wrestling the lorry round steep bends and over the rock-shelves and sand-beds of the plunging, climbing road. We drove between the pillars of an apparently impenetrable treescape, a mine of mahogany and balsa lined with tower-like trunks or slender boles laced with lianas and finned with buttresses. Then it was as if the landscape gasped, let its breath go, and us with it as we saw air fall away to invisible valleys, presenting vista after shifting vista of tree-tops, a pelt on the unfolding flanks of hills, with barer heights beyond and, beyond those, mountains hazy and prodigious. Then, as unpredictably, this dream of distance evaporated and we bored down straighter tracks, deeper into arboreal claustrophobia. How far had we come? How long would it take? How many kilometres to go? To these old European questions our driver answered, every few kilometres, "Not far now".

Once, the road widened, a grass-split dual-carriageway through a village with a core of concrete buildings, like a left-over frontier town. Mostly, clearings contained villages of wood — huts, palisades, granaries, manioc-racks, latrines, fences — or cemeteries of cement. There had been graveyards with spiky crosses by the main road, but the further we went into the forest the more flamboyant the tombs became. They were fantasy houses, temples or shrines painted red, yellow, white and blue, set upon stepped plinths, sheltered by stylish roofs topped with stars or crosses; they had pillars, pediments inscribed with a name and date of death, and balconies inhabited by pairs of figures, male and female, dressed in European-style jackets, ties, skirts and blouses, with hands at their sides or clasped upon their heads. Single nurtured plants grew in front of some houses on otherwise bare earth. Sometimes the boneyards were ruinous, with fallen pillars and toppled effigies, like the miniaturized relics of a great civilization, though most of them were bright and neat. Like sideshows at a fair, these model villages for the dead faced the road, with the forest's thick darkness at their back.

"Not far now," and suddenly we swung off the track through the gate in a timber-yard's palisade. Here the plunder of the forest was ordered, graded and stacked. A team of chanting men with stout poles levered a massive trunk away from its fellows, inch by inch towards the saw-shed. Finished planks and squared timbers were built into walls. Off-cuts kept for firewood made a flush mosaic of ochres. Within the shed a noisy, naked band-saw ripped planks off a great trunk. Breathing a heady cocktail of exhaust, hot sap and sweat, we watched the endless blade unveil each fresh instalment of the grain; watched each plank laid, on spacers, above the last; a tree rebuilt with an airily elliptical cross-section. A white man appeared; his transatlantic *"Bonjour"* made us relapse into English; Bill was a Canadian missionary who had come down from Matadi, with his young son and a local pastor, to buy timber. What they wanted wasn't available here, and he was keen to return to Matadi before the President arrived in town. His air-conditioned Landcruiser looked luxurious and we gladly accepted a lift. The five of us took off on deeply-rutted side-roads through small villages carved out of the forest, to a second timber mill where another ritual of men and song and long levers was in progress around a felled, shorn giant.

The pastor pumped us for information about scholarships to England. Bill found the wood they wanted and, following the advice of hunters on the road, we made a rendezvous with the green lorry. The pastor left us to guide it to the yard, and we careered back to Kinzao-Vuete and the main road. Bill stopped at a village of woodworkers to bargain for a carved *pirogue*-chair. He didn't stop on a long straight through the next village when we struck a dog that walked into our path; it skidded heavily after us with its legs in the air. "Good thing it wasn't a goat," said Bill. "Goats cost. Dogs don't." People hugged the roadside, sheep and goats scattered, and chickens fled dangerously across our path as we rushed towards Matadi. Bill spoke of blood-money, of *ndoki* and of missionaries who had recently suffered mysterious deaths. How, at their graveside, anguished folk among the mourners confessed to poisoning them.

The landscape became barer and more roseate. Hills netted with pink paths grew up rumpled and rocky. Our road ran in a cleft, and the road to Tshimpi airport climbed above us. We came upon soldiers in brand-new uniforms, parties of people carrying paper flags, police posted at intervals along the highway, and bands with motley collections of brass instruments, including that of the Kimbanguist church on a blue lorry. The view opened up, the river way below like a great lake curving grandly away in a haze between steep hills towards the Cauldron of Hell. Upriver, beside the falls that stopped Diogo Cão, mountains grew out of the water. Opposite us, Matadi clambered up from its port and railway terminal to the Belvedere and the monument to the builders of the railroad. Tuckey sailed below us in 1816. Stanley took in this view, before Matadi was born, and saw a vision of his station Vivi, the first capital of the Free State, founded this side of the river above the Lufu tributary in 1879:

> As the eye swept rapidly over the view of massive and glorious sweeps of land and numberless detached hills, with the winding Congo a thousand feet beneath us, the cool breeze fanning our perspiring faces hot from the ascent, we felt ourselves repaid in some degree for the toil of coming. . . . I already viewed the completed station, the broad, well-travelled turnpike road, the marching columns of tradespeople, the stream of traffic, and the incessant moving to and fro of multitudes. . . .

The task — "to temper this obstinacy . . . to quicken that cold lifelessness; to reduce that grim defiance to perfect submission" — was undertaken: negotiations with chiefs, construction of houses, cultivation of gardens, and the pulverization of rocks for road-beds that earned Stanley the old prophetic name of *Bula Matari*, Breaker of Rocks. It was a long, triumphant, tragic tale. When he returned from the interior in 1884, Stanley sat across the river, spy-glass in hand to view his foundation,

> and I confess with regret that I cease from the survey, wishing earnestly that I could sponge out the history of this unhappy place from my tablet of memories. . . . I can only grieve that my memory is haunted by so many shadows of puerile manhood, and of figures of youth without substance.

Improvement there was not, only decay. He resolved to remove Vivi bodily to the larger Chinsala plateau, in readiness for the stern, temperate, ruling hand of General Gordon. Gordon was diverted to

Khartoum and death within the year. Sir Francis de Winton came instead, and by the time Stanley left for Europe, five houses had been built, a banana plantation had been set out, and old and new Vivi were linked by a bridge and a railway, a foretaste of Matadi's future. For it was Matadi, across the river, that thrived.

Had we come here many months earlier, we should have had to take a current-driven crossing in the ferry, but today, flanked by troops and brass bands and flag-waving crowds, we pass on to the new road-and-rail suspension bridge, thirteen thousand tons of steel thrown across the Zaïre and, today, decked with palm fronds. We queue above the water, behind trucks carrying troupes of *animateurs* and *animatrices* in costumes of red, yellow and green, and groaning wagons full of people in their brightest clothes: Coca-Cola and Michael Jackson T-shirts, cloths printed with Mobutu's portrait and the emblems of *Paix*, *Travail* and *Justice*. We grind uphill into Matadi through crowded expectant streets. Bill drops us at the guest-house founded by the Swedish Mission. They'd had a radio message from Boma that we were coming, but we hadn't had the reply that they were full.

The place is packed with Zaïrians, some Americans and Swiss. The hotels in town, if we could afford them, are full because of the President's epiphany. Bill has driven straight on to change and get into his place in the reception line. We're tired; Noëlle is desperate; for comfort, I irresponsibly assure her that something will turn up, but I'm sickened by the very thought of searching for a bed in a city where you need to know how to conjugate the verbs *monter*, *descendre*, *transpirer*. Eva Karlsson brightens a little and offers us "the cave" beneath the guest-house; it's hot and dirty, she says, but there are beds. It looks all right to us: two beds in a cellar, a cellar with a view because the land drops so steeply. We dump our rucksacks, look wistfully at the defunct air-conditioning, and walk down to a terrace set high above the road with a prospect of the parade-ground where Mobutu will appear. We watch the crowds assembling, the military band marching, the choreographed *animation*, while devouring coffee and cinnamon buns. We are faint with hunger and will have to eat in town as, in any case, the kitchen is being rebuilt. Nothing happens. The Guide of the Zaïrian Revolution is three hours behind schedule. The parade lays down its arms, the band its instruments.

At the sound of sirens, everyone reassembles smartly and crowds erupt with patriotic slogans and cries of "*Papa*" as the President's motorcade approaches. The Big Man himself, Mobutu Sese Seko

Kuku Ngbendu Wa Za Banga, *Maréchal de Corps de l'Armée*, stands in a Land Rover, leopard skin hat on his head and chiefly staff in one of his upraised hands. The band brays a Euro-African welcome; the troops parade, present arms, salute; the President of the Republic, and his lady in a white dress, greet a long line of dignitaries and guests; brief speeches are followed by consciousness-raising animation, tribal dancing out of Busby Berkeley; the crowd surges into the arena, to be briskly reproved with batons; the President's party takes to the motorcade once more and surges off downtown, sirens screaming.

Beneath us, roadside stalls resume business, selling Okapi and Ambassade cigarettes, sweets, bananas, bread and little doughnuts called *minketi*. The blocked traffic snakes up the hill once more, the Mercedes of the Bwanas — rich Zaïrians, a few battered taxis and endless overloaded trucks bursting with freight, people and goats, and at last, laden with timber, the green lorry we left in the forest. We wave madly, then retreat to the cave. We climb around the house to fetch water; short work with a screwdriver gets the air-conditioning going, and we are in unaccustomed luxury. Eva and Lennart call to ask us to eat with them and their colleague Bumba-Meli Edo, if we would like. Suddenly, Matadi is a fine place.

It is a city of more than 150,000 people whose port is Zaïre's main gateway to the world. At its core is a decayed European infrastructure, now lacking the sophistication of Kinshasa or Lubumbashi, with multiple townships sprawling uphill over barren slopes or perched upon successive rock ledges. For several days, as black Bwanas and a few whites swept past us in their vehicles, we walked its stony roadsides, skipping uncovered drains, and began to feel a sweaty intimacy with some of its crevices. Perhaps because we weren't richly dressed or jumping in and out of limousines, we weren't hustled and saw none of the aggression of which we'd been warned. Flags were strung across the main streets, the barracks' gate-pillars were draped in green, with a banner stretched between them: *Mobutu Lelo, Mobutu Lobi, Mobutu Libela* — Mobutu today, tomorrow and forever. The soldiers' brand-new uniforms contrasted oddly with the decrepit blackened field-guns at their gates. Everything else was brown and grey; paint peeled off villas; trees were dusty, though in the rainy season they blaze scarlet and yellow between the buildings, and small patches of cultivation green up.

Bata Shoes and Marques et Cie's mixture of groceries and hardware are the nearest Matadi gets to European shops, apart from numerous pharmacies, smart or dingy, offering Valium, 20 pills for 16 zaïres (22 pence or 32 cents), Bactrim, 20 pills for 36 zaïres, Ampicilline, Tetracycline, and the purple-and-yellow Vitamin B complex capsules sold as a cure-all everywhere. The Regional Governor's Bureau was imposing and immaculate but, below it, the cathedral was a sombre mausoleum of greige concrete with a louvred, rotunda-topped tower; weeds sprouted from walls, blank like a prison on one side, and balconied like a decaying palace on the other. Noëlle was almost flattened by a lorry as we crossed Place des Trois Z to the Moorish-style Hôtel Métropole. Within its black-and-white tiled inner court, walled by five stone storeys of pillared galleries, we relaxed beneath well-watered palms in the cool air that irrigated its arches and drank to celebrate the preservation of life.

Music, and not gospel music, belted from the Cabaret de la Mission. The Gondola Club and restaurant, alive and alight late into the night, was silent. Beside it, the steps were busy with souvenir salesmen at stalls full of ebony, ivory, wooden masks, and attenuated African nudes designed for white drawing-rooms. Everything was at a *bon prix*, a joke older than the "authentic" antiques. On the lower steps some roughly chiselled masks of raw white wood were waiting to be finished, stained and polished; even the stallholder admitted that his *mintadi* of carved soapstone were *nouveaux vieux*.

The railway station's great hall was cool and empty, with a first-floor gallery and one position open where we learnt that trains leave for Kinshasa on Tuesdays, Thursdays and Saturdays at 6.30 am, arriving in theory at 1.30 pm. Conrad and Casement saw the start of the railway-building, and Casement travelled on it when the journey took two days. Outside, we leant on railings and looked across the tracks, engine-sheds and warehouses where copper, diamonds, gold, tin, coffee, ivory, rubber, palm-oil and timber are marshalled. On the river the *SS Kananga* was leaving port in a speedy arc to take the President downriver. Two Swiss at the guest-house, who sailed on it from Antwerp, were having a wearing time getting vehicles and other cargo through customs. Papers must be obtained from, then stamped in, numerous offices, a maze designed after the Belgian manner, inhabited by officials hungry for money. When I went down into the landscape of rails, containers, cranes, ships and offices with Kjell, a Swede just back from Pointe-Noire, we queued in a crush of people at the port barrier; we'd been assured, by a bland bureaucrat in a bleak office, that as we had the correct papers, licences for newly-imported vehicles could be quickly arranged at another office within the port.

The Onatra policeman on the barrier demanded a new kind of *laissez-passer*, not required two days before and only obtainable in two days' time. So it goes. And when you get your vehicles out, they may be dented, as we saw, windows may be smashed, and everything unscrewable — mirrors, windscreen wipers and so on — will surely be missing. Patience is a necessity, and is heavily taxed. "Delay here means nothing," wrote Douglas Fraser, "for is not Africa herself a delay?"

In late March 1887, Stanley's party for his third assault on the Congo, the Emin Pasha Relief Expedition, disembarked here. Among its members was Lieutenant W. G. Stairs, one of the advance guard who met Emin Pasha a year later, only to find that he did not want to be relieved. Later still, Stairs was to meet Dan Crawford in the most dramatic circumstances. But here, in Matadi at the outset of the unlucky relief expedition, Stairs aroused the covetous delight of Tippu-Tib, Stanley's imperious Arab slaver, by firing, at the rate of 330 shots a minute, a brand-new Maxim automatic gun. Stanley had attended Hiram Maxim's demonstration in Dulwich and had ordered one at once, specially equipped with a tempered shield to ward off arrows.

Conrad had been in Marseilles when Stanley arrived there to great acclaim after his pioneering voyage down the Congo. On the eve of his own Congo journey, Conrad almost coincided with Stanley in Brussels. In the spring of 1890, on a visit to his homeland in the present Soviet Ukraine, he learnt that a letter for him from the Société Anonyme Belge pour le Commerce du Haut Congo had got lost in Russia. He hurried back to Brussels to find out what it contained; it seems he reached the "sepulchral city" on 26th April, two days after Stanley had delivered his account of the Emin Pasha Relief Expedition at the Brussels Exchange, and eulogized King Leopold II:

> What does the greatness of a monarch consist in? If it is the extent of his territory, then the Emperor of Russia is the greatest of all. . . . But if royal greatness consists in the wisdom and goodness of a sovereign leading his people with the solicitude of a shepherd watching over his flock, then the greatest sovereign is your own.

Leopold led his African flock, by proxy, in a land eighty times the size of Belgium. We can see his minions through Marlow's sober eyes, but for Conrad, in April 1890, the childhood dream and the offer of a command on the Congo coincided.

A few days later, in London, Casement did not miss hearing Stanley, his old boss, lecturing in St James's Hall before Prince Edward and Princess Alexandra. In early May he left for Antwerp and the *SS Kinsembo*. The *Ville de Maceio* had already sailed from Antwerp on the 30 April, and Conrad boarded it at Bordeaux. How narrowly they missed sharing the passage to Congo. As it was, they met in Matadi on Friday 13th June.

Roger Casement knew Conrad's "Company Station" well. In 1886 he had a salary of £150 a year to sort out the Sanford Expedition's supply problems there. In 1886–7 he worked on the survey for the railway. By 1890, Matadi comprised the Société Anonyme Belge's station, four factories and the beginnings of the railway, with 170 resident whites. Joseph Conrad, or Captain Korzeniowski, came fresh to the raw, rocky scene; Marlow's account in *Heart of Darkness* was constructed for a grim dramatic purpose, but gives a real enough taste of it: "mounds of turned-up earth by the shore, houses on a hill, others with iron roofs, amongst a waste of excavation, or hanging to the declivity", the blasting of rock, files of men, some chained and carrying baskets full of earth on their heads, and the appalling encounter with "black shadows of disease and starvation, lying confusedly in the greenish gloom" of the grove of death.

"Feel considerably in doubt about the future," Conrad wrote in his diary. "Think just now that my life amongst the people (white) around here cannot be very comfortable." But this after the warmest comment he made about anyone in the Congo:

> Made the acquaintance of Mr Roger Casement, which I should consider as a great pleasure under any circumstances and now it becomes a positive piece of luck. Thinks, speaks well, most intelligent and very sympathetic.

Herbert Ward, the explorer, sculptor and writer who named his son Roger Casement Ward as a tribute to his friend, amplifies this impression:

> A tall, handsome man of fine bearing; thin, mere muscle and bone, a sun-tanned face, blue eyes and black curly hair. A pure Irishman he is, with a captivating voice and a singular charm of manner. A man of distinction and great refinement, high-minded and courteous, impulsive and poetical.

And another of Stanley's men, Fred Puleston, says the Congolese called Casement *Monafuma*, "son of a king", and *Swami*, "woman's God"; he stresses his gentle, emotional disposition, and tells how, when his fox terrier was savaged by a wild hog, "Casement was unable to control his feeling and wept like a girl."

What of Conrad the thirty-two-year-old with whom twenty-five year-old Casement shared his Matadi room? The nearest vivid descriptions we have were written after Conrad had superficially recovered from the trauma of his Congo travels. Edward Garnett wrote, "I have never seen before a man so masculinely keen yet so femininely sensitive." John Galsworthy remembered meeting him in 1893:

> Very dark he looked in the burning sunlight — tanned, with a peaked brown beard, almost black hair, and dark brown eyes, over which the lids were deeply folded. He was thin, not tall, his arms very long, his shoulder broad, his head set rather forward. He spoke to me with a strong foreign accent. . . . Fascination was Conrad's greatest characteristic — the fascination of vivid expressiveness and zest, of his deeply affectionate heart, and his far-ranging subtle mind. He was extraordinarily perceptive and receptive.

In 1916, Conrad recalled staying with Casement at Matadi for three weeks. It was less than that, for Conrad left for Kinshasa on 28th June, and on the 24th Casement had "gone with a large lot of ivory down to Boma", as Conrad noted in his diary. He had been "busy packing ivory in casks. Idiotic employment." But they made expeditions together to palaver with village chiefs and procure porters for caravans, and they must have got through three weeks' worth of private palaver in half that time.

Casement, the ambitious poet. Conrad, the embryo novelist with the opening of his first book in his baggage. Casement, orphaned at thirteen. Conrad, orphaned at eleven. Casement whose uncles, John Casement of the Elder Dempster line and Edward Bannister of Hatton & Cookson, had helped him on his way to Africa. Conrad whose uncle Tadeusz Bobrowski was his guardian, and whose cousin's widow, "aunt" Marguerite Poradowska, had used her connections in Brussels to get him his Congo contract. Two displaced creatures in the city of rocks. What Conrad then meant to Casement we don't know, but Casement's blithe adventurousness seems to have entered into Marlow's Harlequin, and his talk into Kurtz's mouth. In a letter of 1903, Conrad hints at the impact Casement, "a limpid personality", made on him:

> There is a touch of the conquistador in him too; for I have seen him start off into an unspeakable wilderness swinging a crookhandled stick for all

weapon, with two bull-dogs . . . at his heels and a Loanda boy carrying a
bundle for all company. A few months afterwards . . . I saw him come
out again, a little leaner, a little browner, with his stick, dogs, and Loanda
boy, and quietly serene as though he had been for a stroll in the park. . . . I
always thought some part of Las Casas' soul had found refuge in his
indomitable body. . . . He could tell you things! Things I have tried to
forget, things I never did know.

That two such men should meet in the white society of Matadi was
amazing. On the 24th Conrad noted: "Prominent characteristic of the
social life here; people speaking ill of each other." And on the 28th:
"Left Matadi with Mr Harou and a caravan of 31 men. Parted with
Casement in a very friendly manner." In imagination, I parted with
Casement and Conrad, left the docks, railway tracks and all the
architecture of colonialism and climbed up through the city on the
back roads of the present.

Houses on the rocky hillside to the right, a new one being built on a
massive boulder. A stream in a valley crossed by a bridge. Upstream a
vision of green — grasses, banana trees and palms — confined
between houses and shacks, children skipping on stepping stones.
Downstream more like a drain, rubbish strewn on the banks, acrid
fires burning. A wholesale Marques et Cie, and a makeshift market at
a wide junction. People rooting through heaps of second-hand
clothes. A woman with a stall of knick-knacks under a multi-coloured
sun umbrella in tatters, faded, spiky. The Mama Mobutu health centre
across a dusty space full of mamas and babies. Two manioc and maize
mills, people queuing with roots and grains, whitened men humping
sacks. *Dames couture*. Bars advertised with empty beer bottles ranged
on sills, or hung from tree-stumps. *Dali coiffure*. Spare parts, engine
blocks and suspension members displayed sparsely like sculptures.
Choc Electric. Rows of concrete houses with open drains between. A
Protestant bookshop on a corner and, still further up, seven tiers of the
Mama Mobutu market. Smart cars hooting to clear a passage.
Cataracts of cloth, cheap cottons and costly wax-prints in deep, dark
colours.

A woman with bank-notes tucked into her low-cut bodice stepped
before us, gyrated provocatively, stared crazily into our eyes, before
melting away into the market among sidelong smiles. At the bottom,
a profusion of baskets and basket-makers. Rows of roofed stalls facing
one another on each tier. Music blasting from a clothes shop, stacks of
plastic and enamel bowls, plastic ivory bracelets amongst jewellery.
Tomatoes, beans, rice, flours, fish of all sizes in silver heaps and

bloody joints, golden and black caterpillars, shrimps and tiny prawns. A man pushed past carrying a cow's bleeding head and feet. Frozen meat, chicken in plastic bags. Goats heads oozing, blackened dried fish. Beautiful carrots, onions, fat peppers, chillies and yellow-orange-brown palm-nuts. At the back, the yeasty bloom of all kinds of breads. Tier on tier of colour, smells. Cloud upon cloud of flies. A shifting sound-scape of song, banter and barter. We bought Fantas and a big golden and purple basket, and walked up the shack-lined street to the summit of this particular hill and a view of the corrugated, concrete Cité, flexing in the heat-haze, rising and falling away to the river.

We dropped down and climbed past the noise of hammering and planing from the Atelier de Menuiserie Pompe Funèbre, a cobbler's tapping at the roadside, and small concentrated sounds from a drunkenly-perched horology booth. Views grew broader. A church with a cross-topped rotunda of tall pillars seemed to erupt from the Cité and the monumental Kimbanguist temple squatted on the horizon. Opposite the mission, military maize and manioc were being watered, lorry-loads of troops with automatic weapons rolled into barracks, a woman climbed with a vast bowl on her head piled high with bread, and an antique truck, mottled yellow and orange, full of wood and plantains, crept up the hill, engine coughing, pushed by its passengers. In the compound high above the guest-house a red Volvo lorry was loaded with sticks of furniture and household effects, people and chickens; goats had escaped, chased by a dog; a singing, dancing, clapping crowd gave the departing family a per-cussive send-off.

We ate *mbeekwa*, a pinkish porridge or hummus, laboriously prepared from the kernels of pumpkin seeds. The house and the blushing mango trees were buzzed by swallows small and grey-brown, like shuttles swiftly weaving the dusk. Mosquitoes whined at the windows' mesh. Edo sang Kikongo songs to his guitar, and Noëlle taught him the reformed slave-trader John Newton's hymn, "Amazing Grace". A friend, strangely named Tippu-Tib after the Arab slaver, came to visit him and we heard an awful bed-time story: how he was picked up by soldiers outside Kinshasa and taken into the forest; threatened with knives, guns, bayonets, he was stripped of clothes, money and *carte d'identité*; they talked in code about his fate — "Shall we do twenty-four or forty-six?" — they dumped him, with ten zaïres, by the roadside. From a compound below the mission, staccato drumming throbbed half the night. Wind rose and leaves rattled loudly as they fell. Across the dark river a tide of fire swept up the hills.

On Sunday afternoon, we set out for Palabala with Lennart, Eva and Kjell. It was a road test for a new Landcruiser, liberated from the port, bruised but gleaming because I'd spent two hours washing it and giving myself a welcome shower at the same time. We drove uphill past the woman who had ceremoniously presented us with four extra fruit when we bought ten zaïres' worth of bananas at her stall, past the Appeal Court with its long-unfinished second storey, past a very Mediterranean view of hills and river across a graveyard, and out round the raw edges of Matadi, into what Chevalier called "a veritable African Switzerland". Conrad had followed the route Colonel Thys's railway would take, along the Congo's bank to the mouth of the Mpozo River. The line runs up the Mpozo before crossing it and diving under the Kinshasa road. In the shadow of the blunt cone of a mountain growing above its fellows, we dropped to the railway and swept up past a plaque commemorating its builders. They were three months into blasting and excavation when Conrad was horrified by it all. The first rails and sleepers had accompanied him out from Antwerp on board the *Ville de Maceio*.

It is a cliché that, over 250 miles, one black worker died for every sleeper. The worst losses were here where rock trenches, bridges, retaining masses and aqueducts succeed one another. Of 2,000 blacks employed during 1892, three succumbed each day on average, mostly in the Mpozo valley; whites died too, and thirteen per cent of them were repatriated on a single ship. It was forced labour. Local workers fled into the bush; recruiting on the West Coast became difficult because of the reports that survivors took back; malaria, blackwater fever, dysentery, smallpox, beri-beri and sunstroke, demoralization, disaffection and revolt dogged the grand opening of the Congo basin to civilization and exploitation. Labour imported from Zanzibar, the West Indies and Macao was even less suited to the conditions. Marlow's grove of death was real enough. The first locomotive reached Stanley Pool in March 1898, and the line was declared open on 4th July.

We turned left off the tarmac, where boys were selling tomatoes, grapefruit and lemons. We took pity on them — one said, "I haven't sold anything all day, I am very tired" — then roared up a rough track over two bridges at steep angles. We picked up three boys with a load of palm-nuts and took them to the top. The hill tossed us about. The prospect was of more great hills, pebble-dashed with boulders and riven by streambeds, dry but green, lined with palms. I understood Conrad's laconic entry for Sunday 29th June: "Ascent of Pataballa [sic] sufficiently fatiguing." The plateau was topped with rich red loam which nurtured tall grass, gardens and groves of slender trees.

Children ran, shouting "*Mindele, mindele!*" as we entered the first village. Its substantial houses had moulded arches and pillars, painted faces with holes beneath the chins, angular figures with applied breasts. There was an open-roofed grass church and an old Catholic mission. The plateau boasted graveyards in several styles: in one, cross-topped "cupboards" like reliquaries; another full of simple heaps of earth covered with holed enamel bowls and bottles, and the occasional umbrella frame, objects which last touched the deceased's lips and hands, focusing his effluvia, *kanga mfunya*, capable of transmitting his judgements, *mambu*, to the living. A third was grandiose, with big ornamental tombs, some enclosed in buildings, grills and railings. A fourth held slabs and table-tombs, and one green concrete aeroplane complete with wheels, fins and wings.

We were stopped by women offering black pottery and baskets, and playfully ambushed by children trying to sell *coeurs de boeuf*, or lorries and helicopters with moving parts, beautifully and intricately made of wire. One held out a yellow and black pulsing bird by its spread wings. On the south edge of the plateau stood shells of two mission houses, one with an arch like the entrance to a coaching-inn, both with interior decoration of graffiti and windows affording vertiginous views of a sea of mountains, far-reaching swell obliterated distantly by heat-haze — like Adam's vision, from the highest hill in Milton's Paradise, "to the realm/of Congo, and Angola farthest south. . . ." Here, facing a challenging vista, the Livingstone Inland Mission set up their first station in 1878. When Stanley stepped on to "this fortress-like plateau" in 1884, he described how "the mission has its pupils; and the old chief Nozo has erected a lodging-house for strangers, a miniature caravanserai, the walls of which he has garnished with ancient chromographs for the amusement of his guests". Stanley's relief expedition camped at the mission in 1887, and seventeen sick Soudanese and Somalis were left behind to recuperate. From an abandoned arena of memories, a panorama of hopes, we drove across the plateau.

High grasses invaded the vehicle. Smoke rose beyond a village; we approached a furnace of grass and bracken that had leapt the narrow track; impassable, I thought, in a new vehicle full of diesel. We wound

up the windows. Noëlle shut her eyes. I took a deep breath. Lennart
paused, then accelerated between high walls of flame, a corridor of
crackling, roaring heat. Exultantly we emerged into the air and a
landscape of black and tan. The track was faulted by a deep gully.
While Lennart backed up, and pitched through scrub to regain the
track beyond the fault, we walked to the plateau's northern edge. Far
below, the river stretched as far as we could see, elbowing its way
between grim, steep banks from Inga and Isangila.

There, in life, reproduced faithfully down to the scrub trees in the
foreground, was the view of the Yelala Falls engraved for Stanley's
book of 1885. The water beneath us looked still, like ice, but we could
hear the thunderous rapids. A jagged dinosaur of a cliff dragged its tail
in the water at this end of narrows in which the river ran deep and
dark, or shallow and white over rocks, and creamed around the
hunched backs of islands. This was the river that stopped Diogo Cão,
that Tuckey bypassed on foot, that compelled Stanley to build his road
on the far bank; this, the reason and excuse for the porterage system,
un sentier sinistre, jalonné de cadavres, and for the costly Matadi-Kinshasa
railroad.

We drove steeply down a narrow spine and up to a rugged tor that
seemed to hang above the river. Again we disembarked and began the
long precipitous descent between red boulders and white flints, tufts
of purple grass and scrubby thorn trees. It was a leg-shaking climb;
rocks redoubled the sun's heat; I paused gratefully to drink, admire
Matadi from afar and lust after delicious beaches nestling in the curve
of the river upstream from it. Down, down we went towards dwarf
but antique baobabs, a sloping mass of rock and a horseshoe of white
water cascading over an emerald-green shelf. *Oliveira 1905* and other
names were engraved in bark like tooled leather; plastic sacks and
hemp rope draped the baobabs' branches; green velvet fruits overhung
incongruous iron railings and concrete posts set into rock.

Clothes dry on scrub bushes. Tiny fish, silver and ruddy gold, glint
on the rocks. A man pounds palm-nuts in a natural rocky mortar.
Another slices the heads off small fry over a cooking-pot. A third
fishes from a tiny ledge under the weighty plinth. We clamber down
to water level, to his nets and catch, clinging to his liana rope. The
river that is fifteen miles wide even before it has gathered all its
tributaries, is little more than a hundred yards broad here. It is deep
and powerful. Divers say that vast boulders bound along its bed. Its
rise is a good twenty feet, for in the rock up near the baobabs a deep
pothole has been scoured out by a swirled pebble. Immediately

upriver there is a tremendous overhang and huge unsteady-looking rocks above the precipice. It is dream-like, crystalline and distilled, everything deep golden in the sunlight. An old man leads us to his cave-dwelling beneath slab upon slab of natural masonry. This dim home, inhabited by shifts of fishermen, is furnished with tin boxes, bags hanging from spikes of rock, wooden beds like the bottoms of canoes, clay pots, utensils and blackened hearths. In one particular cleft, beneath massive rock above the mighty river, a man lies on his plank bed in a feverish, blue-black sweat with a transistor radio at his ear. The river's music drowns it.

The cave-dwellers, fishermen and their forefathers, have always known the runes engraved on the rock-face here above Yelala's high-water mark: the shield of Portugal, a cross and an inscription on one rock, with names on two more, five hundred years old and pristine as if they were carved yesterday. But four centuries passed before another white man noticed this *padrão*, the earliest record of white exploration in Congo. Some say it was the Revd Domenjoz of the Congo Balolo Mission who, about 1900, saw what was unremarked by earlier travellers. But, as far as I can discover, the Baptist Revd Thomas Lewis presented photographs of the inscriptions to the director of the Dutch factory at Banana in 1890. He must have stood amazed at the courage of mariners who navigated, rowed, hauled boats upriver against the current, past the whirlpools of Hell's Cauldron and the wrecking rocks, in 1487. I can only imagine his excitement. I know my own as I stand in this powerfully beautiful place. The weight of significance and feeling, that for once amount to the same thing, is overpowering. I see Cape St Vincent, those other rocks at Europe's south-western tip, and the stone compass at Sagres, the *rosa dos ventos*; I see the white promontory penetrating the black river, an act of love, of conquest, and of rape; I can read enough of this document in rock to know a terrible joy and sadness: *Aqy chegaram os navios* . . . "Here arrived the ships of the illustrious King Dom João the Second of Portugal. Diogo Cão. Pêre Anes. Pêro da Costa."

V

THE HAUNTED PATH

There remain comparatively few of those numerous villages which were to be found earlier along the caravan routes. The State soldiers, Zanzibaris, Haussa and Bangala have devastated the country, and what was possibly left has been stolen by Stanley's troops when they passed through last spring. . . . All that remains are the carcases, or skeletons of porters or soldiers, who fell ill during the march. . . .

LIEUT. M. JUHLIN-DANNFELT Letter of 9th August 1887

> For there *is* beauty in the devious path
> That turns from too stern duty, and the wrath
> That only knows to punish, and goes in
> As to its proper goal, the haunts of sin. . . .
> *His* healing robe the leper's hand might pull.
> God! break my heart — but make it pitiful!
> ROGER CASEMENT Fragment

In the end we did not take the train. With Lennart and Eva and three Zaïrians we drove the 220 miles to the capital in half a day, with a stop at Kimpese. Marlow's fictional march, with a fat white companion and sixty porters, took fifteen days and one paragraph in *Heart of Darkness.* Conrad, with Prosper Harou and thirty-one porters, took thirty-six days, including a seventeen-day pause at Manyanga to recover from sickness, and filled pages of his black penny notebook with pencilled diary entries. The old State caravan route ran close to the course of the river; mountains, hills, and the valleys of large and small tributaries made it a tortuous switchback. Casement knew it well. His biographer, B. L. Reid, has him and his porters making the march, June 1903, in two days. In fact he took the train, in service for five years by then. Our road, a rare stretch of tarmac, roughly follows the line, the flattest route across turbulent terrain.

As we sped through a bronze land of grass and rock flecked white with cotton grass, I thought myself spoiled. The most notable feature of one roadside village was the body of a truck propped up on oil drums. What seemed like hanging forests of cedars filled the clefts of hills. Sumptuous clumps of bamboo screened water-courses. I asked the eldest Zaïrian the name of a particular sedge-like grass; "*Matiti*," he said. I wrote it down. Later I checked it; it means "weeds". Wrecked lorries and coaches punctuated the sinuous road, before it ran straight and flat across a plain with few trees and hosts of ironstone boulders. Cuttings and bridges took us through a new landscape of hills and rivers, with long views of golden and dark-maned mountains on the horizon.

Always, north and west of us, I was conscious of the old route trodden by hundreds of traders, missionaries and officials, by thousands of soldiers and porters, from camp to camp, river to river, market to village, mission to State post. At Kenge station I looked towards Congo da Lemba, which Stanley remembered as a flourishing village, but burnt, he noted in 1887, by a State force of Bangalas when they beheaded its chief for exacting tolls from caravans. Marlow saw the other side of that coin:

> a solitude, a solitude, nobody, not a hut. The population had cleared out a long time ago. Well, if a lot of mysterious niggers armed with all kinds of fearful weapons suddenly took to travelling on the road between Deal and Gravesend, catching the yokels right and left to carry heavy loads for them, I fancy every farm and cottage thereabouts would get empty very soon.

At the time, on the third day of his march, Conrad wrote in his black book, "To Congo da Lemba after passing black rocks. Long ascent. Harou giving up. Bother. Camp bad. Water far. Dirty. At night Harou better." Next morning, in heavy mist, they forded the Bembizi, threaded through Mazamba Wood on a steep mountain slope and descended to the Lufu river, a good bathe and a sleepless night. Three years before, Stanley had passed Baron von Rothkirch and a party of Kabindas near Mazamba Wood hauling the shaft of the *Florida*, the boat which Conrad came out to command. Casement's friend, Herbert Ward joined Stanley's rear column on this march. After the revelations of Casement's trial, Ward changed his son's name from Roger Casement Ward to Rodney Sanford Ward; he felt a privileged friendship had been betrayed. Just before his execution, in a letter of 28th July 1916, Casement recalled Ward in happier times:

> when I think of him it is of earlier days when the good things of life were all contained for him and me in a Huntley and Palmer biscuit tin, and we were lugging the crankshaft of the *Florida* over Mazambi Hill, down to the Bumbizi and up again, to the night camp where red ants came. Oh! so long ago. . . .

As the road crossed the Lufu river I thought of strange meetings downstream a century ago, and of Banza Manteka, Conrad's next camp and the site of a notable missionary experiment. From 1878, Henry Richards of the Livingstone Inland Mission had preached the Law for six years, and then the Gospel with no result; so he tried to *live* the gospel, including giving away his possessions to those who asked for them; slowly the people gave back what they saw he needed, and many asked for baptism. Few missionaries lived their faith like this, and the contrast with white traders, officials and adventurers was startling. Even Stanley noticed the fervour of the people's services, and that "young men whom I had known as famous gin-drinkers had become sober, decent men, and most mannerly in behaviour".

Conrad camped on the market place, disconsolate, with a cold in the head, "not well enough to call on the missionary". He marched fourteen miles a day on average and, on 3rd July, near the Luinzono river, he met an officer of the State inspecting the route, and a few minutes later came across "the dead body of a Backongo. Shot? Horrid smell." This became Marlow's "white man in an unbuttoned uniform" who

> was looking after the upkeep of the road, he declared. Can't say I saw any road or any upkeep, unless the body of a middle-aged negro with a bullet-hole in the forehead . . . may be considered as a permanent improvement.

That day Conrad noted "health good" and wrote unusually precise observations: of the oil-palm — Palma Christi — and calabashes suspended for *malafu*, of other caravans and travellers. He heard the fluting and booming of birds, though he saw only pigeons and green parakeets, the magic of mist on the hills and light on the river. On the 4th, after an unpleasant night, he "saw another dead body lying by the

path in an attitude of meditative repose". Two more rivers and the
shocking sight of a malformed albino woman, red eyes, red hair. "At
night when the moon rose heard shouts and drumming in distant
villages. Passed a bad night." Noëlle and I recognized exactly the
range of amplified emotions, everyday enchantment and fear, these
entries struggle to convey.

The party crossed the swift and deep Kwilu river by canoes on the
5th, traversed steep hills and ravines, and Conrad "fell into a muddy
puddle — beastly! The fault of the man that carried me. . . . Getting
jolly well sick of this fun". On the night of the 6th, Conrad and Harou
kept mosquitoes off with large fires round the tent. On the 7th, they
by-passed Lukunga and the exquisite mission station where Casement
had written: "Give back the Elgin marbles; let them lie/Unsullied,
pure beneath an Attic sky. . . ." Conrad was busy with immediate
African detail:

> route very accidented . . . walking along the crest of a chain of hills . . .
> walking through long grass for $1\frac{1}{2}$ hours. Crossed a broad river . . . $\frac{1}{2}$
> hour's walk through manioc plantations . . . walking along an undulating
> plain towards the Inkandu market on a hill. Hot, thirsty and tired . . .
> About 200 people. Business brisk . . . left in search of a resting place. Row
> with carriers. No water . . . No shade. Tent on a slope. Sun heavy.
> Wretched . . . Night miserably cold. No sleep. Mosquitos.

A three-hour march under an overcast sky on the 8th brought a
glimpse of the main river and the descent to Manyanga. This was
half-way to the Pool, a staging-post and recruiting centre for the
Société Anonyme Belge, where fresh porters were engaged.

We drove through scrubland with cattle, past passengers and produce
clustered around lorries at the roadside, piles of sacks of manioc, and
villages adorned with finger-like cacti. Soon after an electricity sub-
station, we crossed the Kwilu river and, across lumpy hills and lush
gardens, saw the Bangu mountains. Beyond them was Manyanga and
the Zaïre; this side, at their foot, Kimpese, our staging-post.

For centuries, the best trade-route from Mbanza Kongo (São
Salvador) to Mpumbu (Stanley Pool/Pool Malebo) was the Mount
Bangu road through Kimpese. When Wilhelm Sjöholm came here in
1896 he was shocked by the sparse population and quoted local
wisdom, "Where the white man settles, the people die". The railway
created a deserted landscape, and of those who worked on it "never
more than one third returned with their lives". Of the village of

Kongo, preserved by the State because it was the site of a sixteenth-century Catholic mission, he wrote, "It was very peculiar to see a village which had been spared from the white men's pillaging expeditions". People gathered around mission stations where destructive press-gangs were inhibited in their work. Elsewhere, as Gustav Palmer said, "the porterage system gnaws like a cancer and breaks multitudes of the country's strong men". In 1899, yet another Swedish missionary, J. E. Lundahl wrote, "Sometimes it feels as if we wander through an enormous cemetery, when we see heaps of skeletons". Of Kimpese in 1903, Casement noted, "The country a desert — no natives left".

After leaving our Zaïrian companions at the hospital of Kimpese's thriving Institut Médical Évangélique, we took coffee and pastries with Benkt and Ingela Bryngelson, before driving on to Kinshasa. It seemed months, rather than weeks, since Benkt had flown us from here over the Inga Dam and downriver to Moanda. We'd spent five nights at Kimpese, which until then had been only a name, a mythical place where my sister and her husband, Ann and Peter Scott, had worked in the 'Sixties.

The town of Kimpese, meaning "kingdom of cockroaches", was a straggle of rough brick houses and shacks along the main road, with a Catholic enclave at the far end. The grandly-named Hôtel Escale and Dancing Club Sexy-Box offered their delights. The smartest building was an unfinished butcher's, with few chickens and even fewer joints of meat, but boasting a tiled first floor. Shops ranged from a fragrant bakery and dark, basic general stores to the crumbling Alimentation Ya-Ya where you could buy Benedictine mustards, tarragon vinegar or Grand Marnier. Most trade was done at market stalls under corrugated canopies. Boys hawked bowls full of bananas or chimed Coca-Cola bottles to encourage a thirst. Music blared from a jacked-up *fula fula* in noisy competition with the record-shop across the street. A man prepared to treat himself, slowly mixing a tin of condensed milk into half a bottle of Fanta. Kids buried their faces in the orange flesh of paw-paws.

Eastwards, Kimpese peters out shanty-style, with onion fields on the right and the I.M.E. to the left, the mission laid out spaciously among hedges of variegated croton, mango trees, spiny-barked kapok trees and feathery cassias with pipe-like surface roots and yellow pom-poms of blossom in the rainy season. What started as an orthopaedic unit has grown into a large complex of wards and staff training schools, with three operating theatres and probably the best pharmacy and pathology laboratories in the country. Women cook for sick relatives in outdoor kitchens and spread washing to dry on the grass. Hedged paths are crossed and re-crossed by sellers of fruit and manioc, and by boys offering mortars, manioc sticks and spoons carved from white wood and decorated with poker-work.

In a grove of trees there is a church designed by a Swede, with a steep roof, so they told us, to shrug off the snow. Where the ground begins to tilt towards the railway track, there are houses for Zaïrian, Swedish, North American and British staff. There is a guest-house for patients and visitors where we ate with four Zaïrians and one English missionary doctor from the north-east. When the white doctor had left the table, and the pastor from Kananga was looking tolerant, the man from Gecamines at Matadi complained, "*C'est trop calme. Pas de whisky, pas de télévision. Ce n'est pas normale. Et tous les livres en anglais dans un pays francophone! Ce n'est pas normale.*" I hadn't seen the uneasy black/white cultural compromise in quite those terms before. In the room next to ours, he tried to make up for it all with smuggled bottles at night and Kinshasa-music from his transistor radio at dawn.

It was not always so calm. When my sister Ann, her husband Peter and their baby daughter first came here by train from Leopoldville, a few days before Independence, machetes were brandished, stones were thrown and people spat at whites. Then, on 30th June 1960, Lumumba declared, "From today we are no longer your *makak* (monkeys)!" At the garrison town of Mbanza Ngungu, then still called Thysville, troops rose up against their Belgian officers and scoured the country for victims. Peter was stood up before a firing-squad in the mission compound. But for an elderly Congolese, no one moved. He came and stood in front of Peter, saying, "You'll shoot me first." The soldiers hesitated. They lowered their rifles, shook Peter's hand and patted him on the back, deciding to believe that he was not a Belgian target. The old man, whom Peter had not seen before and never saw again, had melted away.

At an American mission to the west, men were beaten up and women raped; a girl, made pregnant as a result, has lived in an asylum since. The United States' fleet, standing off the coast, sent in helicopters and air-lifted white women and children, and most of the men. Peter was one of the few who stayed, mostly in Kinshasa. On reconnaissance missions to Kimpese, he found their house untouched, and the baby's nappy, changed just before the airlift, still lying on the bathroom floor. Ten miles up the line, at the cement factory from which Peter and Ann got their bread, a helicopter pilot was shot out of the sky by rifle-fire and, it is said, eaten. Such episodes, and stories, were repeated throughout the country, but in general missionaries suffered less than other whites. By September, amid uncertainty and turmoil, they were welcomed as a stabilizing force. My sister flew back with my niece, the first white child to return to independent Congo.

On a Saturday afternoon, we walked down through manioc and soya gardens to the railway-line. Two waggon-loads of people waited on the siding at the new cement factory. We crossed the tracks beneath the power-lines from Inga. Like a great pink sculpture set against the blue-grey backdrop of the Bangus, crushers, grinders, blending silos and furnaces stood beside mountains of rock blasted in the dry season. We climbed an avenue of mango trees above a steep scarp screened by bamboo and, for 15 zaïrcs, entered the cement factory's swimming-pool. To the plash of water, and the pluck and smack of tennis in the neighbouring court, we relaxed at tables shaded by *paillottes* and swam in cool water on a shelf of land between the mountains and the plain.

Nearer the town, at the community agricultural development project, we saw the kind of grass-roots work that, if repeated throughout Africa, could make a huge impact on the continent's food supply. Gerry Knights, an Angolan-born Canadian, showed us his experimental manioc plots on an eight per cent slope, where run-off was filtered through sacks and the eroded soil weighed. Downhill ridges, and traditional planting on mounds of earth and burnt vegetable matter, both lose four times an acceptable level of soil. Contour ridges are acceptable, but both green mulching and the use of forage ground cover gave no soil loss at all. Other plots demonstrate the virtues of available fertilizers, manures and mulches. In citrus plantations, shoots of orange, tangerine, grapefruit, tangelo and other crosses are grafted on to resistant lemon root-stocks and sold in their thousands each year. Individuals, sent here by their villages, return with proven, practical husbandry skills to pass on to the community. In this way, soya was introduced into Bas-Zaïre.

Twenty-eight thousand eggs per day, and thousands of chicks per annum, used to be sold from the chicken unit; but in the 'Seventies, under compulsory local control, lax management and corruption created such bad debts that the chickens had to be sold. A handful of Rhode Island Reds have been kept, amongst the redundant graders and incubators, to maintain the blood-line, together with three generations of newly-bred rabbits. There was still hope. Terrible screaming arose from the pig unit; two large white sows were being despatched to the Sugar Factory up the road. Each was wrestled to the ground and, while one man stood on its face, the others tied its legs and then all heaved it into the back of a Land Rover. That sound, that smell and the overcast sky made me homesick for North Devon.

In the workshops, carpenters and tin-smiths produced high-quality utensils, such as buckets, watering-cans, and brilliant tools and low-technology machines: wood-and-bicycle-wheel hand-ploughs, weeders, seed-drills for maize and soya, pedalled rice-threshers and winnowers, and hullers for soya and peanuts. Such a huller transforms two days' labour into a one or two-hour job. Thermostatically-controlled, paraffin-heated incubators are built to aid village chicken-breeding, and screw-thread mills for *mpondu*, manioc leaves, are popular among Matadi flat-dwellers where pounding is unpopular. I was very excited by all this creative energy, but the prevailing attitude was one of realistic pessimism tempered by a little hope. History is hard. When Gerry's father left the project, he prophesied that theft and corruption would rule. It was so. Tractors and big mills remain but the best hope is in the agricultural school and the low-tech workshops. Even so it is uphill work: against clannishness which undermines wider co-operation, against corruption, and against the sense that, despite all the innovation and motivation for good, one might not leave anything behind.

One morning we made for Kivuvu, "place of hope". In a steep hollow below the nursing school we crossed a narrow footbridge where women washed themselves in the stream and pounded clothes. Above, near the I.M.E. workers' village, a man was carrying a glass bidon, wrapped in cloth, on his head. He unveiled his golden liquor and held a one-sided Kikongo conversation with us, before we found a crippled French-speaking boy listening to a radio with an aerial rigged up to the roof of his hut. It was simple, the boy said; the man smoked out bees from trees in the forest and took the honey to brew mead. Very, very good mead.

Soya beans rattled in their pods like maracas as we threaded through gardens to the ochre railway cutting. We walked along the costly sleepers and turned up towards Kivuvu and Peter and Ann's old house, where we were welcomed by Citoyen Nkelele and his wife, he in a pale blue *abacost* suit and she in dark but vivid floral cloth. They were surprised we had walked, but covered in smiles when they heard who we were. We sat and talked of past and present. Dramas with thieves and pythons, that thrilled me as a teenager, had been played out here. Ann had given birth to three children in the I.M.E. hospital and brought all four up in this house, between working as a physiotherapist with leprosy patients; Peter had worked on construction and maintenance work for the Leprosy Mission.

As the director, Nkelele visits his twenty-three clinics each month, and attends conferences in Africa and Europe. Treatment now takes place in the community: leprosaria are things of the past. We walked past the orange grove Peter had planned and down the avenue of palms and mango trees he had planted. We saw the drainage ditches and the bridges he built, and entered the leproserie's ghost-town. Most of Kivuvu had been built by the colonial government before *les événements* overtook it. The day before Peter faced the firing-squad, its Belgian architect was shot. Concrete paths linked obliquely-angled duplex houses, haunted by a handful of men, women and children. Cold hearthstones stood on porches. One woman lay on a mattress on the grass beside a charcoal forge in a tin drum, with bellows driven by a bicycle wheel. Peter's water-tank still stood high on its framework; his power-lines ran between their poles, though the generator he installed may soon be obsolete. They plan to bring mains power to Kivuvu, and equip it as a school for community health workers: no longer a refuge, but a source of hope for the villages. Only five to ten per cent of the population are susceptible to leprosy, and only twenty per cent of sufferers are contagious, whereas tuberculosis is on the increase. The little leprosy hospital was silent. The mountains loomed behind. In the middle distance smoke curled from a village of mud-brick and grass.

I heard a rhythmic creaking and left the track to find out what it was. In the shade of trees on a pale carpet of pulp, a man was tugging at a paddle-like lever in a dug-out trough. He was crushing sugar-cane and letting the juice run out into a black tin underneath. He decanted it into white plastic bidons where it would ferment for four days: cane beer and spirit. "*Trop fort*," he said. His red shirt and digital watch hung on a branch behind him. Like Nkelele, he had a most charming face, and a lithe, impressive physique despite greying hair. Mukanda Raphael Soda was in his fifties and had seven children. *Soda* means "soldier", and he had served as a corporal in the Force Publique for six years before Peter, "Petrus" he called him, took him on to work on the draining, the building and the planting of trees and pineapples. Now he is a driver and decorator. In the sweet-smelling air, he smiled when he said that he didn't drink his brew himself, but had to earn some extra cash somehow. We were sorry to leave him. Yes, dear Soda, we would be sure and tell Petrus that the generator is still going strong.

I am not so sure that I will tell you everything. Did I forget to mention the crimson bougainvillaea outside Gerry Knight's office? Or the look of passionate amnesia in the eyes of the woman who trails round the hospital in the wake of "her husband", a British doctor, and her rival, the doctor's wife? Or Noëlle's abdominal pains and fruitless tests in the clinic? Or the white man and his black lady, constant companion or *deuxième bureau*, who stayed at the guest house until her Belgian husband came to sort them out? Or the trainee doctor out from London who was bitten by a snake, fortunately not a lethal one, with no serum in the place? Or the languid, sweating men and women dying of AIDS? Did I mention the maize crop, the hard-working Angolan refugees, the preaching, the growth and the fervour? We live our lives in detail, in particular. We cope with it all by making patterns, loose and tight routines. We sleep to forget, and after the forgetting and the dreams we wake with an idea of tomorrow, boring or stimulating, perhaps a vision. Otherwise, all the pressing facts would suffocate truth. For the traveller, if he can make patterns at all, the kaleidoscope is shaken, shaken, shaken. As André Gide said, in *Voyage au Congo*:

> in a country where everything is new to him, he is stopped short by indecision. Being equally interested in everything, he cannot cope, and begins to note nothing, since he could note everything . . . happy the specialist! He hasn't enough time for his limited domain. If I were to live again, I would be happy to study nothing but termites.

Did I mention the soldier ants? No. Did I say that when we took off with Benkt in the Cesna, we used the air-strip that my brother-in-law originally cleared? No. Forgive me. Now I am dreaming Zaïre, remembering and forgetting it. Lennart and Eva are ready to go, on to the Pool. I am dreaming Congo. Beyond the Bangu mountains, Joseph Conrad and Prosper Harou are leaving Manyanga after seventeen days of recuperation there.

They took plenty of hammock carriers because Harou was lame and neither was strong. It was hot, and uphill, through country thickly inhabited for once. On the third day, Sunday 27th July 1890, they arrived at the Baptist mission Conrad called "Sutili" — Lutete, or Ngombe Lutete; the station had been transplanted there from Manyanga in 1884 by Thomas Comber, George Grenfell and Holman Bentley. Here, Ndonzoao Nlemvo, the first Congolese Protestant Christian, was baptized in the river Tombe in 1886. His marriage to his first wife, Kalombo, is claimed as the first Christian wedding in Congo. For it he wore a white singlet, a loincloth and a leopard skin. A Belgian official asked, why not a suit? Bentley replied that he did not want blacks to transform themselves into whites. Nlemvo helped Bentley with translation. Soon after the Kikongo bible was published in 1905 he went blind. People said that whites had cut the strings of his eyes, because in Europe he had seen factories and much *mindele ndoki*, "white man's magic". He died and was buried at Ngombe Lutete in 1938, after years' more work at Mbanza Ngungu (Thysville) and at the mission of Kibentele, "people of Bentley", founded in 1921.

It was in the spring of that year that a young convert, baptized like Nlemvo in the Tombe river, began to heal the sick in Bas-Zaïre. His name was Simon Kimbangu and his title, Prophet and Doer of Miracles, set him in the line of religious rebels that stretched back to Francisco Bullamatare. He was strict; he prohibited polygamy and sorcery and preached the law of Moses. He declared, "Follow God alone, and not me," but his followers were won over by miracles. Most people said, "It is the whites who have killed Christ. We have nothing to do with it. Whites who kill a white? — old tribal quarrel. Leave us alone in our village." Christ was seen as a *mundele* from *Mpoto*, not as a Jew from the Roman colony of Palestine. But Kimbangu, like Kimpa Vita, preached a black gospel. It spawned minor prophets, mass meetings and demonstrations. Whites felt threatened and, in June 1921, Kimbangu's sect was banned and his arrest ordered. His escape was hailed as a miracle, but in September he gave himself up to the Force Publique. He was denied a martyr's death; the prophet's sentence was commuted to life imprisonment. Driven into the bush, Kimbanguism assimilated traditional elements and grew increasingly anti-white. For thirty years, from his prison cell, Kimbangu saw his cult develop, under the triumvirate of his sons, into a doctrine far removed from his original vision. He died in 1951, but Kimbanguism thrives.

Another erstwhile Baptist at Ngombe Lutete was Roger Casement. Between working for the Sanford Expedition and the Congo Railway Company, Casement was out of a job. Holman Bentley needed help because 1887 had been a bad year for Baptist missionaries. At least six died, including the pioneer Thomas Comber, and A. D. Slade, "a splendid all-round man" who succumbed to blackwater fever after only eight months. Bentley took Casement on to replace Slade as manager of transport, building, planting, accounts etc., until the end of the rainy season 1888.

His treatment of the natives is all that can be desired. . . . I managed also
very delicately to get an assurance that there had been nothing in his
manner of life out here which would cast reflection on us. . . . He speaks
very definitely of his conversion . . . which he dates from the early part of
this year.

It may be that, two years later, Conrad left the government road and
went to the mission at Casement's suggestion. It looked "eminently
civilised and very refreshing to see after the lots of tumbled down
hovels in which the State & Company agents are content to live".
Bentley and his wife were away in the south, and Conrad stayed only a
few hours, enjoying an "hospitable reception by Mrs Comber". That
is, Annie, who had arrived in Congo the previous month, married
Percy Comber at Matadi, and died four and a half months after
Conrad passed through. Six months of marriage. Six months of
Africa. Her gravestone at Banana Point is a cross inscribed "He
knows".

The tarmac led us past an edifice of sweet fat sacks at the Sugar Factory
junction, and along beside the oil-pipeline and its intermittent
pumping stations, an artery so often drilled and tapped that tankers
roll along the road instead. On the undulating plain the swell of fires
shimmered and shook the hills beyond. It was like a dream carrying us
towards night. Near Mbanza Ngungu, old Thysville, the dream may
drop you underground into miles of rocky corridors, caverns full of
bats, and grottoes in whose lightless streams swim blind, translucent
fish. A subterranean cemetery holds the bones of the chief
Mdombolozi Finzolwa, who was born, according to the inscription,
in 1684.
    At 2,500 feet, we surfaced in Mbanza Ngungu, a high town of
antique villas on stilts, of elaborate ironwork, balconies and walk-
ways. We stopped abruptly for the lowering of the flag, during which
ceremony anything that moves risks arrest. Early coloured lights
glimmered outside bars in the garrison town. We looked up to the
belvedere and down, through fragrant eucalyptus trees, to railroad
workshops and oil-rigs. Lush valleys twisted away, between mud
houses perched on multiple spurs of yellow and red earth, to vegetable
plots and paddy-fields of rice. We snaked down into a country of
blue-green and lime-green grass and climbed again through dry grass
fires and shadowy villages. In one, men sat under roofs of luminous
purple bougainvillaea. We drove on into darkness through the long

market town of Inkisi, with its unlit streetlamps, and met the railway where a ponderous freight-train of wagons and tree-trunks blocked our path. Then we crossed the Inkisi river and left Kisantu's botanical gardens to the night.

Two days from Ngombe Lutete, Conrad and Harou crossed the Lunzadi river "by a very decent bridge" and met M. Louette escorting a sick agent back to Matadi. He bore bad tidings: "All the steamers disabled — one wrecked." They passed a skeleton tied to a post and a nameless white man's grave — "heap of stones in the form of a cross". From one steeply wooded bank to another they crossed the Inkisi river's rapid waters in canoes. A quarter of a century later, in Berlin, Casement boasted that he was probably the only white man living who had swum the Inkisi:

> I used to swim all those rivers, *plein des crocodiles*, Kwilu, Lukungu, Inpozo, Lunzadi:– but the greatest of these was the Nkisi, about 100 metres broad, and swift at canoe crossing, because the great fall of the Nkisi was not far below.

There in 1887, Casement had camped beside A. J. Mounteney Jephson, a distinguished and thus coveted distant relation on his mother's side, who was struggling to bring the Relief Expedition's boat, the *Advance*, up to the Pool. Jephson gives a fresh view of Casement's "Huntley and Palmer biscuit tin":

> We bathed and he gave me a very good dinner — he is travelling most comfortably and has a large tent and plenty of servants. It was delightful sitting down to a *real* dinner at a *real* table with a table cloth and dinner napkins and plenty to eat with Burgundy to drink and cocoa and cigarettes after dinner.

A half-brick, thrown up by the truck in front, shattered Lennart's almost-irreplaceable windscreen and showered us with glass. We slithered through Madimba on a sandy road. Lorries loomed with or without lights and, on a gravelly stretch of roadworks, a dark one slid downhill sideways and just missed us. Lennart had to drive on hard, but later, just before our return to Europe, we came back with the British Ambassador and his wife, a Rear-Admiral and an international team from the Royal College of Defence Studies on a country-hopping tour of Africa. We felt we knew the road well. Lorries skidded towards us as usual.

At a flower-strewn table, in Kisantu tropical gardens, we ate *nsusu*, chicken, cooked in *mwamba*, palm-oil, with chips. The hanging, climbing, tumbling orchids were waiting for the rains: a few exotic, enigmatic blossoms. Trees lined the Inkisi river, that Casement swam long before Friar Gillet turned inhospitable marshes into a bit of Eden: all the grand palms, scented *Hopeas*, funereal cypresses and vanilla, clove, cinnamon, camphor, cocoa, mangosteen, banyan, wild fig and tulip trees. In the small zoo, a melancholy baboon, a frustrated lynx, a comatose crocodile, verbose parrots. The military posed self-consciously beneath giant bamboos, or in the woodland fringe, for "jungle" photographs. A charming gardener plucked grapefruit blossom, with its huge fragrance, for Noëlle. Over lunch, a Ministry of Defence man presented her with a flower; a Yugoslav colonel proffered a whole bunch; a Pakistani captain smiled.

Beyond the Inkisi, Jephson met Casement again and shared a midday breakfast — "how I tucked into his oatmeal cakes!" They camped together for three nights, waiting to cross the rain-swollen Luila. Jephson was feverish as he ferried Casement over on the river in April 1887; he dismantled the boat under hot sun and sent his men ahead. Luckily, he caught up with Casement, who dosed him with quinine and had him carried, barely conscious in the cool of the day, to his colleagues.

On 30 July 1890, between the Inkisi and the Luila, Conrad dosed the feverish, vomiting Harou, with ipecacuanha, quinine and lots of hot tea; his fever had gone by 4 o'clock, but he had suffered terribly from the jerks of the hammock; expecting "lots of bother with carriers tomorrow," Conrad "made a speech, which they did not understand. They promise good behaviour." Or, as Marlow says, "I made a speech in English with gestures, not one of which was lost to the sixty pairs of eyes before me." The next day was "infernally hot" and Harou was "too heavy — bother!" and very little better. Bathing in the Luila, Conrad himself felt seedy. The first day of August began cold and misty. They made long ascents and steep descents until it grew very hot and "the aspect of the country entirely changed. Wooded hills with openings. Path almost all the afternoon thro' a forest of light trees with dense undergrowth".

One hot day we crossed Conrad's path, when we dropped down from the main road on a sandy track through woodland, scrub and grass. We slithered and bucked over rocks. At one moment we were cramped by dense green foliage, at the next tawny hills rolled to the horizon. Mfuti, or Crocodile Hole, was a collage of white sand, black rocks and grey river. Sharp sand squeaked and sang underfoot. *Pirogues* whose grain was grey and weathered were beached beneath live and dead trees. A sluggish stream carved its way down to a lagoon at the near bank. The river was low, the boulders its dry bed, its offscouring. Like redundant components of its mill, these rafts and carcases of rock were strewn or heaped, dull or shiny as if tarred or glazed, cracked open or whole like great dark eggs, a still-life of the river's power. I clambered, leapt, listened to the suck and surge of water beneath. They mystified by their immobility; the river mystified by its motion. Upstream it was a snake of rapids running back to the great falls below the Pool; downstream it rushed to the Zongo Falls and all the cataracts between here and Manyanga, and between Isangila and Inga where the great dam squats, in the crook of the river's elbow, above unshootable rapids; here, under our noses, eddies and countercurrents played over unseen channels, standing waves built up and subsided, everything shimmered and shivered with the elusive flexing of musculature, of a great river's dream-sleep in its deep and narrow bed. We climbed and swam and picnicked and watched the rounded hills of Congo-Brazzaville under an overcast sky. A group of Zaïrians visited and went away. Since then, people have been shot and robbed at Mfuti. That day, however, we left happy.

Conrad intervened in a row between his carriers and a man who said he was an official: "Blows with sticks raining hard. Stopped it." A chief brought a boy with a gun-shot wound in the brow and Conrad gave them some glycerine to dress it. He felt rather seedy, he wrote, and "Harou not very well. Mosquitos — frogs — beastly! Glad to see the end of this stupid tramp." His Congo Diary ends here. The tramp continued for another fifteen miles to Kinshasa, where he must have arrived the next day, Saturday 2nd August, fifty days after he disembarked at Matadi.

From Matadi on 18th June he had written a passionate letter to Aunt Marguerite, adding, "I leave tomorrow on foot. No ass here except your very humble servant. Twenty days of caravan." He therefore planned to reach the Pool on 8th July, almost four weeks earlier. But delay, and sickness at Manyanga, added up to the crime of tardiness which the Société's Kinshasa manager, Camille Delcommune, seems to have held against Conrad from the start. Their dislike was mutual. Conrad wrote to Uncle Tadeusz on 3rd August expressing, as we know from the reply, "deep resentment towards the Belgians for exploiting you so mercilessly". On his second day in Kinshasa,

Conrad was smarting and ready to resign. His uncle begged him to calm down "lest it should affect your liver" and to weigh the implications of breaking his contract. "Unless your health becomes affected you should stick it out."

Eventually, Conrad took intricate revenge in his portrayal of Marlow's manager, a commonplace, sinister, "flabby devil". Marlow has a three-month job salvaging and repairing his tin-pot vessel before he can take command and steam upriver. In fact, the broken-backed *Florida* had already been salvaged by Delcommune and the *Roi des Belges*. Kurtz dies because of the manager's delays. But, on the very day of his anguished letter, Conrad embarked on the *Roi des Belges* as a supernumerary to learn the course. On 4th August she steamed out of the Pool. Without delay, with no time to rest, he set off on the real voyage, to which his "stupid tramp" had been a mere prelude.

Seventy-five miles on from Kisantu we saw, through Lennart and Eva's smashed windscreen, the carpet of lights that Kinshasa spread out beside the Pool. The long river-passage began down there. We narrowly missed crashing into the back of a Mercedes, but found our way to food and bed. Alone together, Noëlle and I looked into each other's eyes, asking where we were, who we were. We seemed to recognize ourselves, and made hot love to feel out and confirm that knowledge.

Part Two

TO THE FALLS

CONGO

Ubangi

Mob
Lusengo
Mankanza

Basanku

Lulonga

Lulonga

Ik

Bolenge Mbandaka
Bamania
Iyonda

Irebu

Bikoro
Gombe
L. Ntomba

Zaïre

Lukolela

Inongo

L. Mai-Ndombe

Yumbi

Bolobo

Tshumbiri

Mushie

Kwamouth

Mswata

BRAZZAVILLE

Langa-Langa

Pool Malebo

Kwango

Kwilu

Luker

Kasai

KINSHASA

VI

JOURNEYING DEEP

The Congo has been, and could have been, nothing but a personal undertaking. There is no more legitimate or respectable right than that of an author over his own work, the fruit of his labour. . . . My rights over the Congo are to be shared with none; they are the fruit of my own struggles and expenditure.

KING LEOPOLD II *Speech of 1906*

O mother, how unfortunate we are! . . .
The white man has made us work,
We were so happy before the white man came,
We'd like to kill the white man who has made us work,
But the whites have a fetish more powerful than ours,
The white man is stronger than the black man,
But the sun will kill the white man,
But the moon will kill the white man,
But the sorcerer will kill the white man,
But the tiger will kill the white man,
But the crocodile will kill the white man,
But the elephant will kill the white man,
But the river will kill the white man.

Porters' song of 1888

Three times we come to Kinshasa. Three times we leave it. Each time it is a different city. Each time we see more, more clearly. After London and Lisbon, it is both broken-down and hopelessly ambitious, as if in a love-hate relationship with the dust. After Bas-Zaïre, it has style and sophistication, a vigorous sense of its African self, flirting with — and asserting itself against — imported attitudes, a rebellious soul rejecting the dogmas of the "big men", the black bwanas. After our travels in Equateur, Haut-Zaïre and Shaba, however its façade may soar, the body of the city squats in the grey, gritty sand, its spirit blasted by incorrigible corruption.

Shall we mourn the villages Stanley found on the south bank of his Pool: Nkunda, Nshasa, and Ntamo? Shall we greet Leopold's town and applaud its only begetter's "opening up to civilization the only part of the globe into which it has not yet penetrated, piercing the shadowy darkness that shrouds entire populations". Shall we mourn Leopold's harsh light, the loss of the old order, the old tyranny?

Shall we welcome the imago Kinshasa that emerges, colourful and free, from the cracked chrysalis of Leopoldville? Shall we echo President Mobutu's appeal for vigilance, thrift and work. . . .

so that Zaïre, our beloved country, which has been a prototype of disorganisation, shall become a model of organisation; so that Zaïre, which has been the apple of discord among African countries, shall become a centre of cohesion and agreement for African comprehension and solidarity; so that Zaïre, which has been bled to death by the systematic plundering and exploitation of which it was a victim, shall become the unconquerable barrier to all attacks by imperialism and the spearhead of the liberation of the continent.

Or shall we simply walk into this capital, product of clashing cultures and conflicting ideologies, remembering Richard Burton's words elsewhere: "It is always a pleasure, after travelling through the semi-republican tribes of Africa, to arrive at the head-quarters of a strong and sanguinary despotism."

No, that kind of irony leaves the traveller with blood on his hands. It's too easy to abandon oneself to the place, and too presumptuous not to. At dawn I stand on the balcony, this privilege, and look across Avenue Trois Z to the Supreme Court of Justice. I am talking about judgement. In front of the court a bronze woman sits on a plinth and abandons herself to grief, head on arm on knee, in memory of the martyrs of Independence. Are the bronze cheeks of Wuma's sculpture wet with tears? From here, the régime's opponents are judicially marooned on the island of Bulambemba, or exiled from day and night in underground cells. Wuma's woman weeps for justice, they say.

The big man on trial today, for attempting to smuggle a fortune overseas, is weeping diamonds.

Behind the court, in a little tree-shade by the roadside, women are cooking eggs and selling them with bread and cans of drink off a wall. Some men stop to eat this breakfast at two rough tables and, between the tables and the women, one man presumes to dance. There is presumption in abandonment. Exuberance issues from pain as well as joy, and is good fortune. Justice is a privilege. I am trying to see straight, but words warp in the growing heat. I am a white man eating mine with bread and tea on a balcony.

It is overcast but warmer than it should be in the dry season. We walk heavily down Boulevard 30 Juin towards Place du 27 Octobre and Place de la Révolution. Triumphal monuments are in the recent ruinous style, grey and spiritless. In their shadow on a great traffic island, market-women with twig-brooms brush rubbish and brazier-ash off their pitches of grey dust. We buy eggs there for ten zaïres each; change, in filthy small denomination notes, is unravelled from the knotted corner of the vendor's *limputa*; we have no bag and there is a loud, laughing, argumentative fuss to procure one from another woman's stall. We buy six bread sticks for fifteen zaïres. A man in a blue *abacost* warns us against the salesmen who patrol ranks of paintings propped up in the sparse grass, and undercover stalls piled with masks, wood-carvings, green malachite and ivory, the thieves' market, *marché des voleurs*. We want bananas not tusks, and he leads us past men touting watches and key-rings, begging boys and tattered elders, to where a group of women thrust fruit and their hard-selling, grinning faces at ours. We get a hand of twelve for twenty zaïres, and notice that our guide gets three bananas' commission. What *are* things worth? What is the world worth?

Here, haggling at ground level, we could be in any village. We are in old Nshasa. Behind us, the boulevard runs its high-rise way past the copper-coloured, copper-roofed SOZACOM building (Société Zaïroise de Commercialisation de Minerais), past the great white Banque Commerciale Zaïroise and the Post Office, all the way to the golf course in fashionable Gombé; as Avenue Colonel Mondjiba it continues towards old Ntamo, old Leo, and the President's enclave on Mont Ngaliema. Before us, an interminable wall hides the railway station, a waste of tracks between us and Pool Malebo. We skirt it and cut through side-roads to Shopping.

Shopping is smart. Hot and dusty, with none of the style of those

who slide their limousines into the white-walled car-park, we pass
into its chilly air-conditioned atmosphere. Here, amid almost shocking cleanliness, are five men waiting to take charge of our bags. A
blonde girl, in a white cat-suit and high-heels, sifts through the
toiletries and perfumes. A poised West African figure, in lilac robes
and head-dress, flows amongst the garden furniture. An expansive
commissaire surveys rank upon rank of choice wines and spirits. A fat
white diplomatic wife eases off her gold sandals beside a refrigerated
counter full of imported meats, sausages and cheeses; she sighs and
plumps for *chèvre*. A quinine-sallow, white-haired man gazes at fresh
herring and kippers, at Moanda squid and *capitaine du lac*. And an
English poet seizes upon the brand of Belfast-made tobacco he smokes
in his pipe. That, at least, is cheaper here than in England. Outside, the
flag of the MPR, Mouvement Populaire de la Révolution, hangs
limply above the limousines. It would take some revolution to make
Shopping a people's store.

It is not far to the heart, or hearts of Kinshasa, the Cité areas that swell
successively along their artery, Avenue Kasa-Vubu. They are dense
grids of streets and alleys, some of whose names will soon be more than
names to us: Lac Moero, Lubumbashi, des Lokele, Lisala, Bangala,
Lukolela, Bolobo, and so on, and on and on. The Cité is where most of
the city's three to four million people live. The central market, *grand
marché*, not so far from the Memling Hotel and downtown Kinshasa, is
the Cité's Shopping: a concrete expanse sheltered by hangars where
country meets city with currency of vegetables and fruits, fish from the
river, meats from the forest, spoils off the backs of upmarket lorries,
cloth and jewellery, fetishes and cosmetics. Deep in the Cité is the Stade
du 20 Mai, temple of football. Here Mobutu exhorts his people,
though, for many in his capital's underground society, MPR stands for
Mort Pour Rien, "death for nothing".

Avenue Kasa-Vubu is main street of an alternative world where
clothes, coiffure, music and sex are kings and queens; here SAPE —
Société des Ambianceurs et des Personnes Elegantes — reigns. *Abacost*
means *à bas costume*, down with European-style suits; here the rule is *à
bas abacost*. Here Franco and Rochereau are out-of-date; the music
belting from the bars is from Papa Wemba, Zaïko Langa-Langa,
Choc-Stars, and Victoria Eleison. Here are hundreds of clubs where
les anges noirs, not black Bwanas, meet. Here are bar/funeral parlours
where families laugh and cry, drink and dance the night, and the wake,
away. Here you give banknotes and jewellery to the best dancers.
Women display basins-full of *minketi*. Boys stand by small edifices of

concrete blocks, plinths for bottles of petrol filched from military depôts or drilled from the Matadi-Kinshasa pipeline.

Féticheurs offer healing in their "surgeries". *Parisiens* hawk forgeries — money, passports, visas. *Londiniennes* sell their bodies, despite the government's campaign to foster the dignity of women; some recall the *petites* in Muamba Kanyinda's novel *La Pourriture*: "This type of girl doesn't let herself be pawed by just anyone. You need to be rotten with money and not go on foot. Still, even an old banger saves your face and puts up the birds in Kin." Not "Maman Chantal" though. She has the air of "a high-class cover-girl or of a Hollywood taxi-girl with a scale of charges capable of drying up an oil-well". But cheap *Sidagogues* — SIDA is the French acronym for AIDS — are plentiful; there's many a *labo*, hired room, in which to *cailler*, "congeal", make love on a good bed or *faire un match sur un wemblay*.

In the tight mesh of sandy alleys, this multitude of single-storey houses, squalid and smart, Matonge is "*le quartier plus bruyant — beaucoup de bars, beaucoup de femmes libres*". So says Badi-Banga who guides me there to the low white house of Tamba, the sculptor. Tamba is away, but a relative opens the gate. The living-room is rich with rugs, low tables of objects, sculptures, mirrors, figurative montages. Air-conditioning drones. An antique fetish figure wears hi-fi head-phones. The workshop is full of power-tools. In the yard and the *atelier*, cats play among bronzes. A new cast of *Lovers* and an abstract of flat planes and parallel plates wait to be polished. On the ground, an intriguing plaster maquette melds the styles, and plants grow out of Tamba's still-life ferment and scale the house.

I flag down a taxi and clamber into the back, along with a vast fragrant mama and a thin clerk. The driver swerves into a filling-station at once and, with us as security, gambles on a pint or two of *essence*. The taxi is gutted; the springs of both seats and suspension are pancaked; the upholstery's stripped; the doors' inner panels are missing — naked mechanism which won't wind the windows down; the dashboard is a memory — just wires and the remains of instruments. The driver connects two loose ends, presses the starter and I'm off to fetch money in a raucous, rattling, oven-like carcase of a car. The horn works, and the brakes, thank God. The bank is in the Galeries Présidentielles, among shops in which European clothes, shoes and jewellery are sold at West End prices. They glow and glitter modestly behind plate-glass. The escalator to the first floor is unmoving, stuck fast like the economy. I climb.

The bank officials are helpful; my paperwork mounts on successive desks; the exchange rate is better than I'd feared. A girl, with intricately plaited hair, soft lips and hard eyes, piles bundles of fifty and hundred-zaïre notes on the cash-counter. She's sorry she has no five-hundred-zaïre notes today. Later, I'm glad, because few people upriver can change them. Now, I sweat, filling my carrier-bag with three months' money. At revaluation, before they printed many large denomination notes, I'd have needed a wheel-barrow. One of the bank employees leans against me to breathe that his friend would give a good rate for sterling. No thanks. Black market money is not the temptation that it was before the IMF leant on Mobutu. You could get five times the official rate then, and I'd have needed a *charrette à bras*, one of the barrows that the Bayaka, that old war-like tribe, trundle down every thoroughfare in Kinshasa.

I feel guilty, carrying this much money on the streets. Then I see black Bwanas in Mercedes, and think of Mobutu's supposed fortune of three or four billion dollars. It's only £1,500 under my arm, but I'm ripe for the picking. Noëlle meets me and covers the money with some of her shopping. There is a small crowd in Place Salongo, gathered around what might be a street-hawker or a side-show. We mingle with them. A policeman leans on his long stick. At his feet a man lies crumpled, and naked but for a rag someone has thrown over his genitals. His skin is very dark, midnight brown. The soles of his feet are tan. His blood is very red. It leaks from his head over his shoulders and gathers, a glossy puddle, in the dust. To explain everything, a man mutters "*Voleur!*" in my ear. This is justice. Blood runs down the thief's cheek like vermilion tears.

We sit down to lunch with Jake, a geologist whom I met at the bank. His house is being repainted primrose, and the corrugated roof grass-green, for its owner, the ambassador to Tanzania, soon to return home. Jake is flying back to England, having just finished a two-year project drilling for water in Equateur and Kasai. His servant, the good Baptist Albert, serves avocado, roast chicken and chips, iceberg lettuce salad, white wine, yoghurt and apples. Jake makes us feel we may survive. He gives us advice, contacts upriver, and a big map of Kinshasa. Now we know where we are. When I tried to buy maps, I wove my way on foot to the Institut Géographique, where they had run out of them. For a price, they could offer grey photocopies in a few days' time. . . . Jake's map is a much-coveted prize.

Julie, from the Bank, picks us up after work and speeds us along the riverside of Beau Rivage and Gombé, past Kallina Point. In *A Personal Record*, Conrad describes the Point as "a specially awkward turn in the Congo between Kinchassa and Leopoldville". There, in October 1890:

> I failed in being the second white man on record drowned at that interesting spot through the upsetting of a canoe. The first was a young Belgian officer, but the accident happened some months before my time, and he, too, I believe, was going home; not perhaps quite so ill as myself—but still he was going home. I got round the turn more or less alive, though I was too sick to care whether I did or not.

Kallina, Conrad's "Belgian officer", was an Austro-Hungarian lieutenant going, not home, but upriver, not months but years before, in March 1883. Now, the Palais de la Nation is grandly disposed on the Point. Here was the focus of the 'Sixties cold war in Africa, a focus cruelly sharpened by events in Thysville, Stanleyville, Kasai, Katanga; a focus held in the cross-lines of Washington and Moscow's telescopic sights, and in close-up by the CIA, the KGB and the UN.

Here President Kasa-Vubu sat it out, amongst the "tribes and bribes", while Prime Ministers — Lumumba, Ileo, Adoula, Tshombe — came and went, until Colonel Mobutu staged his bloodless coup on 24th November 1965. When he briefly took power in September 1960, *Pravda* declared, "Events have shown that Mobutu was just a soap bubble. The power of the puppet colonel did not last twenty-four hours. . . . Mobutu is already a yesterday for the Congo." Before the Palais, the statue of the white king on his white horse has long gone. Mobutu has been in the saddle for more than twenty years. Into the river, that simmers off Kallina Point, the CIA station chief Lawrence Devlin dumped the deadly virus that the agent "Joe from Paris" smuggled into Leopoldville to add to Lumumba's toothpaste, just as Khrushchev was pounding his shoe on the desk at the UN in New York.

At Place de Ngaliema, near the railway terminus in old Ntamo, a policeman is trying to control the traffic that floods from the Cité up Avenue Kasa-Vubu to meet the traffic coming into town on the Matadi road. A crazy woman is wandering across the junction, arms outstretched, wearing nothing but strips of rags for a skirt and an expression of outrage. Her pained eyes, her open mouth, her heavy breasts rebuke the tide of civilization.

The Bateke at Nshasa gave Baptist missionaries a hostile reception in early 1881, thinking them Stanley's forerunners. Pierre Savorgnan de Brazza, the French Italian who gave his name to Brazzaville, had warned them against Stanley. Chief Ngaliema of Ntamo was, in contrast, quite friendly and not as interested in belonging to France. He started out as a chief's slave, bought for one plate, but enriched himself by ivory trading. Stanley entered into blood-brotherhood with him in 1877. By 1881, he was powerful enough to give Stanley trouble, but *Bula Matari* succeeded in founding a station just west of Ntamo and, in April 1882, christened it Leopoldville. Soon, Thomas Comber founded the Baptist station of Arthington on Leopold Hill. The *En Avant* was launched at Ntamo Bay at the end of 1881 and the *Peace* from Arthington in June 1884.

Heirs of those pioneering craft are now repaired at the Chanimétal Shipyards. We pass them, and climb Leopold Hill, now Mont Ngaliema. Julie takes a wrong turning and we hurtle towards the gates of the Presidential Domain where *Yeoman of the Guard* soldiery hold sway in green uniforms with épaulettes and cuffs of red and yellow, and leopard-skin hats with plumes of red, yellow and green feathers. Happily, they are amiable tonight and grin beerily as we turn and make off. Later, we shall penetrate those gates, but now we make for the viewpoint. Under trees in the Presidential Zoo, I can see one lion and one okapi. The sun is a red ball over the river. A soldier leans on the balustrade, like a man in a theatre box, smoking. Steps lead up to a monument, a sinewy warrior with a spear who, with flanking figures beneath a colonnade, has taken Stanley's place. He faces Brazzaville. Lights sparkle through honey-coloured haze. Cicadas scratch treble night-music above the bass rumble of rapids beyond Île des Mimosas. The river is big. Upstream, the great crescent of Île Bamu is set in the Pool. The sun drops out of sight. The Pool holds its silky light. Far off, invisible, the river feeds it. The dream we are waiting to live.

Stanley returned in 1887 with the Relief Expedition. He had to work hard to talk the Baptists and the Livingstone Inland Mission into lending their boats, the *Peace* and the *Henry Reed*. Chief Ngaliema complained of the change in white traders, how imperious they had become. Stanley decamped to Kinshasa to superintend the launching of the hull of the Sanford Expedition's *Florida*, that Conrad was supposed to command three years later. On the last day of April she was dragged down the slip by two hundred men and fastened to the *Stanley* at the Dutch factory's landing-place.

In his War Office Army Book of 1901, Casement drew a plan showing the site for the proposed British Consulate: beside a large Euphorbia tree on the bank of Stanley Pool facing Route de la Gare. It came to nothing. In 1903, as work began on the consulate building in Boma, Casement had great difficulty getting a passage upriver. He kept his eyes open and was appalled by the native hospital in Leopoldville: three mud huts — two roofless — and seventeen people dying of sleeping-sickness — one woman fallen in the fire — "all lying about in the utmost dirt". Next door was the State shipyard: "here all was brightness, care, order, and activity". In a State store, he found a dead body and some fifty cases of guns for the ABIR rubber concession. He reported that most of the Bateke had abandoned their homes, for the French side of the river, one night two years before. "Where formerly had stretched these populous native African villages, I saw today a few scattered European houses." By this time, Arthington had moved to Kinshasa, and Casement went to stay there. After four weeks he took up the offer of a berth on the Société Anonyme's vessel, *P. Brugman*, as far as Tshumbiri.

We have been given an introduction to Citoyen Ngundu La-Botali, Sous-Directeur d'Armement, ONATRA. Though we have been told that all the boats are upriver, he is the man to get us a berth. Worn stone steps lead up to the peeling balcony of the port offices; people stand or lean or sit there in attitudes of passive importunity, that passes for patience, waiting for a crumb or a ticket to drop from ONATRA's table. Inside, a dim staircase leads us up to grubby offices: dark green paint and dark brown doors. Clerks do not seem to think that the Big Man is there, or will see us. We knock on his door, enter and greet him loudly, looking him in the eye, gripping his hand firmly. He is a big man. He carries weight. And he is helpful. "Yes, there is a boat. Not a big boat. But if you must go soon there is a boat tomorrow. Then not for two weeks. Really. Come back at three this afternoon. I'll confirm it and you will pay me for the tickets." We know about promises and payments, but we have to trust him. His French is elaborately courteous.

In three days' time we have a dinner date at the British Ambassador's residence. We walk to the Embassy on Avenue de l'Equateur to cancel it. The Americans have an elegant Embassy on Avenue des Aviateurs, past the Revlon Beauty Salon and the ancient RAC cinema. Then they have a cultural centre and a large anonymous fortified building, heavily guarded. A shuttle-stop bus links the three. The British have two floors above a bank, but the welcome is warm and our invitation becomes one for drinks tonight. In his office, the Ambassador shows me the registers of births and deaths kept by

Roger Casement, H.M. Consul at Boma. Births to upriver missionaries and the wife of a Congo Free State agent, balanced by deaths of
missionaries, aged between thirty-three and forty-one, and a
twenty-eight-year-old clerk.

What courage and desperation, what vocation and ambition
brought them out here to give birth and to die. The British, even in
Kinshasa today, are a singular breed. There are the young diamond-
dealers who offer us water-skiing on the Pool. They travel out, loaded
with money and stones, to trade over and under the counter in Kasai,
or for gems smuggled from Angola. They pay their way. They
complain that their phone has been cut off again, the line sold by some
get-rich-quick clerk at the Post Office. All they can do is buy it back.
There is the old hand, whose watchman rushes across the street with
an upraised stick when he sees me trying the gate one night. He lets me
in and barely restrains the dog from laying into my leg. The old hand,
bald and thin in baggy khaki shorts, presses his nose against the
mosquito netting before admitting me to the house. Mobutu is on
TV, brandy is on the table, the *deuxième bureau* is on the sofa, and we
have good talk, though not with her because she speaks no English
and little French. There is the wife who lives holed-up in a flat out at
the smart suburb of Binza, terrified to leave it because of her fear of
black men. A watchman we get to know is highly amused. In
England, in winter, there are no leaves on the trees, he tells us, and no
fruits. Winter or summer, you never see the sun. Here in the rainy
season, when we are in our houses, you *blancs* sit out and go pink.
When a mosquito bites, you come up in red bumps. And your shirts
are sopping-wet with sweat. It is very funny.

At three o'clock we present ourselves at Citoyen Ngundu's office.
He gratefully tucks our money — 2,912 zaïres — into his breast
pocket, but can give us no tickets. Is it any wonder we sweat? "*Demain
matin, monsieur et madame.*" In *Children of the Country*, Joseph Hone
describes his recent, fruitless attempt to do the river journey. An old
hand tells him that the passenger boats don't work any more. "It's all a
dream — travelling upriver now." He looks at the place-names on the
timetable. "Just names. . . . Words, not deeds." I wonder too, but, as
Conrad said, "A book is a deed," and I've got to do it.

We walk to the Baptist Mission, New Arthington, now CBFZ —
Communauté Baptiste du Fleuve Zaïre. Among the buildings there
are two old houses, the oldest in Kinshasa, transplanted from Old
Arthington. We have a package to deliver to the OXFAM people who
live in one of them. The bungalow's floor is supported by iron stilts,

each with a cup for kerosene to drown ascending termites. The prefabricated Scots pine structure is in remarkable condition. The corrugated-iron roof balloons along the ridge to allow air to circulate freely. Inside there are cats, a dog and a shrouded billiard table. On a wide balcony, overlooking a fine garden and the river, there is tea.

On the riverbank, among ferns and tall grass, stands the oldest monument of all, the boiler of the *Peace*. The twin-engined boat was seventy feet long, divided into seven watertight compartments. She drew eighteen inches when loaded with six tons. She was carried from Matadi in eight hundred packages, of which only three were too heavy for a man to carry on his head. These, including the steam separator, were slung from poles. The lightweight boiler was a masterpiece of innovation: a massive horse-shoe pipe linked to a steam chest by ranks of curvaceous tubes between which the furnace's flames licked. Steam could be raised from cold in ten minutes; useful if the war canoes put out. Wire-mesh arrow-guards could be folded down from the sun-awning to protect the steersman and the engineer. The men sent from England to assemble her died on the march from Matadi, and George Grenfell, who had watched her construction and trials on the Thames, rebuilt her with nine West African artisans. On the brink of the Pool the shapely boiler sits like a sculpture celebrating Grenfell's charting of the great river. Beyond it the water glimmers grey-lilac. Not far out, wrecks of later river-boats are beached on a sandbank, rust-red stranded hulks.

The watchman lowers the Union Jack. The sun sets over Brazzaville. We sip drinks on the Ambassador's polished verandah and joke about the wrecks. Beautifully clipped green grass is equipped for croquet and set with beds of exuberant flowers and shrubs. Fan-shaped traveller's palms, oil-palms, flame-trees and jacarandas are silhouetted against the dying light. Mosquitoes and small bats buzz us; huge fruit-bats squabble in the trees; frogs croak beside the swimming-pool. Perhaps we should fly east like Joseph Hone. Across the road the river-bank drops steeply, planted with manioc and lit with bonfires; the continuous sound of rapids is oddly comforting; music jangles from the Chinese Embassy next door. Patrick Eyers tells us of two Canadian pilots flying to Kisangani; because the control-tower was silent, they flew on for two hours, then ran out of fuel and crashed in the forest. We'll take the boat after all. He gives us background information and advice, an ice-block for our film, the offer of space in the fridge for all the exposed film that we can safely send back to Kinshasa, and a warm invitation to stay when we return. We are encouraged. Patrick Eyers drives us back to the flat in an air-conditioned Land Rover and wishes us *bon voyage*. The new moon lies on its back. We do too, but don't sleep much.

At 8.30 am Citoyen Ngundu marches us through the Gare Fluviale. Knots of men part to let us through, minions click their heels, bow, grovel, as they greet the Big Man. We by-pass the ticket queues completely. Here we have power on our side. Ngundu warns us that the price may have risen since yesterday. Oh yes. But no, the clerks inscribe the old price on our tickets for Bolobo. *Merci citoyens, merci mille fois*. In crazy taxis, we rush about town to collect our rucksacks, deposit keys, leave messages, say goodbyes. In the crush back at the port, there's a noisy competition to carry baggage. Passports and health certificates are inspected by officious officials at a barrier. Beside them, people queue for tetanus injections, a long line, one needle. Noëlle has a tetanus certificate; I haven't. I think hepatitis, AIDS; but my cholera and yellow fever papers are enough. We clamber on to the *Goma* and pay off our porters.

Men were welding pipes beside oil-tanks on the quay. Among large cranes on rails, *Les Titans Belges*, was a small one with a wooden cab, supplied in the 1940s by Stothert & Pitt Ltd., Bath, England. Loud last boardings and transactions continued as, on time, at noon, the *Goma* edged out. Goods and money were thrown, men leapt between boat and quay, then swam, then only *pirogues* could reach us, and shouts of farewell. Beery water frothed. Two barges were shunted and lashed side by side at the *Goma*'s bow. Police from a launch boarded, departed, re-boarded, searching and checking, as people rushed to find pitches on the barges and spread their cloths, padlocked trunks, utensils and trade-goods. We shoved at the river's weight, through flotillas of water-hyacinth, past the wrecks on their grassy sandbank; Île Bamu's long shoreline of palms lay way off towards the horizon. Way beyond, on the Congo side near our exit from the Pool, white cliffs shone. In 1903 Casement noted:

> Hippo downstream. Saw three pelicans feeding — close to us. Also saw a beautiful Egyptian ibis, Black body, white wings — a lovely fellow in full flight over us for his Home in the woods below Dover cliffs — white-winged too!

While Gide observed in 1926:

> There are counter-currents, strange vortices and back-flows shown up by the islets of greenery in their wake. These islets are sometimes

enormous; the settlers amuse themselves by calling them "Portuguese concessions".

I gazed into the golden eyes of the water-hyacinth's pale violet flowers. Gide did not; with lily-like leaves and air-filled stems, it was introduced from tropical America by an anonymous donor in the 'Fifties, and has spread aggressively ever since. It is still called *Congo na sika* — new thing on the Congo.

In the tatty saloon we ate boiled potatoes, steak, and onion sauce off a white tablecloth. The powerful freighter *Lubumbashi* drew alongside and transferred sacks of supplies to our kitchen stores. The engine-room deck was slippery with oil, but men from the barges scooped up all the spilt rice they could from it, and from our rusty deck above. Two cabins astern of us a *commerçante* struggled to get baskets through the deck gate, into her cabin or on to its roof below the wooden awning. She was surprised and thankful when I helped. The sun, and its path on the Pool, made an inverted crimson exclamation-mark. The great waters were mother-of-pearl, flexing, lilac pink and opalescent green. A glowing shack stood on the bank, with long poles leaning on the grass roof, criss-cross at the ridge. Before this spiky dwelling a boy rode, unmoving, in a dug-out. Far across the vastness, many slight canoes were paddling into dusk.

As the horizon vanished to port, the bank to starboard grew higher. The boat's searchlight picked out trees and way-marks; moths and mosquitoes seemed to fluoresce in the swathe it cut through darkness. The engine-room lights whitened the water-hyacinth and cast huge men's shadows on the water. On deck a Muslim prostrated himself on his mat. The bank disappeared; a tributary ran incommunicado into the night, but there were lights above; it was the N'Sele river, and the Presidential Domain where MPR Congresses, held in luxury, point Zaïre's path and where a satellite communications station keeps her in touch with the world. I had never felt so out of touch, or so in touch with the immediate. Riding alongside us were two dug-outs getting a tow. The larger had an outboard motor and a heap of sand to weigh the propeller into the water; in it men undressed and washed with scrupulous modesty; they shrouded themselves in white cloths and lay down in the bottom, like corpses in a coffin. I could have stood on deck all night and watched the darkness go by, but I'd have been bitten to death.

I try to fix the holes in the netting at the two small windows and the vent in the wooden roof of our cabin. The walls and floor are iron, rusted, stained and still retaining the day's heat. It is a small oven smelling of rats' piss. On our sagging cots the sheets are clean, and we hang up mosquito-nets for safety. There are two washbasins; a tap on each gives out tea-coloured river-water or nothing at all. We take off our sandals and practise beating hell out of enormous ruddy-black cockroaches that sprint beneath the beds. They explode like custard-bombs under our assault. We lie naked under the nets and sweat. The engines throb. We shudder. The engines slow. Shouts and bells as soundings are taken. The engines grind faster. Slower. Shouts and bells. On and on through the night. We were strongly advised to go first class or *de luxe*. We are going first class.

A small sound nags at my ears. In my torch-beam a grey-and-white rat is prospecting among our luggage and pausing to wash itself. Feeling very naked, I give it the run-around and find the hole by which I think it has escaped. I plug it, but it hasn't. As we lie, sweating, it climbs the rags of curtains at the window. It panics, I chase it around our trap. At last, I think it's gone. I plug the hole again. It's not the rat, so much as the soundings and slowings, the stories we have heard of wreckings, of people grounded until they starve, that wear Noëlle down. I sleep now, but for her the darkness seems to outlast its appointed twelve-hour span.

In that darkness, the *Goma* with its antenna of light feels its way out of the Pool. She passes the tributary, the "black river" at the mouth of which, Casement noted, "Rabinek died, 1st Sept. 1901 — the day I left Congo for Loanda I thought the last time." Gustave-Marie Rabinek, an Austrian Jew who had been in Khartoum with General Gordon, had been nursed through rheumatic fever by my great-aunt Grace Crawford at Luanza on far-off Lake Mweru. The document by which the Belgians granted him the rights to all the rubber in Katanga was witnessed by Dan Crawford. The way his monopoly was broken became a *cause célèbre* in England, for Rabinek was arrested aboard a British steamer on Lake Mweru. He smuggled a letter out, hinting that he did not expect to reach the appeal-court in Boma alive. His long last voyage ended too soon, as predicted. To Noëlle, in the noisy noisome blackness, our eventual destination, Lake Mweru, seems very much more than two thousand miles away.

At first light I could see both banks of the river, the first rocky outcrops on the Congo side, on the Zaïre side the first villages. Wrapped in a towel, the Agent Administratif à Bord rebuked me for taking photographs. Didn't I know it was illegal to photograph the river? It's the State border almost as far as the equator. Strategic targets must not be photographed. Of course, a permit might be arranged. A few minutes later, I emerged from his dim cabin with a piece of paper in exchange for a pile of paper money. Mist made everything pastel, held the day's colour in reserve, the sun pale gold on the water. The first smoke seeped from village kitchens below dark wooded slopes and the parchment-coloured hills of the savanna. Occasional trees burst with orange or pink blossom. Each mud-and-grass house and kitchen stood in a *lopango* or plot of beaten earth. Palisaded gardens thrived above inlets marked by crosses or diamond-shaped signs. Dug-outs lay there half-hidden, or put out with parcels of *kwanga* — manioc bread — wrapped and cooked in canna leaves.

The paddlers stood in their canoes upriver, waiting to pounce. As the boat neared, they judged their moment and paddled strongly in, tossed by the bow-wave, stroked aggressively to keep the boat within reach, then grabbed for the lower-deck rails and hung on grimly, dragged through water, until they made fast with liana-rope. They bailed madly to keep their cargo clear of the water they had shipped. Folk from the barges bartered for *kwanga*, and spread goods on the open decks or under improvised shelters of cloth or plastic sheet: onions, ginger-root, chilli peppers, heaps of rice, salt and sugar, and kerosene lamps made from recycled tins. With larger tins on strings they drew water from the river's surface. As the sun lifted higher above the savanna it was incandescent orange. Mists rose, unveiling brand-new colours, new beginnings, virgin water, virgin territory.

It does feel like that. That old romantic ecstasy. Noëlle was not so ecstatic. She had gut and bladder pains. With our camping gas, which we bought at SEDEC in Kinshasa, we boiled a lot of water and filtered it with our small pump filter. I ordered soda-water from the steward so that Noëlle could drink something alkaline. Waiting for him on deck, I put on sunglasses against the glare. Men by the saloon and on the barges ironed shirts and trousers with big flat irons full of glowing charcoal. Laundered cloths dried on the steel decks. A dug-out moored alongside; in it a ghetto-blaster, silent, and smoked fish sold by a rangy lad in yellow trousers and an orange Michael Jackson T-shirt. Suddenly I thought, will the steward recognize me in dark glasses? Then remembered I was the only white man on board. We laughed about that. Noëlle drank soda-water, but could not really enjoy the only three-course meal of the whole river journey: a sort of cabbage soup, beef stew with rice, and tinned fruit salad. We tried to shade the windows and door, while keeping what little air that moved moving. Noëlle dozed in the heat. On the shady side of the boat, two women slept together on a mat, turning in unison. Water-hyacinth and papyrus sailed past. One heathy hill followed another, lapping, overlapping. Rife fingers of trees, grass and reeds poked into the river. It was not yet the impenetrable forest I'd imagined.

At 2 o'clock we passed an elegant villa and, soon afterwards, a village and the glistening white but broken-backed wreck of a river-boat slumped in the shallows. At 3, everyone roused from their cabins as we mated noisily with our sister ship the *Gundji*. The dug-outs we towed abandoned their moorings to avoid being crushed as the boats clashed with the clamour of greetings and mutual trade. We parted and made upriver towards Kwamouth where the *Gundji* would branch off on the mighty Kasai. At 5 o'clock, the river broadened and we skirted an island for the first time since the Pool.

The second Congo notebook of the apprentice river-boat captain Conrad is concerned only with details of navigation:

> When about the middle of the open snatch steer right across to clear Ganchu's Point. Pass the point cautiously. Stones. . . . Sandbank always covered in the bight. . . . The landing must be approached cautiously on account of stones and snags. . . .

But on the Zaïrian bank lies Mswata from which Conrad brought back "the lightest part of the loot I carried off from Central Africa", the story *An Outpost of Progress*, written in 1896, three years before *Heart of Darkness*. "All the bitterness of those days, all my puzzled wonder as to the meaning of all I saw — all my indignation at masquerading philanthropy — have been with me, while I wrote." At Mswata, Stanley had palavered to some purpose with the chiefs Gobila, Gandelay and Ganchu. He left Lieutenant Janssen there to establish a station. Conrad's agents Kayerts and Carlier do not have Janssen's experience. They patronize Gobila and alienate him by inviting a slave-raid; he leaves them alone, without friendship or food; Kayerts shoots Carlier and hangs himself. When their superior — Conrad must have been thinking of Delcommune — finds them, Kayerts is "putting out a swollen tongue at his Managing Director". As Conrad says:

> Few men realise that their life, the very essence of their character, their capabilities and their audacities, are only the expression of their belief in the safety of their surroundings . . . the contact with pure unmitigated

savagery, with primitive nature and primitive man, brings sudden and profound trouble into the heart.

In his story *N'Gobila des Mswata*, Paul Lomami Tshimbamba makes the chief a hero who will not submit to *Bula Matari* and his lackeys, "black strangers". He annihilates them by starvation, clearly solving the difficult equation of dependency. Lomami concludes, "Here the role of the narrator stops, the eternal liar, to whom falls the atavistic mission of peddling and perpetuating the legends of the soil." Conrad says of his own cathartic tale: "For a moment I fancied myself a new man — a most exciting illusion," and naïvely adds, "it is true enough in its essentials. The sustained invention of a really telling lie demands a talent which I do not possess."

The truth is that, as we passed between Ganchu's Point and N'Gobila's Mswata, a high wind got up. The broadening river became choppy and lightning tore down the darkening sky behind us and to the west, or flickered on and off like an electrical filament. Distant beaches were blonde streaks between angry grey water and threatening sky. The truth is that, in July 1883, a gale blew up here. Lieutenant Janssen had helped Abbé Guyot to found the first upriver Catholic station at the mouth of the Kasai, and was bringing him down to Mswata by canoe when the storm struck. Eleven Congolese and both whites were drowned. I could see rocks and caves on the nearer shore and lightning flying upwards like fireworks. Noëlle made it to the saloon for an omelette, then went to bed. I talked to a biology student who wanted a scholarship to England. His father had been a Baptist pastor, but converted to Kimbanguism. He assured me he was still a proper Protestant. I drank beer with an ONATRA policeman called Teri. The ranch we were passing was smart, he said, owned by a Zaïrian colonel who employed three Portuguese to run his cattle. "Are you enjoying your trip?" he asked, looking concerned. "Yes," I said. "Why?!" he responded, "This is a very bad boat."

Well, I'm not thrilled with the loud-mouth big-shot who dines at the next table and studiously ignores us; nor with the stinking stained latrines whose floors swill with muck; but the crew are kind, the passengers mostly friendly and the river is, well, breathtaking. Here are the lighted bungalows of Kwamouth, the lights of a modest promenade, the canoes putting out in black water; the Kasai, in daylight, is brick-red this side where the waters from Bandundu and Ilebo empty and, where the waters flow along the north bank from Lac Mai Ndombe, indigo. But I won't see it. We pause, and then press on a short way before burying our nose in the vegetation of the bank.

The engines quieten; just revs enough to light the boat. The barges nestle beneath trees struck by moonlight. The storm has passed.

Teri explains that in the darkness we will not risk the dangerous rocks ahead. This is mixed news for Noëlle who, with pain and sickness and lack of sleep, has re-discovered her fear of water in a big way. To stop is good, but the rocks loom. She feels she can't go on. Should I continue without her? How would she get back? We are in anguish. Should we abandon the trip? What if her kidneys are implicated? Better to press on to Bolobo and a doctor. She, a more seasoned traveller than I, is filled with shame, but more with horror. My turn will come, but for now it is she who wants to die. The seductive river has brought "sudden and profound trouble into the heart". I'm torn, utterly, between her suffering and my own enchantment. At least there is relative silence. Sleep may come. Mosquitoes storm the deck-lights. Men moving past the bright engine-room play grotesque shadow-puppetry on the foliage. Water laps. Tears flow.

VII

A MUDDY HOLE

These meddlesome American missionaries! these frank British consuls! these blabbing Belgian-born traitor officials! — those tiresome parrots are always talking. . . . And that British consul, Mr. Casement, is just like them. He gets hold of a *diary which had been kept by one of my government officers*, and . . . is so lacking in delicacy and refinement as to print passages from it.

MARK TWAIN *King Leopold's Soliloquy*

B.M.S. Bolobo is a regular town — lots of people there . . . Called on Miss de Hailes at her Hospital in afternoon. She complains of State exactions bitterly upon the people. Went to the Clarkes in the evening a blessed gathering — all silent & all diligently damned . . . Basokoo splendid types. Two magnificent . . . At State beach photoed pier & Loango — about 9"

ROGER CASEMENT *Diary entries July 1903*

Sleep had done Noëlle some good. She smiled bravely and shut her eyes once more. I was in turmoil, but excited. Even if we had to cut our journey short at Bolobo, today we'd pass Tshumbiri, the village where agent Klein, Kurtz in *Heart of Darkness*, was buried in a muddy hole. The grave of a great white myth.

On 18th July 1890, while Conrad was recuperating at Manyanga, the *Florida*, which he was due to command, grounded and almost broke her back on rocks near Mswata. She was towed to Kinshasa by a fifteen-ton wood-burning stern-wheeler, the *Roi des Belges*. In August, the *Roi des Belges* steamed upriver once more, with the manager Delcommune, three agents, an engineer and Captains

Conrad and Koch aboard. Ludwig Koch must have pointed out the place near Kwamouth where his friend and fellow Dane, Johannes Freiesleben, was buried. He must also have shewn Conrad the village of Tshumbiri where Freiesleben had been killed on 29th January 1890. Conrad was Freiesleben's replacement.

I stood at the stern rail watching the wake unfurl into a dull, misty morning. Terns swooped and climbed above it, almost stalling in the *Goma*'s back-draught, almost brushing my nose. I checked on Noëlle who was catching up on sleep. Music lured me to the bow. On the biggest barge, a choir formed around the flag-pole; as one man led with the words of the National Anthem, the rest swayed and clapped, then joined him in magnificent rich harmony, "Forward! proud and full of dignity, a great people, forever free." The flag climbed into the heavy air:

> Tricolor, inflame us with sacred fire
> To build our ever lovelier country
> About the River Majesty . . .
>
> Emblem waving in the breeze, revive the ideal
> that binds us to our ancestors, our children,
> Peace, Justice, and Work. . . .

The song brought me near to tears. It was not the words. It was being with this music in the middle of this river, approaching a crucial goal. It dissolved the strain of the days and nights. I was alive here. I took my account of it back to Noëlle to revive her a little. I ate a breakfast of ham and bread and tea. Loud-mouth from *de-luxe*, with his beer-belly and his gold jewellery, didn't bother me; in fact, he asked after Noëlle.

The river grew broader. Flying the Congo flag, the enormous steamer *Brazzaville* bored downriver. Rival patriotic shouts were exchanged, acquiescing to the notion of statehood, inky lines drawn on now-dusty papers in Berlin in 1885, in Brussels and Paris. A line on a map split tribes once united by a river.

First signs of Tshumbiri were fishermen who came downstream and joined us to sell fish; they'd get a tow upriver and then go home with the current. Silver-pink scales glittered, amongst furled nets with balsa floats and stone weights, in the bottoms of dug-outs. The fishermen argued vehemently, but it's a buyer's market. Men and women shouted, brandished notes over the lower rails, and threw rags on to the fine fish they claimed. I had prayed that we should not pass Tshumbiri at night. Now, in full sun, here it was, hills rising behind it, a landmark on my map. People stood by rocks at the bank, or washed at bathing-places; set back a little was a town of mud-brick and grass roofs, with public buildings of cement and corrugated iron. The biology student pointed out the *Zone* — government shacks — with flag flying, the school, the Baptist church, the pastor's house. I scanned the ground for the small graveyard. I could not see it.

At least the town was intact. Not so, in Conrad's time. In January 1890, Johannes Freiesleben had landed from the *Florida*. He had greeted one of the chief's wives and given her child two brass rods, the currency of the time. Grenfell noted: "The chief saw nothing but bad in the gift and got angry and sent the woman back." Freiesleben saw no reason to retract it. Palaver became argument, the chief was knocked down, and his son shot the captain in the guts. The engineer pushed off at full steam leaving his captain dying. Slippers, clothes and watch found ready owners. His hair was cut off and woven into a fringe around his face. His hands and feet were severed.

Marlow says that Fresleven died in a squabble over two black hens; "he probably felt the need at last of asserting his self-respect in some way. Therefore he whacked the old nigger mercilessly," and the chief's son speared him between the shoulder-blades. Marlow met his predecessor: "the grass growing through his ribs was tall enough to hide his bones. They were all there. The supernatural being had not been touched. . . ." Conrad did not meet Freiesleben, whose mutilated remains were collected by the punitive force that, in March, burnt Tshumbiri. He was buried at the mouth of the Kasai with military honours. Of the blackened village Marlow comments, "A calamity had come to it, sure enough." I saw an unburnt town, but could not pick out the graveyard. The boats don't stop there any more. I thought that huts and trees under a hill would be the last I'd see of it.

Things change after Tshumbiri. The backdrop of sandy hills becomes higher, stonier. The deep river, with treacherous reefs, doubles its breadth and grows shallow, insidious with sandbanks. What Grenfell called Lone Island presages the myriad islands to come. What seem to be shores are islands, what appear to be hills are trees thickened by haze. Between these illusions, there are real hills on far horizons. Against them the islands seem to shift. "Portuguese concessions" of water-hyacinth and papyrus do move, and among them a floating island of logs, inhabited by people and chickens, shunted downriver from the Central African Republic by an asthmatic *petit-pousseur*.

Often we slowed to negotiate sandbanks. There was much trading with dug-outs that still reached us. The barges, like huge shop-counters, steadily offloaded soap, cloth, T-shirts and sugar. A scuffle on a barge became a chase, a scrum of shouts and blows, "*Voleur! Voleur!*", and two men struggling into their canoes with broken heads. Both paddled hard to escape the wake, then stood in midriver, disgraced and defiant, with blood running down their arms and paddles, muddying the water. They diminished and vanished like jetsam among the islands.

We had no idea that there was a nurse on the boat. Loud-mouth, in his little blue shorts and his straining yellow shirt, went to fetch him. He visited Noëlle, with papaverine and an immaculate bedside manner, no charge. She slept and steadily improved during the afternoon. I slept too. It is hard now to distinguish the dreams and the river. I think the river dreamed us. There was a shifting, sliding water-scape, and us at its centre watching ourselves. There was troubled water over sandbanks, V-shaped ripples opening from hidden snags, surging wake, cold *Primus* beer in cloudy glasses, a hot breeze struggling to stir the heavy foliage of cottonwood, twisting calamus and feathery palms; there was crimson blossom flickering in the canopy, and flecks of blood on the decks. There was a shot. It was getting dark. Just aft of the kitchen a crowd surrounded a man sitting on a trunk. Another thief, they said, shot in the head. The bullet had winged his scalp. While the nurse swathed him with a turban of white bandages, ONATRA policemen stood by. He would not escape.

We moored at Litimba: once heavily wooded, the first of a chain of villages that used to stretch beyond Bolobo, now a Commissaire's timber-yard. Rocks in the channel ahead were not to be chanced at night. Could we send a message to Bolobo? On the wooden awning above the cabins, Noëlle negotiated with the captain. Wearing a white *dashiki* of *broderie anglaise*, he sat on a deckchair before a crescent of women. They giggled; frogs croaked. He received us in the cool of his court under a high moon and stars. He and his chief wife spoke fair French. He summoned a runner who, for 100 zaïres, would take our note. Deferentially he accepted both money and message and disappeared. Downstairs, blood seeped darkly through the thief's bandages. The hot cabin drummed with the generators below. Teri's friend had lost a gold medallion; with my torch the three of us searched decks and scuppers, round and round, with no success.

On waking, the most magnificent spectacle. The sun rises as we enter the pool at Bolobo. On the immense broadening sheet of water, not a wrinkle, not a light bruising able even slightly to tarnish its surface; it is an unbroken shell where the purest reflection of the pure sky laughed. To the east some long clouds that the sun crimsoned. . . .

The prose gets purple but, at five-thirty in the morning, André Gide is right. We begin to pass Bolobo town, the *Zone*, the mission, more town, until we stop offshore. We heave rucksacks down into a dug-out full of plantains. The bandaged thief has jumped ship overnight. Soldiers board the boat in a rush. They were firing across the river yesterday. "Washing our guns," they said, "since there has not been a war recently".

We climb over the rail and down into the dug-out, shakily. Deftly, with a minimum of paddle-play, our boatman reverses out of the ruck and strokes us shorewards. Midway, we meet a canoe carrying a white nurse and a black pastor, Joan Parker and Lunkebila Kanda. The runner reached them. They step in with us. On *terra firma* we greet them properly among a fascinated crowd. Lunkebila humps Noëlle's rucksack. Now we are in Africa; not wide-eyed in the city or, on the boat, gliding through my dream, Noëlle's nightmare. Grasses catch at us, heavy with dew like night-sweat. Like fever, early morning mist and smoke lift sluggishly from the township.

I stumble on a root, fall on my hands. *Teneo te, Africa*. A cock crows, a guinea-fowl screams. Beside a dovecote on stilts, doves shift and turn like so many weather-cocks on the ridge of a grass roof. The house's mud walls have been eroded by rains and rubbed by goats until its wattle ribs show through. Children run between houses crying "*Mindele, mindele!*" — Whites, Whites! Bolder ones breast thin hedges that border each plot and greet us, "*Mindele mbote*". Grasshoppers click and scrape in every register, drums insist Africa, Africa, Africa, and wailing — a tidal ululation breaking antiphonally on an unseen shore — tells of two deaths in the night. Women crowd around the huts where the dead lie; their upraised voices mourn and implicitly deny responsibility, *ndoki*, sorcery. They identify with the loss.

The Lingala word *lilaka* means both a mourner and a corpse prepared for obsequies. In the past the identification could be more exact: a big man's wives and slaves were buried with him. Holman Bentley and George Grenfell tell how eight people were sacrificed for Chief Ibaka's funeral here in April 1889. Small pigs scuttled around wooden palisades that defend gardens. Sheep, dun-coloured and coarse-haired, rustled the parchment-like tatters of banana trees' lower fronds; higher, among the broad and long green leaves, fruit shivered heavily, strings of yellowing tusks finished off with a pendant of deep purple and a tassel of black. The track followed the riverbank once more, beside houses of brick or concrete with corrugated roofs, *pai-pai* and mango trees.

We passed under the canopy of an ancient tree whose fibrous trunk marked the boundary between the Moye and Bobangi towns of Bolobo. Roots like gnarled lace clutched at sandy ground. Not far behind it stood the derelict shell of George Grenfell's second Bolobo house, deliberately built, in 1894, on the fighting-ground. This was the spot where palavers took place between the tribes, where mutual law-making was sealed by sacrifice. A slave's arms and legs were broken before he was buried up to his neck. Digging a post-hole for this house, they found just such a vertical skeleton. We walked a simple path; in the river, women washed clothes on an upturned dug-out and soaped themselves white; a man watered bean plants in his garden behind a palisade of twigs; but I felt, at once, the depth of this soil, the depth of these eyes, the history in the blood.

Down there, cadavers of the ancestors, swathed massively in layers of cloth, rest on the knees of slaves and wives. Down there are the entrails of accused sorcerers tried by ordeal with poison from the shrub *Strychnos*, their gall bladders scrutinized for symptoms of *ndoki*. Inside a hut that crumbled long ago, a corpse stinks because the head wife, who must go down with it, has run to hide in the Moye towns. It is a stench to provoke a war.

We walked on the brink of darkness. A woman climbed the bank with a shining galvanized bucket full of water on her head; she retied her *limputa* and greeted us, "*Mbote*"; she ascended the path that rainy seasons had turned into a gully, strewn with old paving and roots. We followed her a little way; her head was held high; the bucket glided, floated, gleaming in the shadows between the dark bulky green of mango trees. Here was Joan, the nurse's bungalow, with its small detached kitchen and its water tanks fed by guttering. There would be time for many words. We sat down to breakfast: *pai-pai* and grapefruit, home-baked bread, tinned margarine, local peanut butter and Joan's marmalade. It was utterly delicious.

We slept in the doctor's house. The doctor was on furlough. The house had just been broken into, even though it was a squat for Randy, a muscular Peace Corps worker from Wisconsin. We walked down the riverbank to the *Zone*, on the site of the old State Post, to register our arrival. We climbed broken-down steps into a tiny bare brick office where, after sitting a long time on a thin plank, breathing the smell of bat-droppings, we surrendered our passports. We located the Zaïrian stores and the *pharmacie* owned by a Portuguese widow recently married to a man who had another home and wife in Kinshasa. In the *wenze*, the daily market, we prospected stalls of cloths and clothes, cigarettes and pills, maize and manioc flour, brown sugar and peanuts sold by the glassful, bread and *kwanga*, smoked meats and fresh fish hounded by flies. Noëlle bought plastic sandals. We were grateful for the stallholders' smiles. Less so for the continual greetings chanted by our ungainly escort of children.

We greeted a greenish *guenon* monkey tied to a stall and examined a bizarre mixture of goods: cigarettes, eggs, safety-pins, cowrie shells, big cats' teeth, red feathers, the leg of a cock, fetishes. With a gruesome expression, their purveyor rubbed a pink stone above his eye, and smiled, suggesting a cure for headache or madness. Under a spreading tree a brick oven's open doorway flared, a furnace raked out and filled with fragrant dough. Back at the doctor's house we found Randy, triumphant at scaring off another thief. Nothing was missing. Randy camped among books and papers, stores for his *Santé Pour Tous* project, and body-building equipment made of scaffold poles and concrete blocks. His Peace Corps companion, Diane, was a feminist back home in San Francisco; out here she cooked, washed and ironed for Randy and, at night, discreetly abandoned her house up the hill for Randy's bed in the room next to ours. Now, she lit the black cast-iron Donnybridge stove, made in Dover, England; it stood four square on curved feet, 190 miles upriver from Dover Cliffs. There was food to prepare, water to boil and filter. She coaxed it. The house filled with choking woodsmoke.

I sat on the verandah, between cement pillars, and kept watch on the river: a kingdom of iridescent water, the distant ripple of Congo's hills, sandbanks colonized by fishermen's grass huts, dug-outs in the stream making downriver or, using the counter-current near the bank, paddling up and mooring just below the house; boys, tumbling in the water of the men's bathing-place, welcomed them. Yesterday, soldiers were shooting over the river. A week ago, Congo police in a fast boat swooped and picked up a Bolobo man accused of stealing wood from a timber-raft stranded on a sandbank. Soon, the Congolese would shoot four Zaïrian "spies" on an island out there. Tonight, two men stood in a dug-out, the paddler in the stern letting the craft drift as the man in the bow unleashed his net like a lasso.

Stately women walked the river path with bowls of produce, or climbed the bank balancing water on their heads. Each paused for an instant, to adjust her load beneath a magnificent Borassus palm. Its trunk rose like a swelling pillar. Swifts flew vertically up and down it, snapping at insects between earth and sky. Immaculate fans of foliage radiated lines of force in which the sun was caught, in which the river-scape cohered. It could have been the centre of the world.

A very old woman clambered on to the verandah, bent over a staff and an old brown plastic basket of jam-jars. I greeted her, or her greying, thinning scalp. Her dress, for all its rich pattern, was soiled and smelly. She grasped my hands and, lifting sightless eyes as far as she could to heaven, sang me a hymn in Lingala to the tune of *Auld Lang Syne*. She was begging for kerosene. Later, Joan introduced us. She was Mama Liyombe, born about the time George Grenfell first called here in 1884. She had known him and called him Tata Talatala. *Tala* means "to see" or "lamp"; *talatala* means "glass", "mirror" or "spectacles". Grenfell brought light here and was called Father Spectacles. Blind Mama Liyombe still saw him clearly and pinched the loose flesh of her forearm to tell me that his wife had the same colour skin as her. She was proud of that.

On his way upriver in May 1883, Stanley found that two of the men of Bolobo Station had been murdered by Chief Gatula. He blamed the white men — "unfledged Europeans fresh from their homes, brimful of intolerable conceits" — as much as the black.

> As the European will not relax his austerity, but will very readily explode his unspeakable passions, the aboriginal native does not care to venture into familiar life with the irascible being.

In July, the Station was burnt and Stanley's boats were fired upon. Stanley responded in kind, and sent for the Krupp gun from Leopoldville. The Bolobo chiefs were sobered by a demonstration of its power. By the end of the year the Station was again in ashes, fired by a dying man greedy for glory, and the Krupp's gun-carriage was in ashes. Of Bolobo in 1884, Grenfell wrote:

> There are in all eighty chiefs! The chief characteristics of Bolobo people appear to be drunkenness, immorality, and cruelty, out of each of which vices spring actions almost too fearful to describe.

They were still very hostile to whites in 1887; the *Peace*, with Holman Bentley's family aboard, was threatened; but Bentley showed the warriors his wife and his baby. They were invited ashore.

The baby was passed from hand to hand through the town until its white dress was reddened with camwood dye and blackened with soot. Whites were not unnatural beings. They mated and bred like men. Sir Harry Johnston wrote that "the Bentley baby practically created the Baptist mission station of Bolobo".

Grenfell installed James Showers, a native of the Cameroons, here in March 1888. On the fighting-ground between the Moye and Bobangi towns, he erected a small mat-covered school-house/chapel with walls made from the arrow-guards of the *Peace*. Grenfell made Bolobo his base. It was a home for his second wife Rose, a West Indian he had married in the Cameroons, and their children. One, Patience Grenfell, completed her education in England, but returned to teach here and at Yakusu. On the way downriver from there in March 1899, she developed blackwater fever and died two hours after reaching home. The shell of that home, with its two storeys, its attic rooms, its sagging roof and its collapsing balconies, is the subject of debate; it may not be long for this world. Patience's bones are safe enough, under a stone in the small missionary graveyard.

Randy returns from hospital. Grunting and groaning, he works out with his weights. Then he knots himself to meditate. Out here, the moon rises over the town and the sun gilds the river, then bleeds into it. Randy and I wade in at the men's bathing-place, just downriver from where dishes are scoured and fish gutted, and where Noëlle, Diane and Joan wash with the women. The water is murky mahogany which soap turns frothy coffee. Randy's physique looks grotesque among the lithe bodies, and we both look absurdly pale, but everyone enjoys themselves.

At 6.30 the hospital generator pumps light into the mission houses. Noëlle and I eat with Joan. The World Service of the BBC feeds us the 7 o'clock news. It is unreal. This small world, great world, is enough tonight. We descend to the doctor's house in thick darkness just before the generator shuts down at 9.30. We light oil-lamps and swat mosquitoes. Fire-flies, moths and bats dance in the living-room. Our film is in missionaries' fridges, our money is locked in Joan's cupboard, our bedroom has netting at the windows. There is a foam mattress on a high slatted base. We fall on to it, and sweat, and listen to frogs and crickets, distant drums and the pulse of music from the bar beside the *Zone*, until we fade.

We returned to the *Zone* to see the Big Man: an interview by committee, under Mobutu's portrait in a high blue office. Would I pass the test? Noëlle explained about my book. The Big Man returned our passports, smiled and said, "I am here to give you protection. If you have any trouble, come to me night or day." He was away four days later when a messenger grimly handed me a *convocation* from the *Sous-Commissaire du Zone*. Scenting trouble, Lunkebila came too. The man painstakingly entered every detail from our passports into a ledger. Then he asked for money. Lunkebila talked calmly, firmly. The man insisted. I agreed to pay, so long as I had an official receipt. The man said the bookkeeper was away. I said we'd pay when he returned. We left, and heard no more. Over coffee, Lunkebila explained how rarely officials get paid, how sorely they are tempted.

At church we were welcomed and, thanks to Joan's coaching, I made a short speech of greeting in Lingala. Four choirs competed in praise of God with complex rhythms and compelling harmonies, by turns swaying, standing, sitting, backed by an orchestra of drums, tambourines, double gongs, friction-drums, rattles, scrapers and an antelope horn. The collection was a dance to the pulpit for children, men and women in succession. Outside the hot, crowded church a man went swinging past, raving; his deep shouts and high-pitched screeches pierced me to the marrow. A woman paraded to the sound of bells at her back; she wore a crown of woven palm-fibres stuck with red feathers; her indelibly sad face, her arms and legs were covered in white spots applied by the *nganga* to win her husband back, or curse him.

She let us take her photograph at the hospital. There, what seemed like squalor passed for comfort and care. The State had taken the hospital over for years, then handed it back. Staff struggled to restock with drugs and re-establish standards amid peeling walls, pocked floors, battered beds. Pigs roamed around the shelter where relatives cooked food for their sick. Grass burned outside the dispensary. We heard how, in 1964 when the rebels were approaching Bolobo, soldiers had discarded their uniforms and moved in as patients, or fled across the river. In maternity a serene woman sat on a bed with the one survivor of triplets; its face was dusty pink, anointed with a pale stone; if that didn't work, she had baby cream and powder as well. We talked, and contributed to the bowl of money and string ordained by the ancestors to succour the spirits of multiple births. Outside we were greeted by an old man who, from a boy, had worked for the mission; an epileptic, he had fallen in the fire years ago and lost one arm. "If it wasn't for the missionaries," he said, "I wouldn't be here now."

In the old hospital here, Casement listened to complaints against the

State. I thought of his photographs, whether of atrocities or of beautiful men at the beach, and of the words Mark Twain put into King Leopold's mouth: "Then all of a sudden came the crash! That is to say, the incorruptible *kodak*. . . . The only witness . . . that I couldn't bribe." Grenfell and Casement talked late into the night of 22nd July 1903, "Fire at our feet to keep mosquitoes off," and again at dawn. Grenfell was a member of Leopold's 1896 Commission for the Protection of Natives, but realized its inadequacy from the start:

> If the Authorities are really in earnest about rectifying abuses they can do it without a Commission of Missionaries, and if they are not . . . it will require a Commission with a very different constitution. . . . Not one of the Commissioners resides in the districts where the cruelties are re- ported! I think I am nearest and I am two hundred miles away!

His very worst fears were confirmed by Casement's findings. Before H.M. Consul steamed away in the early morning, Grenfell officially reported the birth of his daughter Caroline Mary in 1883, so that Casement could register it, twenty years late.

Upriver, downriver, and inland to the high rocks, we walked through the town on a web of sandy, grassy lanes. A man extolled the medicinal qualities of plants in his plot; a woman gave us a loofah from her tree; a man dug a pit in the sandy soil, four metres deep at twenty-five zaïres a metre, for a latrine which would be hidden by a palm-leaf shelter; a basket-maker squatted on a stool, his swift fingers making fine work of dark brown fibres; at a rough bench under a frangipani tree an ivory-worker turned out delicate armlets and necklaces with a vice, a fretsaw, a drill and a file; an ebony-carver sold us figures of fishermen, a string of beads, a pipe. We were welcomed into the luxury of an elder's house: corrugated roof, cement floor, locally made furniture and a paraffin fridge. We entered the small darkness of a bare hut, with a mud floor and a filthy cloth screening off sleeping-quarters, where a withered mama with pendulous breasts fingered delicious peanut butter from an old spoon into our margarine tin. Men lounged in chairs beneath trees. Women grated and pounded manioc in wooden utensils, and plucked grass from their roofs to light fires.

Thursdays were for *salongo*, communal work. Those who couldn't buy themselves off slashed at grass, cleared débris, brushed the streets. Noëlle helped Joan mark nursing examination papers in French. I worked on the fridge until it no longer emitted plumes of black smoke. With a pliant branch, I rodded blocked drains that swarmed with huge red cockroaches. We found an unusual number of people with long knives crowding the stores.

Père Charles showed us round the Lazariste mission: the big generator, the wood-shop, the manioc-mill where whitened men worked in a powdery haze feeding noisy green machines, while folk queued for their flour. He invited us back for a meal, so one dark night after rain, we picked our way between puddles and invisible people towards a supper of cheese, sardines, bread, jam and bananas. Père Charles doffed his beret and tugged at his greying beard; he was a faithful man with no illusions, but he looked hard-used; he had suffered a *crise de malaria* the day before, and refused young Père Yolek's Polish vodka. He smoked cigarette after cigarette and talked of popular Catholic Lingala *versus* Protestant Lingala, older and rich in Bobangi. He spoke of the astounding growth of the church, of Zaïre as the potential leader of spiritual revival in Africa.

We visited the bar by the *Zone* and sat under trees within high white walls. We drank Primus, danced on a raised concrete floor, and watched the men, with slight and profound motions, signal their intentions towards the *bandumba* or *femmes libres*. Sometimes men danced with men, and sometimes with themselves, admiring their style in a full-length mirror hung on a pillar for that purpose. Randy talked glumly of the trade in *femmes libres'* "compulsory" venereal health certificates. We felt our way deep into town to an altogether dimmer bar under leaning palms; there they strummed the rough bottles with bottle-tops; regrettably, in our honour, they substituted French pop for Kinshasa music. Then the generator ran out of diesel and the lights went down. Bottle-music was all there was to dance to.

I had itchy feet, not for dancing, but because a jigger was buried between my toes. Joan gouged out the egg-sac with a needle; the large crater healed incredibly fast. Casement never attended one of Joan's singing, dancing bible-studies. No silence or sense of diligent damnation there. Student nurses, VD and abortion cases among them, sang of divorcing the Devil and marrying Christ; then with Joan — *mama na biso*, our mother — we all danced out into the moonlit garden. That night a child, hospitalized for a lumbar puncture, was spirited away to the *nganga*. A woman died, and wailing and drumming beat at our ears.

One morning I carried some sweet manioc — *mondele mpako*, white man's tax — up to the house of Simon, a young English missionary. Blind Theodore was playing his mouth organ. A man with a withered arm greeted me with his left hand. We were preparing for a feast at which we'd meet two of the local elders, one of them Bolobo's historian. Simon was laying on a spread of fish-stew, *kwanga* (manioc-bread), *mpondu* (manioc leaves like spinach), *likemba* (fried plantain), rice, sweet potato and pineapple. He greeted me with the news that two other guests, Ndebe and Omango, planned to go down to Tshumbiri at the weekend in an outboard-motor-powered canoe. Would we like to go too? Would we?!

Four mornings later, Noëlle and I were ready at eight. Niko, the boatman, had fixed the motor into the slot in the rear lip of the dug-out and loaded reserve tanks. There was a high wind; pied crows blew from palm to flailing palm. The river was choppy. There were paddles in the bottom of the canoe in case the motor failed. Ndebe, Omango and Simon took their time. Soon after ten, we loaded our gear and, sitting in line on five stools with Niko standing astern, launched out into the river.

Each wave we slap throws up spray and soaks us. The dye from Noëlle's new *limputa* stains her legs green. From down here, at water-level, the horizon recedes even more dramatically than it had from the boat: shifting islands, water-hyacinth, reeds, grass, trees, like incidental scenery in a steely world of water. We are a speck of flotsam. We pass Litimba's timber-yard and crooked crane, rocky headlands heavy with trees, walls of reeds with tiny inlets, sometimes marked by stakes, through which dug-outs appear and disappear, making to or from half-hidden houses. Now we can see whole settlements of huts on stilts, with tall frames for drying nets and fish and manioc; now, low sandstone cliffs, baked earth with a tree or two and huts with woven screens; now, beaches and bathing-places, men, women, clothes on rocks. The wind drops. Omango cracks two coconuts together and drains them over the side. He splits them in his hand with a keen machete and shares the succulent white flesh between us. Refreshed, we seem to be floating past English parkland, studded with great trees and backed by greige hills. We leave behind the tall white buoy that marks the end of the upriver islands, and see our destination, Tshumbiri, spread out on the slopes.

At a quarter to one we disembark. The reception committee, that was ready for us at ten, rapidly re-assembles. The welcome is fulsome. Officials at the *Zone* cannot see us because the Presidential boat is imminent. We process up to the pastor's house, a stylish brick building abandoned by the American Baptist mission in the 1930s. From a circular path around a bed of shrubs, a stairway climbs to the verandah. There, men hold back a horde of boys and girls while a choir sings to us. The pastor, frail and wracked with fever, has risen to greet us but, unknown to us, soon takes to his bed in the rear of the house and relapses into sweats and incontinence.

We are marched by our hosts and a hundred children in a cloud of dust up the hill behind the village. We survey the place celebrated, justly, by Stanley for its beautiful women, and remembered for its roguish chief with his charms, his snuff, his peace-pipe and two score wives weighed down with brass collars. Down there, beside the gleaming river, Freiesleben was killed; the village was a punitive expedition's bonfire; the *Roi des Belges* paused overnight by charred ruins to inter Klein beside missionary graves. If Conrad was like Marlow, he remained on board. "The voice was gone. What else had been there? But I am of course aware that next day the pilgrims buried something in a muddy hole." For me, this poor village, where whites hardly come now, is haunted by the shade of Kurtz. It holds the dry bones of a potent myth. A helicopter zigzags over the river. From the hill-top we watch a fast white boat, with Mobutu on board, ascend the river and pass Tshumbiri without stopping.

Drumming shook the *Zone* office in which we faced two wary officials. Luckily, I recognized the soldier in attendance; on leave at Bolobo, he had walked around Grenfell's house with me, so I greeted him joyfully. The drumming ceased, passports were returned, and the men requested us to take their photographs. We snapped them, and the drummers and *animatrices*. If they couldn't dance for Mobutu, they wouldn't dance for us. They posed like serious sirens, until Noëlle enquired after their misery and they broke into great laughter. The officials sent the gift of a sheep up to the pastor's house. In the village, among tall cacti and drying manioc, a proud man presented us with an egg. He set up his camera, a small tea-chest with a hole, on a wooden tripod. He had no plates. From his mud house he brought a faded portrait he once took and the treasured lens. Beside him stood a girl in a silver lamé jacket; sadly exquisite she was, with coiled hair, voluptuous lips and a sensuous, mournful gaze; the infant at her back looked over her shoulder with the same deep eyes.

We gave the egg to the noble beauty who was our hostess. Beside a kitchen that was linked to the verandah by a gang-plank and flanked by sugar-cane, bananas and coffee trees, women pounded manioc; within its smoky interior they cooked *kwanga*, *fufu*, *mpondu*, rice and mutton. Inside the house, paint was peeling, plaster was falling and there was a faint smell of vomit. Black lathes dividing the high ceilings were punctuated by wasp-nests, sand-coloured volcanoes. For us there was an antique, mesh-sprung bedstead covered with woven mats, foam rubber and a bedspread. In the next room our host stood, beside an enamel bowl of water on the floor, holding a towel. Washed, we sat on an assortment of chairs and stools at a table almost covered by blue-check oilcloth and laid with remnants of European crockery, cutlery and glass. They wanted to make us feel at home. Niko, for one, tugged voraciously at the grey mass of *kwanga*. It had the taste of sour cheesy bread, but I found its glutinous texture hard to swallow. *Fufu* was lighter and whiter and more to my taste. The meal was good, with bowls of spring-water and grey coffee. We asked after the pastor and discovered how sick he was. The man in charge of the medical post here had sold off his stock of drugs: there wasn't an aspirin among four thousand people. If we'd known we'd have brought something. Noëlle dispensed tablets for dysentery, all we had with us.

Outside, some of our escort are still waiting. One little boy has a charm-string tied around his head; one youth wears a loose tweed jacket for a shirt, but his cheeks and temples are decorated with the parallel cicatrizations of the Bateke, though skin-carving was banned, despite authenticity, long before he was born. As it gets dark the children bid us goodnight, or simply drift away. The men gather. From the verandah I watch fire carried from hearth to hearth, silhouettes of people and huts, while a male-voice choir sings for us. They sing *us*. Deep, breathy, punchy bass to lyrical contra-tenor, the singers' pentatonic melodies and subtle harmonies weave their way amongst complex rhythms and pauses achieved with perfect *ensemble* whether their leader is swaying, dancing out front or sitting down with them. Song after song, the music grows around us like a twining thicket, a forest of sound in the night. It goes on and on, and persuades us we should be here. It is a gift, not a performance. It is being in music. "*Oh! Merci mingi, citoyens, merci mingi.*"

Our Lingala won't go the distance. We take the songs with us to the river. Ndebe says it is best to bathe in the dark to avoid an audience. *Mindele* washing would be an irresistible novelty. At every rut, Omango warns, "*Malembe, malembe*" — gently, gently. We wade down a stream and on to a small island at its mouth. Water-hyacinth is slimy underfoot. Warm water caresses our nakedness and cools the blood. Reflected stars ride the current. Downriver, a boat probes forward with its antenna of light. As we float, the air is alive with fireflies, the rushes at the bank are thick with them, their greenish lazy flickering.

★

The *nganga* greeted Sunday's dawn white-robed. We clambered up to a perilous lavatory seat, and washed in a bucket on a three-legged stool behind a woven screen in the half-darkness beyond the kitchen. Breakfast was grey coffee in a tureen, condensed milk, sugar, corned beef and bread. Still the *nganga* paced to and fro before his house, before his acolytes, as if disturbed by a persistent Christ, or by visiting *mindele*. Of "Chumbiri", in March 1877, Stanley wrote in his diary:

> A native accused of witchcraft was drowned according to doom today: arms tied behind, and a wooden gag in his mouth, thrown into a canoe and paddled into the river and tossed overboard. As he was tossed the executioner cried out to him: "If you are a Magician, cause this river to dry up and save yourself." After a few seconds he rose again and was carried down the stream about half a mile. A huge crocodile, fat with prey, followed him slowly and then rushed on him and we saw him no more.

Le fleuve runs on, though crocodiles have all but deserted the main river. *Nzambi* alone can dry it up. A boy climbed on to the verandah outside our room and picked two drumsticks, wound with wild rubber, from between the lips of the talking drum, the *lokole* there. He made a good noise on the hollowed trunk, announcing church, but could not talk the bitonal talk, the code phrases, the formal poetry spoken by the thick male lip and the thin female one. He banged it like any old tam-tam.

When Casement first came here in August 1887, the line of villages comprising Tshumbiri had a population of four or five thousand. But when the *P. Brugman* left him here for four days in July 1903, he was depressed to find no more than five hundred souls, abandoned sites, and the "State telegraph post in midst of old Chumbiri village — gone all — alas". In his report to the Foreign Office he noted that the remnant peoples of the riverine towns were required to keep the line and the telegraph road clear, though they found it hard to feed themselves far from home and had not been paid for a year; to provide wood for local wooding-posts, where steamers fuelled up; to furnish weekly supplies of goats and fowls, requisitioned by brutal means if necessary. Life and trade had withered. Canoe convoys to the Pool, of slaves, ivory, dried fish and other products, had been suppressed or taken over by white agents. The old slave-trade had disappeared, but all villagers were enslaved by the State.

Casement's gut reactions were confined to his diary:

> Glad to change clothes twice daily . . . I do not like Chumbiri at all, neither place nor climate . . . Soup boiled susu for change and custard . . .

Very glad to be leaving Chumbiri — chicken, chicken, custard, custard
every day — come Sunday. . . .

Nsusu is the Lingala word for "chicken". Between Tshumbiri and
Bolobo, on the *Henry Reed*, "We had boiled susu again for change, also
custard aboard." Always dismally ironic, that "for change". For the
change of vessel, he had the American Baptist, Arthur Billington, to
thank.

What change would Billington the founder see in Tshumbiri's
church? Or churches now, Catholics and Kimbanguists as well as
Baptists: no longer a few hard-won converts outfacing the *nganga* and
the *bakulu*. No white leaders. Women and boys carrying chairs on
their heads down to a packed brick church, choirs' songs pouring
from glassless arched windows, children dancing their collection up to
the front, followed by the men in crisp shirts and pressed trousers and,
lastly, the swaying crocodile of women in their most glorious *limputas*
and blouses or *libayas*, heaping up piles of dirty notes before the pulpit.
We were welcomed, and Mama Noëlle's name gets a laugh. Then,
after more hymns, Simon began to preach in fluent Lingala, provok-
ing more laughter, responses, deep sighs.

We creep out of the humid church into hot dry sun, on narrow paths
through acres of grass that *salongo* disciplines to ankle-height. Mango
trees cast islands of solid shadow. About 150 yards from the river,
small trees, gnarled stumps and squat white pillars mark a tiny
cemetery where a handful of stones remember missionaries. I cannot
see Klein's name. The Belgian authorities asked the mission to locate
and maintain his grave, but nothing much was done until long after
the whites had gone. For four years prior to Independence, the
Congolese pastor received four hundred francs every six months for
its upkeep. No longer. But here is "Jessie Ann — the beloved wife of
— Arthur Billington — May 31st 1889 — Aged 37 years — *Bwemba
Congo*. . . ."

Georges Klein's body found a resting-place, Conrad's "muddy
hole", not far from Jessie Billington's sixteen-month-old grave. His
mother sent a wreath, care of George Grenfell, Bolobo. Like the
flowers, the stones that marked it have gone. Is it on the left as you
look from the river, a slight mound just outside the graveyard? Or just
within it, beneath a squashed circle of rocks? Or is it on the right,
under a scattering of bricks in the grass beneath a *pakapaka*, "paddle-
wheel" or star-fruit tree? The elders palaver on our behalf, the boys
poke in the grass or suck at the fruits' yellow fins. All at once a green

snake starts at our feet, the boys shout, side-step, rain bricks down on it, and the one wearing shoes jumps and crushes it. Has the death of a snake cost the desecration of the relics of Klein's grave? No, the elders conclude, it is the first spot, not far from Jessie Billington's headstone, just out of bounds. I stand there on the barely perceptible mound. I want to shout the fiction out loud, "Mistah Kurtz — he dead!" But I keep quiet.

Ndebe and Omango are amused by my search for the unmarked grave of a man who never lived. D. H. Lawrence couldn't "forgive Conrad for being so sad and giving in". But Conrad was here, facing horrors that he could not quite transmute into literature. He confessed that, out of mental laziness, he had made Kurtz too symbolic. For mental laziness read pain. Facing that, he faltered. It is well that all white myths and histories for which the people have no use should vanish, as if flushed away by the rains. Klein's name is erased. The station moved uphill long ago, leaving the graveyard stranded in vacant land. The two-and-a-half-hour service has ended, and again we are quite surrounded by our curious escort. We all move off towards the pastor's house, where water and a towel and the midday meal await us. I whisper as I walk, "Mistah Kurtz — he dead."

VIII

A MOVEABLE EQUATOR

Slept well for two hours, but then lay awake curiously uneasy . . . imagining that distant voices among the leper houses meant danger. Lights flashed: I lost my torch and lay among illusions as thick and disagreeable as a DDT cloud. When at last I slept again I dreamt all the time of one person.

GRAHAM GREENE *Congo Journal*

She will be the last
to leave the swamp
dressed in white fibres
shod
with spurs of gold
from the python's kingdom
to be acclaimed
by the daughters of Africa. . . .
SÉBASTIEN BONTALA *L'Aurore du Trésor*

There is no chance of a quick escape from Tshumbiri. Casement was late leaving on the *Henry Reed*, because of a crewman's love-life: "Delayed in starting by the Infallible Cause of all Delay & Every Miscarriage since Eve first upset Adam's apple — curst Woman!" At our landing beach, women washed themselves, their daughters, clothes and cooking-pots beside an upturned whale-boat. Exchanges of gifts slowed us, then a speech, a song and a prayer. Our *pirogue* was low in the water because three extra men, a woman, her baby

and a chicken swaddled in leaves had asked for a lift to Bolobo; but
Niko kept close to the bank, and the river was mirror-like. Even so,
we felt the weight of it against us; sometimes water-hyacinth clogged the propeller and we drifted backwards until the outboard
roared. We branched off on what seemed like tributaries but were
just channels between islands and the bank's buoyant vegetation. It
was very hot. Acres of reeds oscillated languidly as our wake hit
them, the brilliant green sabres of multitudinous cavalry.

A sharp turn led up a reedy corridor to a small settlement where
friends of Ndebe lived: a family from Kinshasa, fishing for the
season, living in skeletal huts among palms and *pai-pai* trees, snug
against the afforested cliff. Ndebe wanted a talk, but everyone was
excited: the old man, the women, the children, a dozen dogs and
puppies, the goat, the chickens. Our epiphany had to be celebrated.
There was a shouting, barking, bleating, squawking commotion
over catching a chicken. The birds ran. Three sons deployed a
fishing-net. Their quarry flew up into the trees of the cliff. "They are
chickens and we are men," said the elder. "Should we not be able to
catch them?" The lads climbed the cliff, beat among the bushes. One
handsome black cock flew to a tall palm. A flung stick knocked it
down, stunned. As the old man tied its feet together, its red comb
began to quiver and it crowed wildly. Its captor, squatting, presented it to Niko and pronounced, "We Zaïrians must work." He
pinched his skin, "You *mindele* come from *Mpoto* where there is no
sun, and get burnt working for us." He pointed his chin at our tans,
"This is not your proper colour. But we need doctors and pastors.
So, *bongo*, if it were not for missionaries, should we not be as the
chicken, who needs no pastor and no doctor. . . ."

Ndebe needed a talk, but the chicken-chase had stolen our time:
we had to get home in something like daylight. Niko chose channels
least clogged with hyacinth and read the water for sandbanks and
snags. Now and then one of our chickens clucked, thrashed its wings
and almost made it into the water, miraculous water, blinding white
to the horizon between grey islands. Fishermen seemed to stand on it
and give back greetings. Pied kingfishers flashed above the surface
and white egrets came to rest. Hyacinth glowed lilac. Faces behind
me gleamed, singing. I passed back peanuts wrapped in a canna leaf.
We cut across the face of the water, overhauling rafts like shanty-
towns, a little nearer to Congo's conical hills, the dark rim of the
cauldron.

Kites wheeled above us. I had stood on Klein's bones; Kurtz lay upriver. Perched on a hyacinth raft, a metallic blue dragonfly and a small orange butterfly met us. How far had they ridden so far from either bank? They might have travelled from the Falls. A week ago, a century ago, they might have buzzed grass roofs of the Inner Station. Halfway between, Gide unfurled his butterfly net above darkening water. Darkening? He noted its ecstatic colour, mother-of-pearl shivering long after the crimson road sank. At my back they sang *When the Saints* in Lingala; I joined in, trumpeting, and drumming on the sides of the *pirogue*.

This was the way to travel. River versus road. One day we had driven south from Bolobo with Alan and Janice Brown, English missionaries, in a Land Rover equipped with spare diesel, drinking-water, spade, rope, winch. On a rutted mud track we bucked between trees, flame blossom, Hoya shrubs like giant jasmine, through sand, wet holes, across crude log bridges. Women on the six-mile walk home from their gardens, baskets on their backs stacked with manioc or firewood, ducked into tall grass, swamped in suffocating dust. Anthills like huge fungi, men carrying monkeys or felled stakes. Gardens of manioc at each stage of its three-years' growth. A long savanna detour to avoid major mud-holes amongst the trees. Litimba, with its mud-huts and machine-sheds, its generator, its crane and its broken band-saw over a pit; lack of maintenance, hulks of timber and of lorries, a parable of Zaïre, of paralysed riches. A ranch, shifty cattle in long grass, a village where a man crossed a stagnant stream with a bicycle shrouded in bananas.

At the ranch-house, an ex-forestry post, a shrivelled man showed us a tortoise he'd brought from the forest for the pot. The foreman picked us star-fruit, and I savoured the sharp sweet flesh, like orange and gooseberry, of its waxy fins. A silky-brown bull with black points and big horns feinted as if to charge, but we pushed past and risked returning on the main road. It was a causeway through forested marshland. Four-wheel drive and Alan's skill got us out of glutinous pits, through miry ruts that threatened to topple us. It was the dry season on the through route to Mushie and Kinshasa. In a dark wood we picked up a beautiful woman with a heavy load, while a toothless man on a bicycle plucked Hoya blossom for Janice and Noëlle.

All that had been inland. Now we glided through dusk, a chill wind populated by swifts. There was no moon; high, extravagant cirrus was the last light thing to die. We ploughed a dark furrow between darker islands of hyacinth. After Litimba's crane we held our breaths, knowing Niko had to negotiate *l'Escale d'Enfer*, the hidden rocks. Then there was a light, and all eleven of us sighed "Bolobo". Light became lights, bar and mission. We slid between men in the water, and our prow grounded gently in the mud of the fire-fly encrusted bank below the doctor's house.

We had missed Mobutu. He'd disembarked from his Japanese-built steamer and promised Bolobo a generator to light the whole town. He had invited *les blancs* aboard for drinks and dispensed money: twenty thousand zaïres to the Baptists, fifty thousand to the Catholics. He'd looked fit, not wasted by rumour's leukaemia, and at ease, having just despatched six Libyan-funded assassins.

Randy roared in, vaccines, condoms and machete strapped to the rack of his motorbike. He was mad because a microscope had been stolen from an outlying dispensary, and the nurses arrested. He took it out on his weights before going to the *Zone* with Dr Lusaisu to bail them out. He worried that they'd lose face. The people feared he'd close the unit. An old woman wanted the clinic moved from her house; her nephew — just back from exile for misdemeanours — was suspected. We went to bed, slept deeply.

Night and day we were tied to watching the river. Soon I slept light. Amid night-sounds of creatures, drums, and wailing, or during long sweaty love-making, I started at the throb of engines, grabbed trousers and sandals and ran to the bank. Usually it was a barge or a *petit-pousseur*, a Congo boat or an ONATRA one going down. Then I'd smoke a pipe, light a lamp, make tea, read about the madman who was chained to a mango tree near the hospital because he'd have demolished the brick buildings. Noëlle slept. Unlike her, I was badly bitten; shoulders, back, calves and ankles itched; my buttocks were lumpy and as blotched with red as the two hemispheres in the high days of Empire.

From the verandah I heard the plashing of night paddlers and the first nets being cast. Gusts of wind, crashing in the banana trees, died as the dark was diluted. Towards six, two men came to collect the Government doctor who was staying with us. The three of them had driven from Mushie the day before, six hours. I made breakfast. They said it would get colder and, didn't I know?, it was snowing in Kinshasa. Dr Mwemba smiled. Last night he had looked me in the eye and opined, with irrefutable authority, how hard it was for the *blanc* to understand the *noir*, for were not the African and European world-views irreconcilable?

The microscope was located over the river. The thief was brought home. When I went to the *Zone* to buy sugar and *pili-pili* in *le grand marché*, he had just been beaten and locked in a cell. The market-woman chased me with three zaïres' change I didn't know was due. Standing amongst heaps of forest leaves, padlocks, watchstraps, gourds, whitening creams and Trebor mints, I thanked her. Over the river, they expected ten thousand zaïres for the return of the microscope. There was much talking to get to the *mama na likambo*, "mother of the palaver".

We thought we might hear the end of it. We tired of false alarms and packing for nothing. A merchant who sold me a T-shirt and whisky said there'd be no boat for at least two days. Père Charles had no news from Kwamouth. Then, at dusk, I saw a boat. Alan said no, it was cargo. We sat down to eat. Lunkebila came hot-foot to say it was a passenger-boat for Mbandaka. We ran downhill and packed, said rushed, heartfelt farewells, leapt into Alan's Land Rover and piled into an overloaded dug-out at the "beach". It was dark and wet and we hung on, water lapping at our hands. Noëlle shook. We circled, waited, made for the boat, stepped unsteadily from canoe to canoe and, after hands from above grabbed our rucksacks, hauled ourselves up the side of a greasy barge. Lunkebila followed, and saw us settled. We'd miss him. There was no hurry, for this boat, the *Gundji*, carried a cargo of cement that Alan had given up for lost. It had ridden the river for eighteen months and took half the night to unload.

The *Gundji* was similar to the *Goma*, but better appointed. We were received with aggressive, boozy *bonhomie*. First-class was full, but we could have a *de-luxe* cabin for the same price, because there was a problem with its water. Yes, yes, we'd take it anyway. It had armchairs as well as beds, a bathroom, and air-conditioning that hummed. It felt like luxury, like cheating. I bailed out the bathroom floor into the bath, and installed a bowl under the incontinent pipe. Noëlle sprayed bed-frames to discourage the cockroaches that proces-sed along them. I sprayed for mosquitoes and shut the door tight. Fellow-passengers greeted us at the rail. Beyond the tedious unload-ing of cement, barge to *pirogue* to bank to lorry, beyond the deep darkness, we held on to luminous memories of Bolobo.

Twice, just upriver from here at Mabwa, we had swum with dear Joan. We'd walked through long grass, eight feet high and topped with plumes, toothed spirals, heads of gossamer. Under a tree bank before a carpet of water-hyacinth we'd baked yams in a camp-fire and beaten out the spreading flames with leaves. Up to our necks in soft water we'd watched passing traffic and Congo's far bank which seemed to move upstream. We baked in sun, while over there black clouds let down their drapes and lightning ripped them to tatters. Three kinds of kingfisher worked the water. The undercliff forest at our backs was an orchestra pit: weavers, sunbirds, wax-bills, hoopoes, white-tailed flycatchers, yellow-vented bulbuls. The trees, the air, fizzed with colour. A pair of blue-headed coucals, with buff breasts and rufous wings, mated on a branch, flaunting dark tails. Men beat out a tattoo, patching a split dug-out with metal; children with machetes chattered up the river-path; women came to meet the early catch, and mothers turned their babies' heads, for luck, to view the *mindele*. Fish nibbled our skin; one bit my nipple hard; a sharp-beaked bird snatched a fly off Noëlle's shoulder.

Chill morning. Many islands. Fishing-camps on stilts. Women on the barges fed their young from opulent breasts, long dugs. A fey, sad-eyed boy walked the deck; his bare legs, beneath a long grey-green gabardine, had all the balletic resignation of a pierrot. A wiry lad stood or sat all day, awkwardly, outside the *agent administratif*'s cabin; then we noticed that he was handcuffed to the rail. The suave *agent* himself, in his towel, his shorts, his snazzy pullover and slacks, his epauletted uniform, flaunted his ghetto-blaster and his status. Our neighbour, a Catholic planter with gold-rimmed spectacles and shabby black gentility, talked to us quietly: his Kimbanguiste wife, his acres of *pai-pai*, pineapples, coffee, hens, ducks and sheep on the Equator. The lugubrious steward Boniface, with his white mackintosh, his huge nose and occasional gleaming teeth, prowled about or anxiously played cards. Ingratiating youths begged water, money, books. A big mama sat at her cabin door, and, each time we greeted her and enquired after her health — "*Mama mbote, ojali malamu?*", grinned hugely, vibrated with mirth and babbled away in Lingala as if we understood every word.

Trade was brisk and voluble. On the barge *Bayaka*, a man and woman argued ferociously over the price of *kwanga*; they jostled, shouted, threatened; she raised a knife, he jumped into his *pirogue* and cast off, brandishing a stick; his mate, paralytic with laughter, tried to paddle him out of trouble. The afternoon was quieter but, as Gide wrote, "the countryside in its varied monotony remains so attractive that I can hardly leave it for a siesta". A man in an orange shirt sat on one of the capstans, his naked daughter between his knees; he soaped her from head to foot with water from a bucket; he made her blow her nose into his hand and flicked the snot into the wake; he washed his hands and cleaned her nose and ears with his little fingers; he rinsed her and hugged her dry with a cloth; he dressed her and greased her hair with his palms, over and over; he took the comb from his hair and teased hers; he held her head between his big hands as she clutched a little chrome-framed mirror and examined herself; she smiled and glanced up at me, large-eyed. I fell in love.

Easily. Already I was in love with the turgid, tea-brown river. I was in love with the monochrome vegetable anarchy of the banks, the tall trees that now and then stood proud of the many-textured, liana-threaded, shadow-grounded green. I could have fallen for a girl on the starboard barge, where the vivid market was spread out; she emerged from its bowels through a dark hatch; she wore a simple *libaya* and *limputa*, her hair was neither coiled nor ridged nor drawn out into points; but she walked upon beautiful feet with such vibrancy of buttocks and breasts; I watched the delicate tension in her neck as she swung a can on string over the side to drag up water; I saw strong pleasure in her face. On the barge's rear superstructure, men stood by a redundant wheel, or lay on mattresses, prevented from falling by a sack of flour tied to the rails. Some of them watched her too. I thought of the men who went to Bolobo hospital complaining of what they had caught from "a woman of the boat". The thought made no difference. I lay with Noëlle, her *limputa* hanging at the door like stained glass. I loved her. And I thought of those I loved in England. I thought of love and faithlessness. And grief. Wouldn't I grieve for this river? Why must we always pass through? Not all, and too much, of what we love loves us in return. However much we stretch moments of ecstasy into hours and years, must the chain always slacken or break? Who did she love? We lay close, and again I wanted to stretch this love, this journey, this life to its limit. We must have passed Yumbi, a border-town between the regions of Bandundu and Equateur. Noëlle could have fallen for a Polish priest from Yumbi. He had visited Bolobo, and we had shared words, sparkling water and immaculate bananas with him at the Lazaristes' table. He was weathered, gentle, humorous, that young father from Yumbi; he knew what love was. Noëlle asked if he'd spend the rest of his life out here. Modestly he replied, "*Peut-être. Pourquoi non?*"

The sunset was extravagant that first night in Equateur. We photographed it. A sharp-tongued man summoned us to the *agent administratif*. If the messenger was stony-faced, the *agent* was adamantine. He shouted about the law, about our crime, about confiscating our cameras. We explained that the captain had given us permission to take pictures, of the country and the river. Not people, that was forbidden. We did not mention the Congo border, behind which the sun dropped. He said it was more than his job was worth. I wondered how much that was, and could we afford it. Frustrated and angry we retired to our cabin.

I woke at 6.30, surrounded by islands of papyrus, reeds and palms. Banana trees signalled a settlement. Huts appeared, women squatting at a hearth, children waving, a girl up a tree watching, and a man standing at an ironing-board with a pile of clothes; he paused and blew at the embers in his iron as we throbbed past, our wake juggling his moored dug-out. Lianas strained at the ones we towed. This morning they brought green sheaves of manioc leaves, black-scaled *ngolo* fish, large silver *nkamba* with a pinkish sheen, yellow-fleshed *mboto*, and half a dozen other species. I saw the captain descend to our deck, a short man in a tangerine kimono, portly and dignified. I roused Noëlle and her best French. The captain's squashed eyes creased even more. He understood. "On this boat I am in charge. Please photograph, you are welcome. And please visit the bridge."

> Going up that river was like travelling back to the earliest beginnings of the world, when vegetation rioted on the earth and the big trees were kings. An empty stream, a great silence, an impenetrable forest.

So says Marlow. But only now, as we approached Lukolela, did the equatorial forest begin. Gone the savanna, gone the hills. The world had other measures here. Its height was the height of the canopy, its depth the depth of the swamp. In June 1883, Stanley saw, in "a clearing cut out of the finest forest I had yet seen", the first of the Lukolela villages that stretched for five miles. E. J. Glave was installed as chief of a station hacked out of forest on the ironstone ridge that rises from the swamps. At school in Yorkshire he, like Conrad in Poland, had been seduced by the map: "The tentative way in which the geographers of that day had marked down localities in almost unknown equatorial regions seemed to me delightful and mysterious." In the real world, Glave was cadaverous after working at Leopoldville, but three months' struggle with the jungle put three stone on him. "Petted by the natives," says Stanley, "he was beloved by his garrison, and was on excellent terms with himself." What a contrast with Conrad whose "steamer toiled along slowly on the edge of a black and incomprehensible frenzy".

Grenfell met Glave at Lukolela in 1884. Two men took two years to clear enough mahogany, redwood, teak, cottonwood, and plane for a mission site; a photograph shows the first mission house, a hut of sticks and shaggy thatch under giants of a forest full of monkeys, great apes and leopards. From 1890, the Revd John Whitehead consolidated his work on the Bobangi language there. A dictionary, the gospels, and a hymn-book rolled off the mission's pioneer printing-press. At the Antwerp Exhibition of 1895, Congolese printers and binders showed off Lukolela's wares. Enlightened Belgian Socialists protested, in a pamphlet, at the training of "dirty niggers to take the bread out of our mouths".

When Casement disembarked from the *Henry Reed*, he saw what clan disputes, migration across the river, sleeping-sickness, the rubber tax and other State exactions had done for Lukolela. "Whitehead and Mrs. W. met us and I walked into villages and saw the nearest one — population dreadfully decreased." Six thousand in 1891, 352 in 1903. In his *Congo Report*, Casement quotes Whitehead's protest letters *in extenso*: a catalogue of horrors, forced labour, food tax, the need to press always further into the interior to tap *caoutchouc*, the infamous red rubber; quotas for ever inflated, chiefs chained and beaten for not fulfilling them, a boy forced to drink from the white man's latrine bucket, brutal punishments, humiliations, murder. "The pressure under which they live at present is crushing them. . . ." The place that Stanley found famous for its extensive trade, its tobacco coils, fine timber and wild coffee was almost dead.

We stood on the bridge as the *Gundji* drew near Lukolela. A man was handcuffed to the captain's stool. The helmsman was very black in his electric blue shirt. Grimly he read the river from the bridge's front door, and stepped back to spin the wheel. I sensed he resented us, but the *sous-capitaine* gave us a boss-eyed, smiling welcome. We were peering through view-finders when a horrifying clang made us jump; the helmsman had struck the ship's bell hanging by our heads. We stared at him in shock, and laughed. His face broke open into smiles. The *sous-capitaine* explained how sandbanks moved from month to month, how the yards of charts that lay before him, direct descendants of Grenfell's plotting, had to be continually updated. He erased old marks with a rubber, and pencilled in amendments. Binoculars stood on his chart-table, beside a Lingala Bible open at Proverbs chapter 21: "*Motema na mokonji kati na loboko na Yawe ejali lokola bitima na mai; akobongola yango na epai na epai elingi ye* — The king's heart is in the hand of the Lord, as the rivers of water. He turneth it whithersoever he will." Navigation aids for the heart of the chief— *motema na mokonji*, on the very great river — *ebale monene mingi*, into the *motema na molili* — heart of darkness.

We saw tin-roofed buildings and timber-yards, giant trunks scattered on the foreshore like so many spilled matches. We passed the old Baptist mission, cocoa plantations screened by high trees, the Catholic mission, plantation workers' ranked brick houses and a plantation church. Our barges were ready, arrayed with merchandise, for the *Zone*, Glaves's old State post. There was a lorry, an antique armoured car and two Land Rovers. Tons of cement were ferried ashore by *pirogue* and a fortress of yellow Bralima beer-crates was built on the beach. Fish, *kwanga*, bread and mangoes were ferried out, and smoked monkeys, like mummies or wizened foetuses. We stayed on, for repairs in the engine-room. Brisk trade consumed the afternoon. As we left, a huge pink cloud hovered above Lukolela and, from a small wood-raft propelled by a ghostly vessel with furled sails, a solitary child flashed a torch at us in the coagulating dark.

Rain in the night. We kissed sandbanks. Much jolting, revving, backing off. Loud bells. Tinkling whispers from the long wires and link-chains by which the bridge talked to the engine-room. I imagined the speed indicator, made by Chadburns of Liverpool, registering zero. Remembered tales of stranded boats, death by starvation, cholera. Grey damp dawn, river narrowed, rocky banks like quays. At five-thirty we stopped off Gombe, a barge loaded with a lorry at the beach. Onwards. Tall forest. We cut across to the west bank and Liranga, the People's Republic of the Congo. Overhauled by paddle-boat *Fleuve Congo*, with its phalanx of container barges. Shouts. "Over there you're rubbish!" Islands and settlements on stilts. River widening fast. Dug-outs, with mushroom-like clay hearths, offering peppers, sugar-cane, smoked fish in frames like snow-shoes, antelope meat, great turtles with feet flailing. Three canoes almost sunk in the battle to make fast. Nets lost, and paddles. Frantic bailing with bits of *bidon* and the first wooden bailer I'd seen, beautifully carved.

Invisible behind the islands were Irebu and the inlet to Lake Tumba, a long chapter of history. Morsel: the people of Irebu could not believe that Stanley of 1877 and *Bula Matari* of 1883 were the same man, for Stanley had only canoes and *Bula Matari* had steamers. They imagined that a score of men must turn the *En Avant's* paddle-wheels, or that the secret was in the big pot that the cook — the engineer — tended; it was white man's magic, *mindele ndoki*. Casement got stuck on sandbanks here, and almost ran out of wood. He entered Lake Tumba, and more deeply into his understanding of the white man's black heart. At Bikoro he was shown the State Post, Station and plantation. "Part of the Exploitation of the Domaine Privé. A horrid business." He was tired and sick but took copious notes and depositions. "Interviewed Frank Eteva & drew out a long story from him of recent 'indecents' of State." Evidence from many frightened folk of gross maladministration, floggings, lopping of hands, murders. "Not at all well. Took 9 inches quinine & lay down."

Between the islands we had glimpse after glimpse of the great Ubangi which poured out its *café-au-lait* waters alongside the Zaïre's, their junction boiling; then we saw its great grey tongue, like a sea, and the *Fleuve Congo* churning away into oblivion. In February 1884, Grenfell discovered the Ubangi on his way back from the Equator in a whaleboat. He found wild coffee growing in its delta and took seeds back to Leopoldville. In October, with Dr Sims of the Livingstone Inland Mission, he took the *Peace* 130 miles up the Ubangi before running out of food because of the fear of people who cried "*Bidimo!*" — "Spirits!" — when they saw the *mindele*. Recently, expeditions led by Roy Mackal, Herman Regusters, and Marcellin Agnagna have explored swamps, and Lake Telle just west of the Ubangi, seeking *mokele-mbembe*, a "mythical" monster; sightings suggest a small sauropod dinosaur, perhaps the Babylonian *sirrush*, or the Congo dragon depicted in cave paintings, and described by Lopes and Pigafetta in 1591. There's too much evidence not to take it seriously.

Zaïre was on both sides of the river now. Dead giants poked above a younger, greener canopy. At eleven o'clock it was still dull. I felt faint, queasy, rubber-legged, and hoped that I was not due for fever or dysentery. A fat man swabbed the deck. A woman painted her son's toe-nails with red varnish. Half an hour later, as we passed between vast swamps, the sun tried harder but I went to bed. This afternoon, it shines thickly. Glowing cloud insulates the world. We seem to drive a wedge through solid light. Islands and shores are layers of cut-out grey trees casting shivered shadows into the river's luminescence. The air-conditioner drips a stream on to the deck outside our cabin: its sweat for mine. Always there are the brush-strokes of the bow-wave, lines of force spreading from a magnet, dug-outs like iron filings drawn or repelled across a bright sheet. Suddenly, a huge thrashing silver fish with barbels thumps on to the deck, something live, real, landed from the dream.

Night overtakes me. I retreat among the horrors and beauties of a sick head. Darkness or blindness, time or memory censors so much. So much that we seek is elusive. On this passage to the Equator, Conrad stares for snags that may spear the *Roi des Belges* and rear her out of the water. Casement mourns mutilated villages, dead idealism and "Poor old Ted Glave. His land . . . ah! me Sept. 1887 — what a change." Gide trespasses upon the forest near Irebu, chasing enormous butterflies that "lose themselves in the interlacings of lianas where I cannot reach them with my net". Graham Greene flies to Co-quilhatville — now Mbandaka — with *Heart of Darkness* in his baggage, fearful of failing to find the character, the book he needs. With the other white men I sweat over hidden snags, loves, butterflies, fictions.

I rouse myself at 4.30, when we dock at Mbandaka. Men on the quay huddle round a fire. A dozen pied crows fly between the port's cranes, iron trees. Two paddlers push against a brisk current; they stand fore and aft of a twelve-foot-square net — *likoto* — balanced on their dug-out like an outrigger. Men and women heave bundles and tin chests on to each other's heads. Some sleep on. Two are shrouded, except for one escapee foot, beside beer crates in the bottom of a canoe. A man scrubs our decks as if to scour them of darkness. Slowly, he succeeds.

Humping my rucksack exhausts me this morning. Noëlle wants to dump hers on comfortable *terra firma*. The streets, flanked by white-painted royal palms, are full of people and stalls. Beyond the grim cathedral, behind the bougainvillaea-decked bishop's house and a cream Christ in Majesty on a grey and pink plinth, we find the guest-house and the *procureur*. He is pale and vague and, though Christ's outspread arms looked welcoming, all his rooms are full of black and white *pères* from the interior on holiday. We face a prospect of insecure hotels full of ladies of the night, perhaps the Afrique on Avenue Bolenge, or Hôtel Kenga on the site of Mobutu's old home. We try out the one name we have on the *procureur*. Yes, he knows Dr Kurz. We've no address. Mindful of Christian charity, he lends us a pick-up and a driver.

We'd laughed at the idea of meeting Kurz, almost Kurtz, on the Equator. I imagined him a quinine-sallow medical veteran with a *penchant* for ivory and women, but Xavier Kurz is a young fresh-faced Belgian just back from weeks in the bush, a round of TB and leprosy clinics, and just about to set off again. He pours us coffee, drives off to buy jam, gives us breakfast, insists we stay. He prises the nails out of a small crate of hydrochloric acid that has taken months to arrive. I employ the *salongo* skills I learned at Bolobo, to mend his kerosene fridge. I am glad that his drains are not blocked. Xavier finds an inch of yellow acid at the bottom of cracked bottles, snug in stained sawdust. If he curses, he does it very quietly. He leaps up, as Noëlle empties coffee-grounds down a sink whose waste-pipe is not connected, crying in his best English, "Mistake! Mistake!"

Of his goodness Xavier Kurz offers us Mbandaka and district. A fridge for our film. A room with beds we rid of bugs. A rudimentary kitchen where Noëlle cooks two memorable meals on kerosene burners. Graham Greene in the bookshelf. In town we walk sedately. They are repainting the MPR monument because *Trente Juin* is only ten days away. That green, yellow and red is startling in this town. Many of its buildings are as elegant as the bishop's house but most are desperately in need of paint. Zaïrian names on the storefronts are interspersed with Patel, Soares, Bolodjwa, Houzet. Houzet's is a famous, high-ceilinged, white-tiled butcher's shop where we are greeted like friends and given preferential treatment against our will. Their pork chops are home-grown, their onions are ten zaïres each. Vegetables and everything from the boats are much pricier than downriver. In general stores and ironmongers' we ask for camping gas; our one remaining bomb won't boil all the water we'll need between here and Kisangani. It's unheard of. Then we see one in a window, attached to a lamp with a shade and mantle. But only one, and we must buy the lamp as well at a silly price. No one'll buy it, I say, because the gas will run out, and then what? We'll at least buy the gas . . . oh, forget it. As we leave, we make way for a wizened Zaïrian in a chocolate safari-suit, sharply pressed but overlarge, and a pith helmet the colour of parchment.

A woman begs and nudges us as we drink Cokes on the street. From their pitches of sparse grass and miserable stalls beneath the palms and jacarandas of Parc de la Révolution, luckless folk size us up. We are walking an edge we don't understand. I gaze at all the run-down villas and residences. Great things surely happened here in Mbandaka, capital of Equateur. The place denies it utterly. It forgets. I like it. I like its lost importance, the boulevards of dust between telegraph poles and street-lamps that don't work. I could live here, I tell Noëlle, I could *live* here. I think I mean I could die here. But, even now, we have to begin to plan our departure, that long process. As the man said, about the expected arrival of the Regional Governor, "*Nous commencons à l'attendre au départ de lundi.*"

We get quite intimate with the ONATRA offices: the ticket booths, the radio room, the *bureau* of the *Chef du Zone Ajoint*. When at last we see the big man, he is clearly too big to bother with stray *mindele*. But after reading my papers his demeanour shifts. How do we find Zaïre? Very beautiful and the people very kind. "*Sans blague*?!" he says. A minion radios a distant boat to book our passage. Next day, another runs to fetch our tickets; the big man must talk with us. He wishes we could meet his wife. He gives us his blessing. He wants love as well as power. Thanks make him emotional; he quotes the parable of the sheep and the goats. He wants the kingdom, not the eternal fire.

Gide described the Coquilhatville of 1926 as "this vast and still shapeless town. One admires not so much what it is, as what one hopes it will be . . .". Sixty years on, Xavier drove us to the real goal of Gide's detour into the Belgian Congo: Eala, five miles out of town. The gate swung open mysteriously; its motive force appeared and begged a few zaïres. We nosed down a great grassy dual-carriageway, twin avenues of noble and decaying palms, enveloped by an ordered forest of exotics. Paths radiated from the hub of the garden, a pit with a pond for an ugly, hissing Nile crocodile, resident here since 1953, bloated and soporific on fortnightly meals. Gide was shown an immature nursery:

> the director . . . presented for our amazement the most interesting of his seedlings: cocoa trees, coffee-trees, bread-fruit trees, milk trees, candle-trees, loin-cloth trees and that strange Madagascar banana, the "traveller's tree", whose huge leaves let flow, at the base of their petioles slashed by a pen-knife, a glass of pure water for the thirsty traveller.

We gazed upon denizens of a superannuated paradise, squinted at blossom two hundred feet up, walked beneath gargantuan groves of bamboo, bent to beds of sensitive *mimosa* which shrank at our touch, outstared surreal orchids, plumbed the river Ruki, where the *Gundji* had passed on its way to Boende. Here were palm-like cycads, rooted deep in the geological record; here, the enormous *bosungo* or kapok-tree at whose foot lay the bones of Sergeant Eala. Our guide was a bright-eyed, sharp-featured Zaïrian, a fund of botanical lore in a quilted jacket and green wellington boots. He celebrated 3,200 species, mourned staff cuts, and hoped for international funding to re-vivify this ageing Eden.

He knew he lived in a sobering parable. He showed us the pathetic zoo: one grey monkey, a few sad birds. Haughty coffee-coloured cattle grazed around a strange museum. We entered an arrested world, a hall of knowledge mummified, an attic of the spirit: timber samples, soil profiles from all over the country, and edible, medicinal, industrial, ornamental exhibits from the flora's treasure-chest. Dusty glass-cases held desiccated wonders. Alcohol evaporated from discoloured specimen-jars. Butterflies and moths were impaled abdomens, fluttering fragments to make Gide weep. Pressed flowers crumbled between herbarium sheets. Our guide lifted some from the drawers and flicked their dust on to the floor. *In memoriam* curiosity. Still, he had a curiosity to show us. He unlocked an inner sanctum, introduced "*mon grand ami, Marcel*". Like a shrunken curator, Marcel the chimpanzee toured his domain at our heels, touched us shyly with fine fingers, gazed up at us with handsome imploring eyes.

A tall ebony-skinned girl with ghostly eyes met us, a few miles up the Ruki, at Bamania. Xavier was at ease, but Noëlle and I were sad. After Eala's glorious light, the straggling village felt depressed in the hovering dusk. Dug-outs and a rusty barge were moored in dark water. Under high fan vaulting of a bamboo colonnade, low benches awaited the Sunday market and an old, emaciated couple squatted beside a poor leaf hut. On the verandah of the *pères'* house, Gustave Hulstaert told us that the people used to build entirely of sticks, leaves and lianas. Missionaries first used mud-and-wattle, and the habit spread. Père Gustave was a slim figure in a white shirt, white trousers held up by blue-and-red braces, white socks and black leather slippers. His eighty-year-old face was lively, sallow, framed with sparse white hair and a luxuriant patriarchal beard. He had lived in Zaïre for more than half a century. His eyes looked wise, befitting the authority on Mongo language and folklore: his local name means "the man who knows as much as our fathers".

In the early days — the fathers arrived in 1895, ten years after the Protestants, and the sisters in 1897 — a girl cooking for the missionaries set the roof ablaze: panicking, she cried out, "There's a fire in the kitchen!" "What did you say?" the *soeur* asked. "I said, there's a fire in the kitchen." "No, you said something else." "No, I said it, but in another way, in Lomongo, my language." Amazed, the *soeur* exclaimed, "What have you been speaking until now?" "Oh," the girl said, "the language of the white people." That language was Bobangi. The *soeur* enquired if any whites spoke her language. "Oh yes," she said, "the English at Bolenge." So the *pères* sent one of their number — scandalous thing! — to learn Lomongo at the Protestants' feet.

Père Adolphe was fleshy, with blue eyes, ginger hair, and makeshift bandages on toe and wrist. He fussed around Père Gustave and piled his friend's published works before us. "These people are easy to understand," he said, "though my Lomongo is best understood twenty miles from here". The older man explained that a man may understand dialects spanning 250 miles, and I wondered if my uncle and aunt, who lived 300 miles to the east, would be intelligible here without resorting to Lingala. Lomongo is not an official language, but Père Gustave trusted that educated Mongo people in Kinshasa would ensure its survival.

Surely he would know what distinguishes the black from the white mind. He laughed. What a question! Many books. "When I first went home, my father asked me that, and I explained as best I could. 'Son,' he said, 'those are the difficulties here, tell us the real differences.' Then I saw that it is a matter of class and education, familial, social and political organization. I, a boarding-school-educated man with a vocation, had the same trouble knowing a Belgian worker. The heart, though, is always the same." As he spoke, a man crept on to the verandah with an upraised machete in his hand. Père Adolphe talked briskly to him. He'd come to report that he'd finished his work. Frogs rasped and gargled. Mosquitoes were biting. "It is the heart that prevents our expansion, and the swamp." The swamp, *Balonga bantu*, "blood of the people", intervened between Bamania and Iyonda to the south-west.

Xavier threaded a way home through the thronged streets of a Cité built on swamp, its houses embanked against stagnant roadside ditches. Kerosene wicks flickered on a hundred stalls, music blasted from bars, shadows danced, crowds clustered at roadside televisions. In the headlights' beam, frogs floundered across the dry dust track.

Stanley wanted a Station on the Equator. He found the people of the Ruki primitive and cruel, but the villages below the delta clamoured for the International Association's patronage. At last he settled on Wangata, fractionally north of the Equator, in June 1883. Lieutenants Vangèle and Coquilhat were installed there with forty-six men. Just one hundred days later, Stanley saw for the first time "the realisation of my favourite ideal of a Congo station". He enthused, "We had left it a jungle of worthless scrub; we returned to find an Equatorial hotel — commodious, comfortable, rain-proof, bullet-proof, burglar-proof, and almost fire-proof." The local people copied the clay houses, and on top of an ant-hill the young white men constructed an observatory or *petite casino* in which to meditate, plan better sanitation, and draw up a code of laws on rainy days. It was a little model of imperialism.

But when chief Ikenge died, the *mindele* could not prevent the obsequies, though they refused to sell their garrison as victims. Fourteen slaves were topped with a panga, each head sprung away by a noose tied to a bent tree. Their bodies were consigned to the river. Blood-soaked earth interred the chief. The heads were unfleshed by boiling, and the skulls on poles ornamented the grave.

In the year of Mistah Kurtz, at Equator Station, Grenfell heard the Bangala legend of the origin of death. *Nza Komba* (God) came offering large and small gifts. If the people chose the small one they would live; if the large, they would be rich, but must die. While men palavered, women accepted the large bundle. *Nza Komba* went away and has never been seen since, though *bantu* have cried and cried for the small bundle and immortality.

Ted Glave took over Equator Station on behalf of the Sanford company. Casement succeeded him in 1887, but was disillusioned by lack of trade, and by the company's purely commercial, rather than State, interests. He resigned under a cloud, and went downriver to help survey the Lower Congo railway. He returned as British Consul in 1903. By that time, Equatorville had shifted four miles northwards and, following Vice-Governor Coquilhat's death in 1891, had been re-christened Coquilhatville.

We drove south from it, authentic Mbandaka, capital of Equateur. We pressed through the thick smoke of grass-burning, past the gutted pumps of a Petro-Zaïre station. We saw the fractured water-tower: the reason we had to walk to the port with *bidons* to draw water from a spring. La Voix du Zaïre, a radio station donated by the French, was empty, silent. Mobutu's old secondary school was being rescued from decay. On its fiftieth anniversary the President returned to thank the Frères de l'Ecole Chrétien for expelling him; for pushing him into the army and power. At Wangata, Mobutu's portrait hung in a small shelter labelled *Paillote du Centenaire, 17 Juin 1883–17 Juin 1983, Un Siècle*. Appropriately, *Bula Matari* is commemorated by a great ironstone boulder on a plinth beside a sign: *Ici fut fondé Premier Poste Equateur-ville en 1883 près de l'Equateur Géogr.^{que} O°2'*.

As we approached Iyonda I thought of Graham Greene's search for a character, for the book that became *A Burnt-Out Case*. His quarry was Querry, a world-famous self-weary architect, whose servant Deo Gratias was a cured but scarred leper. Greene, and Querry, used to sit and read on a tin barge by the river. Beyond felled palms and an acre drained by ditches, pillars and white gables supported the red roof of the Sisters' house. Soeur Léontine founded the leprosy hospital in 1945, retired from it in 1984. Querry retreated to the Fathers' house, from whose real-life Superior the fictional one borrowed his interminable cheroots. We passed the house once occupied by Dr Michel Lechat, who lent a little experience of leprosy to Greene's Dr Colin.

Xavier, today's Dr Colin, turns up the long track to the leprosarium which is now a desirable garden-suburb built on the swamp: ranks of brick duplex houses whose arched, white-rimmed doorways stare out like close-set eyes. From the darkness under tin roofs, real eyes watch us pass; smoke corkscrews from beneath cooking-pots. Our footsteps echo emptily down the green-tiled corridors of the sumptuous hospital that was finished in 1959, the year Greene stayed here. In *A Burnt-Out Case*, Querry worked on it, and the raising of its roof-tree was celebrated with "rather sweet champagne". Lepers and their families were feasted under an awning outside the old dispensary. Xavier has an office in the hospital, but its theatres and laboratories are unused; treatment in the villages has superseded it. The dispensary still functions; people queue for *kwanga*, leaf-wrapped parcels of manioc bread, on its verandah; inside, men sit on a platform with their mutilated feet suspended in a soothing solution; others are bandaged by black orderlies; more queue for drugs.

Sister Amanda urges us meet the old patients; some have been here since the beginning — forty years. "We have cared for them too well," she sighs. "They will live for ever." Will she stay for ever? She replies simply, "*C'est l'affaire du bon Dieu.*" Light seeps into the church through open concrete lattice-work painted in luminous colours: it recalls stained glass if you've ever seen it. Before an array of spears, a perfect albino Christ blesses a display of flaming lilies. Now I can feel Querry's unease, or disease, and obey the magnetism that drew him into dark wards where burnt-out cases sit and squat and lie, living with deformity. The air is sweet-sour. Self-disgust in Querry's nostrils. Love in sister Amanda's mouth. Feeling grotesquely intact, Noëlle and I greet the smiling and the numbed faces one by one, shake fingerless hands and stumps of arms.

Tonight is party-night in Mbandaka. Feeling grotesquely stiff, I mingle with the supple young black limbs dancing to Kinshasa pop. Noëlle moves well. We are in another Belgian doctor's house, distinguished by a solar-powered freezer and a bathroom wallpapered with soft-porn centrefolds. I can see no photograph of the doctor's wife. She is in Brussels. But his Zaïrian "wife" is more beautiful than pin-ups: slim, *soignée*, throbbing with sex. Her daughter is fifteen today, a pretty replica, all-black and conceived while her mother was a nun. The ghost of Querry haunts me: trying to elude the white world, women and guilt, he was murdered here for adultery which had never happened. Beer, peanuts, *mboto* fish, *makemba* and frogs' legs sustain us. Xavier, *bon catholique* that he is, enjoys himself increasingly. Is he dreaming of the *fiancée* he will marry in a year's time? At the centre of a ring of clapping revellers, I dance with the lady of the house, and ritually kiss her. The doctor pours more beer, as he preaches a passionate sermon against monogamy with the refrain, "*Ah! c'est un aberration occidentale!*" While, at the back of my mind, Querry seems to whisper, "I am cured of love."

IX

THE GREAT BEND

The Indus, the Ganges, the Irawaddy, the Euphrates, the Nile, the Niger, the La Plate, the Amazon — I think of them all — and I can see no beauty on their shores that is not excelled many fold by the natural beauty of this scenery, which, since the Congo highlands were first fractured by volcanic caprice or by some wild earth-dance, has remained unknown, unhonoured, and unsung.

H. M. STANLEY *The Congo and the Founding of its Free State*

Ah! what a picture, who therefore will be able to tell the horror of it . . .? Hate, death, devastation, the worst human emotions let loose, have as their contrast splendid nature, a dazzling sun unfeelingly pouring down its light and heat in the midst of an eternally smiling country.

A. E. C. HODISTER *Laissez les Nègres Tranquilles*

The sky was bruised. First drops shot the dust full of holes. Then came the waterfall. Every drain, ditch and rut brimmed simultaneously and coalesced until paths became streams, tracks tributaries and roads rivers. Each tin roof drummed and droned its own note. The ochres of the earth, the very crust, seemed to deliquesce, break free from the chains of solidity, and flow. Palm-fronds bent earthwards under the rain's weight, shivering. The smell of soil rose around us, heavy with promise and decay. Absurdly parcelled in yellow and blue waterproofs, we waited under the Bank's verandah among a hundred fellow-passengers for the *Major Mudimbi*. The port's gates were locked. The morass between them and us was deserted. A madman with a push-cart sidled about us, bored into us with his eyes, grinned wildly, scowled. Our fellows both enjoyed his mockery and watched over us protectively. We had said our farewells to Dr Kurz. We were leaving Mbandaka. I didn't much want to go.

I was leaving many mysteries behind. The marsh monkeys, much studied as a link in human evolution. The flux of tribes, the shifts of power. Equator Station's relics, and the wooden sarcophagi, red-stained human forms, in which Wangata chiefs were buried. The pygmoid people I had glimpsed. The seductive road south across the swamps to Lake Ntomba. I imagined Lake Mai Ndombe beyond, that used to be called Lake Leopold II, and the great tract of "private" land, the Crown Domain, that the Belgian king once held. I thought of Conrad passing through his nightmare, of Casement struggling in the face of a great evil. And I meditated upon the aliens who stay: the landed butcher, the bigamist doctor, the learned *père*, the compassionate *soeur*.

And what of the American missionaries who could offer us "no strong drink" but plenty of Coke and Fanta? They had resolved to retire, and probably to die, here. They were building their own Equator Station, a beautiful house with a vegetable garden of lettuce, carrots and peas; four African Grey parrots in a cage over a stream, two guard-dogs, and a forest hyrax which emerged nervously from its hiding-place, snuggled up to Noëlle and licked her arm. It looked like a rodent, but was a hoofed mammal, the only species that lives in trees. Hyraxes are seldom seen in the wild, though their haunting cries echo through the forest. This one cried if not allowed into bed; perfectly house-trained, it climbed on to the lavatory as if it was a pool or stream. From the clipped lawn outside, we watched the sun go down over ten miles of river and talked of the hippopotami that can still be found among the islands. Three *pirogues* and one of Blashford-Snell's power-boats were moored at the bank. I wanted to stay. But upriver was the Inner Station and, way up the Lualaba, the spirit of Dan Crawford awaited me on the shores of Lake Mweru.

The rain stopped. The crowd surged through the mud to one gate and then another. We were borne along with them. Despite much palaver the gates stayed shut. If they opened to let an official out, those who squeezed through were struck over the head. At last we were propelled through, carried on a tide over the great *Colonel Tshatshi*'s greasy barges; they were two-storey, three-deep, bulging with goods, swarming with people and goats, awash with rain and the overflow from latrines. We were led across perilous gaps, lifted up sheer sides, bundled over rails. Enthusiastic assistance made Noëlle lose her footing. We arrived at the *Major Mudimbi*'s modest barges at last, and clambered on to the boat. The cabin the big man had booked for us was not as clean as the *Gundji*'s, but it was above the paddle-wheels, facing astern, a fine view. Noëlle tended her bruises. We changed out of mud-sodden, grease-stained clothes. It was a good boarding, all in a day's work. The *Mudimbi* eased out into the current, but only to let the *Tshatshi* go downriver. For three hours we looked at the cathedral and a line of rusting river-boats and barges, Mbandaka's hulks. As the grey sky darkened, the deck shook, paddle-wheels throbbed and churned beneath us, the port receded and, along the southern horizon, the perfect Platonic Equator ran away from the river into the forests of the night.

On this stretch, in August 1903, a tube burst in the *Henry Reed*'s boiler. Casement was liable for the vessel, but luckily his crew tethered it to a tree, made repairs and raised steam within five hours. Four hours later, in the dark, they moored beside the station of the Congo Balolo Mission at Lulonga. Among letters awaiting him, Casement found congratulations upon his next appointment: British Consul at Lisbon. We had a letter for Lulonga, addressed to Tata Mokala by my uncle, Dr Arthur Wright, known here as Bolengu. He had written it in case we might follow Casement up the Lulonga River to Basankusu and on up the Lopori to Bongandanga. We'd decided to stick with Conrad and the main river, but roused ourselves at three in the morning all the same. The moon was a sharp scythe. Moths were confetti under the deck-lights. Huge ones, orange-and-grey and lime green, rested on our door. Canoes, drawn to the *Mudimbi*'s illuminations, fought the swift current to make fast. Then we saw Lulonga's lights. Lights! Even Mbandaka's generators cut out at midnight. We simply paused in mid-stream. I was glad we weren't disembarking. Lights faded. Hubbub died. Dug-outs sped away, unpaddled, into the breadth of the night. Soon our searchlight picked out the great Lulonga River's narrow mouth, which discharged an inky-black torrent into *le fleuve*. There, between 1939 and 1976, my uncle and aunt had come and gone to Baringa on the Maringa River, and to Yoseki at the further edge of Equateur. Up there, my cousin Ruth, known as Luta, had re-christened the hippopotamus with a frighteningly apt name, "hit-the-bottom-of-us".

A century and more ago, Grenfell celebrated the Lulonga's vegetation: bombax, pandanus, calamus, borassus, teak, gum copal, orchids, banana, and climbing palm growing to two and three hundred feet. He saw villages on stilts, founded on flattened anthills, on islands, or embanked behind palisades of wattle and earth. Casement found dead villages, and relict populations bitterly complaining of the rubber tax. He bought a fine leopard skin, and two dozen Bangala women's dresses for 225 brass rods. He found some sort of relief in the crew's sexuality. He saw the *Ville de Paris* going down to Coquilhatville full of rubber — "she does nothing else" — and wrote letters and noted rubber sentries returning to their white masters with strings of human hands, ears, genitals, sometimes smoked to preserve them: proofs of execution, but often cut from the living when bullets that must be accounted for had been expended hunting. Not even the Bangala employed this kind of punishment before the white man came. On deck, Casement read Bentley's *Plundering of Congo*, and Captain Guy Burrows's *The Curse of Central Africa*. "Horribly true."

I woke to a world of islands: circumscribed forests festooned with vivid, drooping fronds of climbing palm, lit by flowering trees, and penetrated by towering trunks topped with dark foliage or skeletal branches. At their fringes were the bleached leaf roofs of fishing settlements. A canoe came full of writhing eels, another stiff with monkeys. The air grew sweetly acrid; our neighbour on the starboard side was singing to herself and singeing the greige hair off a monkey. She talked cookery with Noëlle as she plucked it of shrivelled fluff. Its twin nipples were set surprisingly close together. Its hands and feet were half-clenched. Its teeth were bared in the rage of *rigor-mortis*. She cut its head off and jointed it for the pot.

We were keen to conserve our gas, so couldn't make much tea. Only beer was sold on the boat, but our new friends Jean-Pierre and Delphin found a cache of soft-drinks on one of the barges. They took our money and came back with bottles and change, to Noëlle's delight. They came from Bukavu, but lived in Kinshasa. Jean-Pierre was studying economics and Delphin was moonlighting to and from Brazzaville. He'd been bringing smuggled bullets upriver, until they were stolen at night off Lukolela.

"The country lives by corruption, little corruptions mostly," said Jean-Pierre. "We have tremendous resources — Lake Kivu has natural gas — but can't be bothered to exploit them. You plan for seasons, we cultivate when we need to. We aren't motivated like you Europeans, we do what we enjoy. The Belgians left the country in a bad way and it's been hard for us since. I couldn't have travelled here during the Rebellion; everyone fled to the forest, but now Mobutu Sese Seko has established peace. But we're surrounded — events in Angola blocked Shaba's copper — so everything goes through Kinshasa. In Kin I can get a piece of paper which permits me to buy coffee in Kivu for ten zaïres a kilo, and sell it back in Kin for thirty. Planters come into Equateur from Bas Zaïre and Kasai to make plantations and move on, but we must take care how we exploit our land. We must plan. We're so rich. The *féticheur* in the forest knows all about plants, but no one's put his knowledge to systematic use. At home, a man who knows can pick up minerals you'd throw away. Things aren't perfect, but Mobutu is strong like your lady of iron; he has given us the plants, and it is for those who come after him to water them." I wanted to forget our Iron Lady. Instead, I thought of the Minister of Education who went up the Lopori to pay teachers' salaries. He got so far and found he had enough cash left to buy a plantation that appealed to him. He was jailed; but was suddenly released, during a re-shuffle, to become Minister of Finance. Anyone who knows about education or agriculture or industry, or even smuggled bullets, knows that there is more money in money. So what was Jean-Pierre's game?

I went down to the lower deck. On the *Mudimbi*, second class was not a myth. There were cabins astern of the engine-room and every spare inch of deck was a stall. The market was laid out on the single-storey barges, *Bashielele* and *Baluba*, and fish and clothes dried on their roofs. The two-storey barges ahead were packed with third-class cabins, and mamas prepared meals of *kwanga* and rice and beans for all those who paid; the shower/latrines above sprinkled me as I entered. It seemed dark inside because outside was so luminous. Clothes and cloths hung in the gangways. The heat clung like wet laundry. The engine-room's diesel. The glowing charcoal. The steam of cooking and ironing. The unmoving air. I lifted a small boy out of a canoe paddled by two women. I asked a mama, at a stall of cigarettes and salt, where I could buy more drinks. Her head was bound with a bloody bandage, and a large figure sitting on a box loomed behind her: a mummified monkey.

I bought bottles, and watched Bolombo go past: mud and frond houses set amongst tended trees on the sandstone south bank. A man talked vividly about fat boas and wild boar in the forest, but canoe dramas cut him short. Below us, a big dug-out overran a small one; shouting erupted; two kids dived in hot pursuit and caught the submerged canoe, the paddles, the plastic cans. They tipped and slopped water out of the dug-out until it could support them. A man hit the wake awkwardly, fell out of his canoe, retrieved his paddle and re-mounted in great style. "They swim well, the *pêcheurs*," said my companion. "It's a tough trade. Despite their skill many die, especially at night. When they trawl they go naked so that buttons don't snare them in the nets if they capsize. Eeh! brave, these men, these boys."

The sunset was amazing. The giants of the forest were silhouetted and submerged by a broad deep crimson band from which spokes of gold splayed upwards through green, aquamarine, blue, towards a moon like a boat in an indigo sea. The islands were set in shot silk. It would be dark before we reached Mankanza — ex-Nouvelle Anvers — where the Bangala gave Stanley his bloodiest fight in 1877. It had been a string of twenty-one towns, famous for trade in slaves and human flesh long before *Bula Matari* came. As St Jerome said of the Scots anthropophagi: "although there were plenty of cattle and sheep . . . they would prefer the ham of a herdsman or a slice of female breast". Here, Holman Bentley saw men with spoils of war: "one carrying a human neck poised aloft upon a spear, the other an arm. . . . One carried the still bleeding trunk; he had slung the other arm through a large wound in the abdomen . . . two others shouldered the legs." It was done peaceably too. In the market, a man or woman was paraded until their whole body was sold, joints marked in ochre on their skins. Then they submitted to the knife.

The chief Bangala chief was Mata Bwyki, "lord of many guns", but by 1887 the most lordly guns at old Mankanza were two Krupps which, with a garrison of sixty men, protected the prosperous settlement known as Bangala. The Société Anonyme's big chief here, appointed in 1889, was Arthur Hodister. He controlled seven subordinate agents, including Georges Klein at the Falls. Klein gave Conrad the story of Kurtz's death, but Hodister was the model for his character and exploits. Grenfell admired him as an explorer; he was a member of the Belgian Anti-Slavery Society, clearly one of "the new gang — the gang of virtue" for whom Kinshasa agents displayed such distaste. In June 1890, Grenfell met Hodister at Bangala and noted how three months' exploration of the Upper Mongala by steamer and canoe had worn him, though for his pains he had five tons of ivory to take to the Pool before returning to the Falls. The *Roi des Belges* followed him, and in mid-August Conrad reached Bangala, the half-way point on his apprentice voyage upriver.

Islands and then darkness obscured the Bangala towns. As of old, dug-outs flocked out to us, seven or eight deep along the length of *Mudimbi* and its barges. By the time we reached Mankanza, I was asleep. When Mrs French Sheldon arrived there in 1905 on a "secret"

itineration, a public relations exercise for King Leopold, the missionary
John Weeks told how the Free State's agent had pulled down Bangala's
old prison, "and made it all nice, because she was coming". As far as I
was concerned, sleep demolished the whole historic place.

At 6.45 I wake with a sense of loss. We are moored at Lusengo, the top
end of the chain of Bangala towns. Palm roofs, half-hidden among
banana trees, ruddy mangoes, *pai-pai* and other trees, outcrop thickly
along a bank bristling with canoes. Occasional palms stand high above
the vegetation, fronds weighed down with strange fruit, nests of
weaver birds. We lie against a graveyard where stone tombs and simple
mounds alternate with pale grey anthills. People stroll along, some
with loads on their heads, but there is no trading. Men gather in the
graveyard and begin to dig, sharing a spade, supervised by a soldier.
The village carpenter gets to work with timber and adze. A deputation
scours the boat collecting money, a thick bundle of five and ten zaïre
notes. I am glad that we, the only whites aboard, are asked to give like
anyone else. Our names are added to a long list. An elderly *commerçante*
has died in the night and must be buried here, far from home and family.
The gravediggers' heads sink out of sight. A woman with huge naked
breasts and a raffia skirt circles around them and disappears.
    Gunwales barely clear of the water, a dug-out loaded with people,
mattresses, bundles and tin trunks, cuts across the river's gorgeous
skin. A skein of water hyacinth processes past. On our deck, the bronze
carapace of a turtle wavers, black head and legs working ineffectually,
tethered by twin fibres like the strings of a kite. A tiny monkey plays on
a man's shoulders; it blinks brown eyes and wrinkles its nose at the
smoke from a big black one being singed. I feel sad. I tell my
sympathetic friend Prospère so. "Yes," he says, pinching his forearm,
"but we are earth. She sleeps. She will wake . . ." and his grand gesture
encompasses the horizon. The *Mudimbi*'s whistle shrieks. Chanting to
the rhythm of rattles the cortège moves from the barges. The
mourners, the bearers of the raw coffin, sway; only the soldier at their
head, with a wooden cross inscribed EWOYO, marches stiffly. They
assemble around the hole, or scramble on to anthills. The soldier's
whistle shrills and stops the chanting. A man in a blue and white shirt
speaks and waves a bible. Ah, that's why there's no wailing; it's a
Christian funeral. All heads bow in prayer. Men take turns to fill the
grave; the mound is smoothed, picked clean of every blade of grass; the
cross is planted at its head. It is almost noon. The *Mudimbi*'s whistle
shrieks. Ah, Mama Ewoyo, you are cold.

A great swirling of paddle-wheels swamped dug-outs, sent bathers scrambling, eroded the bank. Half an anthill slid into the river. Ship's hoses were turned on the canoes, and ONATRA police checked tickets to rid us of hangers-on and *fraudeurs*. People fought, or rushed for sinking craft. We shaved an island so close that they cast off in a panic; one fell on his face in the water, but hung on to his dug-out by his toes; the bow of a big canoe took the paddler from the stern of another. We left an angry armada tossing in our wake. However hard they paddled they couldn't catch us. One canoe was sucked under the paddle-wheels; it bobbed up in the foam, split like a pea-pod.

The river was hugely wide between huge islands. Smoke trickled upwards. Settlements on stilts perched on the islands' narrow tails. Gaunt trees, like forest ancestors, guarded lush watery glades. All day, what seemed to be the south bank was Sumba, the largest island on the river, fifty miles long. A great white cloud blushed pink, and lightning played within it. Impossible. I glimpsed a momentary waterspout like a mirage. Three women watched us from the bank; one spread her *limputa* wide to display her nakedness. Dusk and a pall of smoke brooded over Mobeka. The *Mudimbi* paused by its Poste Administrative of soiled brick and rusty iron. A few shingles clung to the sagging roof of a three-gabled warehouse. Rotted buildings outlived by mud houses whose fires glinted behind palisades. Ten miles away, beyond islands, was the Zaïre's southern channel, the subject of Grenfell's last survey. We pressed past the Mongala's delta. At our cabin door, a green mantis did yoga. On the superstructure above the paddle-wheels, a Moslem spread his mat and prayed. We moored by a village. Our neighbour Dose and his haughty woman, in gorgeous cloths and jewellery, led loud dancing in the bar. Children on the bank danced in the *Mudimbi*'s lights.

We did not start until 10.45 am because so many *fraudeurs* had boarded and stowed away in every crevice: in barges, between cabin roofs and canopy, in and under lifeboats. They were driven out with truncheons and beaten off the boat. Once started we did not stop all day. Hours later, a *fraudeur* found near our cabin was led away in handcuffs, grinning at his near-success. Noëlle chatted with the policeman's wife and her friend from the barges, whose children played together on the deck. The friend bound her daughter's hair into spikes with black thread. Every now and then the policeman's wife picked fat maggots from the playground. Her cabin was ripe with dried fish. My uncle and aunt had once come down the Lulonga, the deck snowy with seething maggots because the cabin next door was solid elephant flesh. I played cards with Dose and Botomba. We each represented a beer, Primus, Castel and Skol, and the beers represented strength, intelligence and style. Dose's proud beauty adjusted her *limputa*, plucked at her blouse and jangled her gold earrings over each of our shoulders in turn. She thawed and grew friendly — she was a friend to intelligence and style — but I didn't trust her eloquent eyes. Strength won, of course, for Dose; *vive Primus!*

We boiled and filtered water, washed clothes. Fragrant smoke wafted up from the lower deck where youths smoked *bangi*, strong marijuana. The engine-room smelt of diesel unadulterated; an engineer ate his dinner off an immaculately greasy floor; he beckoned us inside his great cage, but we could not converse; four engines, two large, two small, roared and clattered; flywheels and shafts spun. We walked above the monsters on steel catwalks spread with drying clothes, fish and manioc roots. Wires, chains, pulleys and bells communicated orders. The searchlight began to scan water and forest, picking out way-marks. Fires flared like beacons on the islands. Smoke billowed from hearths on the barges. Sheet lightning repeatedly profiled the eastern horizon, and threw a panoply of clouds into dark relief. Powerful magic, strong curses. Lightning ripped diagonally into forest, rocketed upwards, forked downwards, flowed horizontally in rivers and tributaries of static; nerves and dendrites feeling out the skyscape, bleached out by blasts of light, thunder-flashes that burst all at once in various heavens, electric blue, rose, sheer white. Above the paddle-wheels' vibrating steel canopy, we perched on a lifeboat's gunwale and enjoyed the scale of the display, the intoxicating coolness. Thunder obliterated the boat's clamour. The wake, and populated dug-outs that cast off into darkness, showed instantaneously luminous and lingered, vivid after-images, on the retina. The storm wrung rain in great drops from a reluctant sky. We lifted hands and faces to it.

Northwards, in the swamp forest beside the Mongala, was the plantation-town of Binga, run by white men who enforced a colour-bar as if the last quarter of a century hadn't happened. Almond trees blossomed, branches akimbo; pink cocoa flowers on trunks and branches produced pods for hacking, scooping, sweating and fermenting into the thick sweetness of chocolate. The stinking rubber-factory caught fire regularly, detonated by volatile gases released in the refining. Happy coffee-pickers of the adverts filled baskets and barges with *Coffea robusta* for instant brands, risking venomous spiders, snakes and scorpions each time they plunged hands into a bush. But a woman could earn money with her own coffee-garden; she could harvest or steal her own palm oil too, cook it over a fire of husk, cast in ashes and mould her own grey soap. Up there, from 1892, the Anversoise Concession had tamed and enslaved the proud Ngombe people.

Southwards was Bongandanga; down there Casement investigated the Concession of ABIR, Anglo-Belgian Indian Rubber & Exploration Company, at the end of August 1903. At the market, men with rubber were guarded like convicts by sentries with guns. "To call this 'trade' is the height of lying." He found villagers tied up. The children were "let go at my intervention. Infamous! Infamous, shameful system." He saw a plantation of a million Landolphia trees the day before his thirty-ninth birthday, and local chiefs and their wives were ordered to attend a "Dance" in his honour. "Poor souls. I was sorry for it, of all the forced enjoyment I ever saw this took the cake." He saw women seized by sentries "on account of the meat". He hoisted his consular flag on the *Henry Reed* and steamed downriver; "sick at heart for the lot of these people and ashamed of my own skin and colour", he laid charges at Coquilhatville, and marshalled denunciations of the whole "atrocious system" all the way back to Stanley Pool.

On 15th September his boat met the *Peace*; he exchanged news with Grenfell and steamed "On to Pool. Stopped at B'zville & then 3.45 on to Leo . . . Wrote F.O. all night." Frenziedly he worked on Foreign Office papers over the next few days. "Not very well. Deaf and eyes troubling. 'Les cloches de Corned Beef, Opera en 365 Actes' — the daily Chop Bell on the Congo." He reached Matadi on 26th and worked late; "X Coffee at last" is pencilled into his diary, then, added in ink: "Richard Coffee took letter 9pm & returned with answer & then we talked & he said Yes — true Massa, a big one and I swear God Sir, — & so to bed at last!" At Boma he inspected the consulate he'd never inhabit. So to Banana, and Loanda. On 21st October, "Wrote to Morel about Congo . . . & to Joseph Conrad."

On 6th November he boarded the *Zaïre* for Lisbon. On 1st December he was in London. A week later, 15,000 words of his report were typed, the papers were full of his Congo journey and he celebrated, "Dick, West End, biggest & cleanest, *mui mua ami*". Grattan Guinness, whose Regions Beyond Missionary Union included the Congo Balolo Mission, and who had publicized the cruelties of the Free State as early as December 1890, called on him. The same night, Edmund Morel, whose *King Leopold's Rule in Africa*

was soon to appear, visited and talked until 2 am. The forces that
would, against all odds, wrest Congo from Leopold's grip, were
gathering. Morel described Casement's impact:

> A long, lean swarthy Van Dyke type of face, graven with power and
> withal of great gentleness. . . . From the moment our hands gripped and
> our eyes met, mutual trust and confidence were bred and the feeling of
> isolation slipped from me like a mantle. Here was a man indeed. . . . I
> verily believe I *saw* those hunted women . . . the blood . . . the hip-
> popotamus hide whip . . . savage soldiery . . . burning villages . . . the
> ghastly tally of severed hands.

A crowing cock woke me. With thirty miles of Ile Esumba to starboard
and many smaller islands crowding us, the river seemed relatively
narrow. Ahead, I could see the Upoto hills, the first for 460 miles.
Butterflies, crimson and scarlet, blue and black, flitted around the
decks. Green lace-winged bugs with orange and black markings
squatted on the rail. Two women bent over a friend's hair, teasing,
binding, twisting it into an elaborate looped coiffure. Noëlle brushed
her own furiously. Like any woman with curly hair, she wanted it
straight. The humidity frizzed it Afro-style. She despaired of a climate
that is not kind to white women. The tropical sun does not tan, and
she felt pale, sweaty, uncool. The hair-dressing reached its climax.
The woman stood, and turned slowly. It was a work of art. She
smiled, smoothed her cloth, looked like a million dollars. To return
the entertainment, Noëlle cut my hair. The women smiled shyly. We
cleared up all the strange straight tufts and left no fetish-fuel on deck.

It was about here that, in July 1890, the troop-carrier *Ville de
Bruxelles* ran on to a snag. Hodister surveyed her, and the *Roi des
Belges*, with Conrad perched on her roof in the flimsy pilot-house
forward of the funnel, steamed upriver to her aid. She had lain
disabled for five weeks, but got underway an hour or so before help
arrived. In *Heart of Darkness*, this abortive mission has no place;
Conrad ignores other vessels and isolates Marlow and his tin-pot
steamer on an anachronistically primitive river, but the impression he
gives is not much exaggerated. On a morning of butterflies and hair-
styling, a glance over the rail took in a river paved with islands, mined
with sandbanks and snags, walled by sunlit forest that brooded over
deep shadow. I say, a quick glance took it in. A longer look could not.
Add to that incomprehension the utter desolation that Conrad had
seen on the banks as early as Tshumbiri. The State was punitive up

here too. Early in 1891, a trader on the *Roi des Belges* described this stretch in a letter quoted by Edmund Morel; for two hundred miles, from below Upoto up to Bumba, "there is not an inhabited village left — that is to say four days' steaming through a country formerly so rich, today entirely ruined".

We paused for trade off Gundji on the south bank, then pounded across-river towards Lisala. ONATRA police appeared on deck in full uniform with truncheons and revolvers. Beyond an island, Upoto stood upon its hill. There Grenfell, in 1884, met a people celebrated as blacksmiths and feared as cannibals, heavily cicatrized on cheeks and forehead, the women naked except for beads. The Baptist mission, founded on the bank three months before Conrad passed by, tried to clothe them and to suppress man-eating. Slowly they succeeded, though the people continued to sell people for meat to the Bangala and Ngombe. Today's station is famous for its views and its mosquitoes. Blashford-Snell's expedition was offered accommodation, but insisted on camping out; its members had to be carried in, red and swollen and stiff, in the morning; their stupidity caused a lot of mirth and not a little fury all down the river.

Across a ravine, Lisala climbed the hill: mud houses, villas, a spire on the horizon. Ochre beaches overshadowed by trees on plinths of roots gave way to the port and welcoming crowds ranked around cranes, diesel tanks, and buildings. We unloosed the barge *Bashielele*. Dug-outs were almost crushed between us and the barge, us and the quay, but slid out in time. Many carried bowls of palm-oil like cauldrons of blood, clear red-orange on top, turbid beneath. Dose the Primus-strong, now a smart electrical engineer, beamed farewell. He swore he'd ride to Upoto on a borrowed motor-bike with our radio message for Kisangani. He disappeared into the crowds. Steps climbed to a green park and dowdy villas. A road swept into a shady square of shops, offices and hotels. A thick-trunked *libanga* — rock-tree — by a brick hospital recalled a blessed ephipany: "This tree commemorates the birth of the Father of the Zaïrian Revolution, Mobuto Sese Seko, born 14 October 1930." MPR pilgrims paid homage at a palm-roofed cabin on Avenue Mama Yemo where the Maréchal spent his early childhood. We hoped Dose would deliver.

Forest reclaimed the banks. The naked river embraced its islands. We went to bed for the afternoon. Towards sunset, the shore was a silhouetted Somme. Thin blades of cloud sliced an orange globe. Behind stark trunks and leafless branches the sky was a furnace. Mosquitoes whined thickly. The praying mantis did robotics. With

Jean-Pierre and the *infirmier* who had nursed Mama Ewoyo through her last night, we praised the dignity of her funeral, the fellow-traders who so fully played the roles of relatives. Men on the barge *Bangala* played a board-game with bottle-tops until the lightning flashed.

At midnight we took the great bend's northernmost curve, began to edge south. At 4 am we docked at Bumba. Dawn came reluctant, dull. In the wheelhouse of a barge astern of us, a family roused themselves and sat on deckchairs by the hatches to break their fast. We detached the *Baluba*; its iron decks, suddenly empty, were swabbed, its rust scrubbed. Rice-hulling plants, fed by Chinese-run paddyfields, and PLZ palm-oil mills lined the shore. Trading houses, like Nogueira et Cie, Grinza and Super Wenze, spelt prosperity for those who patronized the Select Club. Bumba is the biggest port this side of Kinshasa, a town of 52,000 people, compared to Lisala's 30,000. Stanley entered into blood-brotherhood with his fiftieth chief here; the *nganga* "lanced us both until Myombi winced with pain"; Stanley naturally did not flinch. Grenfell noted that "clay houses begin at Bumba", that the people neither filed their teeth like the Bangala and Ngombe nor dressed their hair so fancifully, but painted their bodies in red and black, pierced their ears and twisted the stretched lobes like rope. Bumba was a collecting-point for ivory and, four months before Conrad steamed past, Grenfell protested that the State's agent fired on canoes going downriver with tusks, and on those going up from Upoto, to protect the white monopoly on white gold. Records show that all vessels, bar those of the missions, ascended stuffed with *articles d'Europe* and descended laden with *ivoire*. As late as 1912 a steamer, moored here with mechanical problems, was rushed and six *mindele* captured. Four were eaten. Two escaped into the forest. They were discovered living in the trees like monkeys, mad with fright and exposure. It seems just.

I bought bananas on the forward barge, oranges on deck, hopped over hawsers and hoses, and walked the plank. I climbed the steep bank and met five *mindele*. One of them, Rebecca, a Peace Corps volunteer, was to be our first white companion on the voyage. Suddenly there were balloons and chocolate bars in our cabin. She despatched a man to fetch pineapple, and a woman selling tomatoes to bring mangoes and avocados. She tried to teach us to bargain in Lingala: "Eh! you are a bad woman, have you not a big enough heart to be good to me, for five zaïres will you refuse me . . .?" Her Portuguese boyfriend Jão came aboard to say goodbye. As we got underway, he purred along the river road on his motorbike and stopped beside the gutted, decaying shell of what looked like a cinema. Rebecca waved. Chin on hands on handlebars, he simply watched us out of sight. Rebecca retired to her cabin to weep. Children in canoes came out to play from a neat village of long low houses; they latched on to the *Mudimbi*, cast off, dived and swam for pure joy and devilment. Towards Yambinga the river was twelve miles wide; it merged with the clouds. The Itimbiri tributary, that Grenfell discovered in December 1884, ran away to the east. We were heading south-eastwards now. Rebecca ate with us. How we talked. When beer ran out, she was glad of our filtered water. She talked of love, of the heart's uncertainty and, as lightning turned the cloud-cover fluorescent, of fear; how highly-educated Zaïrians fear thunderbolts, how distrust and jealousy possesses and gnaws at families, clans, the nation; how successful individuals must leave the village to escape poisoning, how they waste away for fear of *ndoki*; how corruption perverts education and health services. Oh how we rose on wings of rationality and liberality! Oh, weak white wings, fluttering over the night's forest.

We made tea at 2.30 am. The boat was slowing and shaking. Goats bleated wildly below us. Rain sluiced the decks. At first light we watched the lifeboats filling, the river's grey pelt quaking in the downpour. When it slackened, I peered over the rail at dull, well-spaced islands. Something stirred by my foot. I jumped. It was the snout of a crocodile in the scuppers. It was only four feet long and its jaws were bound, but it woke me up. It would make a fine dinner, tender flesh with the texture of fish, the taste of fowl. While a man butchered a monkey by the lifeboat, the morning was enlivened by the mating of the *Mudimbi* with the *Libenge*. Panic among the hangers-on. Exultant greetings. Shouts from bridge to bridge. A great hose snaked across to fuel the *Libenge*'s tanks. We approached the round island at the mouth of the Aruwimi; by a reed-spit at the river's eastern lip, smoke plumed upwards from a dug-out's clay hearth.

Here in 1877 Stanley met fifty-four monster war-canoes whose leader carried eighty paddlers in regalia: parrot feathers, ivory armlets, paddles topped with ivory, stroking to the rhythm of drums, ivory trumpets, the chanting of two thousand voices. Spears met musketry. "Our blood is up now. It is a murderous world, and we feel for the first time that we hate the filthy, vulturous ghouls who inhabit it." Artefacts, which "exhibited remarkable intelligence and prosperity", were looted, along with a "temple's" pillars, thirty-three enormous tusks. Skulls on poles and bones at firesides proved, in Sir Harry Johnston's words, that "man figured in these regions as the fiercest of the carnivores". Stanley asked fishermen the name of the river; one said to the other, "*Alu emi*? — does he know me?" Stanley mistook the question for an answer and noted down "Aruwimi".

We slowed, stopped. The *agent administratif* sniggered, "The third captain's drunk. He forgot to turn left for Basoko." We went into reverse, manoeuvred and, with the *Libenge* bound to us by hawsers, broached the Aruwimi's mouth. In 1887 Stanley had brought home Baruti — "Gunpowder" — a man of the Basoko who had gone to England with Sir Francis de Winton. After a moving reunion with his elder brother, Baruti resolved to continue up the Aruwimi with the Relief Expedition, partly for fear of the Arab danger hereabouts. But upriver, he stole Stanley's rifle, a brace of revolvers, assorted prestigious articles and a canoe before paddling back home. Two years later, Basoko was fortified against the Arabs, much to the disgust of Tippu-Tib, who regarded the area as his domain. When Conrad passed, palisades and cannon spoke a clear message. Later, poles and packed clay were replaced by lime-washed brick castellations, a white fortress.

On a headland, a semi-circular emplacement like a set of old teeth guards a vacant flag-pole. Official buildings rot quietly behind extensive battlements camouflaged with long grass. Basoko is a fortress, a vigilant sentinel no longer. In June 1906, Grenfell's Bangala crew steamed here for medical help because their master was racked with a severe attack of blackwater fever. They were too late. George Grenfell died on 1st July, aged fifty-six, and his bones lie in Basoko's graveyard. We saw a spreading green town, with a gate of twin turrets leading to the usual MPR monument, a hand holding Zaïre's torch. A wall once enclosed the market, but half the roof had collapsed and business was done from grass shacks outside it. The port was a high jetty with tiers of people wherever there was a foothold. Dug-outs brought goats, women half-concealed in cargoes of manioc leaves, and pigs which screamed as they were heaved aboard. I was offered one for two thousand zaïres, but turned it down. I was watching the most stylish paddler I had ever seen. He was tall. He worked the water elegantly. Baruti might have been his name, for his paddle was topped with a twelve-bore cartridge-case. Instead, I christened him Mwanje, "Angel". His distinction lay in his dress-sense: white plastic sandals, a white headband like a halo, a slinky white plunge-neck satin gown. How Casement would have relished the sight. How the vision of a Congolese angel would have thrilled Grenfell.

We reversed out and relinquished the *Libenge* with noisy ceremony. One man, stranded on the wrong boat, chased us in a powered *pirogue.* We cut across-river towards hills. The cliff was dramatically clad with sombre forest; then, among palms and bananas, steps climbed to mud houses set on excavated platforms one above the other. Suddenly, among high trees, I saw villas and, down by the river, a palm-oil town, street-lamps, factories, tanks like gas-holders. In the 1920s Douglas Fraser admired Lever Brothers' civilizing role at Lokutu, then Elizabetha:

> No cheap ostentation here; no improvident splattering of lime-wash; solidarity, neat and well planned to the smallest detail. Orderly plantations face the hills. Orderly rows of brick houses crown them — the houses of the natives. . . .

Ruthless cost-cutting wage slavery may be an improvement on slave-raids. Stanley and Grenfell, in 1883 and 1884, both found a depopulated, ruinous shore between Basoko and the Falls. Grenfell saw what he took to be salt-makers' fires, but learned from fugitives that their town of four thousand had just been razed by Congo Arabs in pursuit of slaves and ivory. In 1904, he recalled this period of "native rule":

> I saw the havoc made by the liquor traffic . . . slaves brought down to the white man's store and sold for gin and rum . . . and I have been in the midst of an Arab raid . . . and within twenty-four hours counted twenty-seven burning or smoking villages. . . . I have seen the cruel bondage in which whole communities have been held by their superstitious fears. . . . And I have all unavailingly stood by open graves and tried to prevent the living being buried with the dead, and altogether have seen more of the dark side of human nature than I care to think about, and much less to write about.

Six months before his death he addressed a missionary conference at Kinshasa, and talked of his high hopes of white rule and his bitter, if belated, disillusionment with it:

> I saw the fall of the Arabs . . . and when His Majesty bestowed his decorations upon me I was proud to wear them. But when change of regime came, from philanthropy to self-seeking of the basest and most cruel kind, I was no longer proud of the decorations.

I saw no burning but that of cooking-fires. The sunset gently bruised the grey river and subtly inflamed the forest's greens. The night hid Isangi, at the mouth of the Lomami. For me it must remain in the realm of history and myth. In 1883, Stanley watched twelve thousand people fleeing across river from it. At New Year 1885, Grenfell found Isangi possessed by Tippu-Tib's Manyema forces and men of the east coast; the country was in chaos, but he explored the Lomami 140 miles south as the crow flies; the *Peace*'s mesh repelled flights of poisoned arrows aimed at the supposed slave-raiders aboard. Conrad probably met no arrows on the main river; nor did he meet Hodister at the Falls, because the illustrious agent had embarked on his own exploration of the Lomami. Conrad's boss, Camille Delcommune, must have been furious: his rival had pre-empted his brother Alexandre Delcommune's Lomami expedition of 1891, for which Conrad had been engaged as captain. Hodister and others were supplied by M. Schouten at Isangi. In *Heart of Darkness*, Harlequin is fitted out with stores by Van Shuyten, and it is at Isangi that I imagine Harlequin's abandoned hut of reeds, the tatters of an unrecognizable flag, the wood-stack with the note, "Wood for you. Hurry up. Approach cautiously." And the book *An Inquiry into some Points of Seamanship* "by a man Towser, Towson — some such name", annotated in Russian that Marlow mistakes for cipher. Marlow steams on into dusk, until the manager stops him because of the dangers of night-time navigation.

I wake to the sound of manoeuvring, backing-off, nosing ahead to find a channel. Forward, the man taking soundings with a pole is working overtime. As the sun rises, the mist that annihilates the islands lifts a moment, and then Conrad's "white shutter" comes down again "smoothly, as if sliding in greased grooves". The *Mudimbi* stops. In midstream, in mid-nowhere, in a clammy shroud, we are frozen: a small obstacle in a river that has grown swifter, narrower since Basoko, since Isangi, that boils along beneath immovable steam. Heat from the engine-room has driven Rebecca from her cabin on to the deck. Like Noëlle, she sleeps on, until a stooping hawker belabours me, metaphorically, with miniature axes, spears and knives. They are not inscribed "A present from Basoko", that's all I can say. A man vents his frustration at the delays, then lightens his tone and confides, "*Ma chèvre est morte, dérangée par le brouillard.*" Noëlle is horrified to hear me chuckle, as if at a whimsical remark. His goat *is* dead, deranged by the mist. I am mortified.

    In the interval we enjoy a breakfast of omelette, peanut and banana sandwiches, mangoes and tea. The mist grows brilliant, hot. Layers of gauze lift, to reveal flats of headlands, flats of cut-out trees, black, grey, ghostly. A silver-gilt sun burns through. All at once, the paddle-wheels thrash at blinding water. Twenty goats in a *pirogue* are tipped into the wake and carried away. Paddlers abandon the boat in a reckless chase after drowning wealth. They heave two or three goats from the hungry river, before vanishing out of sight.

The river narrows; cliffs heavy with forest rise pink, ochre, yellow on the north bank. Now we have left the great equatorial basin that, beyond human memory, was an inland sea until it pierced the Crystal Mountains and found the ocean. Early cartographers sensed it and drew vast Lac Zaïre at Africa's heart; a mythic lake replaced by honest blankness, until Stanley linked Livingstone's Lualaba with "Tuckey's Farthest". Here, at Yangambi's bluff, Stanley confronted warriors "in full war paint . . . the bravest we met. Of course such arrogance met with instant punishment . . . we had landed spearmen and musketeers, and in their rear fire was set to the village." In 1883 he foresaw that the terrace of land, occupied by Arab slavers in his wake, would "offer a charming field for European agriculturalists". Yangambi is an agronomical research station still, set in a forest of three thousand species of tree.

A parrot-catcher from Mbandaka, desolate because in the name of conservation his trade has just been proscribed, asks me if we are Belgian. "Oh," he says, "all white people look the same to me." Today, the King and Queen of the Belgians are in Kinshasa. There are military parades in all Zaïre's cities and towns. It is *Trente Juin*, a quarter of a century on from Independence. There's no sign of celebration on the *Mudimbi*. A man with a rattle announces a Protestant Sunday service in the restaurant. Soon, bibles are open, drums are throbbing, folk are harmonizing raucously to the tune of "Count your blessings".

At Yalufa, a long village on the south side, drums are talking. Fish-fences and traps are arrayed at the foot of a sandstone bank draped with nets like lacy underskirts. The decks fill with poker-work mortars and stools, cane-work stools and chairs. Soon we see men in coolie-hats and a grandiose vision at the forest's edge: Lotokila's brand-new Chinese sugar factory, a glistening steel and aluminium town turning out forty thousand sweet tons a year.

Villages climb chines in yellow-green cliffs. Naked kids from canoes scale the *Mudimbi*, dive off the roof again and again. We've not been snared by sand-bars, but we crawl. One engine has died. At 3.45 pm we moor at Île Yaolimela, once called Belgica. Stanley found it inhabited by a clan of the Yakoso; in 1883, "however, not one hut is seen". Over the rail we gaze at eye-sockets of crumbling villas overtaken by forest, the mouth of a white church, the rusting, rotting bones of a rubber plantation. Jean-Pierre scavenges for mangoes in a noble tree. He presents them to us. He pours us banana spirit. It's powerful and vile. He swallows our whisky. It is good. He offers Noëlle emeralds, diamonds, gold. Ah, now we understand. The sky is rose, streaked mauve and overlaid by leaden cumuli. Astern, a solitary searchlight feels its way round a black headland into a river of blood. We anticipate a last night of love on the river. But Jean-Pierre warns Rebecca not to sleep on deck here. She moves her bedding and her charms into our cabin. Her reputation as my *deuxième bureau* is finally confirmed.

X

THE INNER STATION

Yes, this was the very spot. But there was no shadowy friend to stand by my side in the night of enormous wilderness, no great haunting memory, but only the unholy recollection of a prosaic newspaper "stunt" and the distasteful knowledge of the vilest scramble for loot that ever disfigured the history of human conscience and geographical exploration.

JOSEPH CONRAD *Geography and Some Explorers*

First of all a baptism of fire
Peter, Paul, teach us
To contemplate fire the colour of blood.
A baptism of blood is needed
Of blood which purifies our eyes
To decode the Night.

SÉBASTIEN NGONSO *Baptême de Feu*

A ten-mile-long island. A tall radio mast. A pall of cloud. A sunrise of carmine. A bank of cliffs. A river of rocks. We limp, on one paddle-wheel, towards the town at the bend in the river, the Inner Station. *Pirogues* beneath the bank move as fast; people on cliff paths walk faster. We may not reach port by three o'clock. After that, docking is impossible. One engine is lame. The river is treacherous with reefs and jagged islands where fishermen drape nets. This is the way to the heart of the heart of darkness. One blade of light stabs through cloud, then another; they stir the gloomy water to shimmering. We limp. Light grows and grows. The heart will be hot and luminous.

No one celebrates this day: 1st July, the centenary of the founding of the Congo Free State. Five years later, Conrad came here to pick up Klein and ivory. Marlow came to fetch ivory and Kurtz. Out of the mist came a desolate clamour, a mournful shrieking. The pilgrims rushed for their Winchesters. Marlow lectured them; he observed the crewmen's appetite for human flesh, that mocked the very notion of restraint; he negotiated a snag and saw the poleman lie on the deck, the fireman duck. "Arrows, by Jove!" He pulled the shutters to and tried to steady his helmsman, that de-tribalized creature with his blue cloth, gold earrings and filed teeth. Another snag. A fusillade from the pilgrims. Thick smoke. The helmsman let off a rifle and fell back, speared. Marlow's shoes filled with blood. He blew the steam-whistle. Silence. He slid the helmsman's body overboard to prevent its being eaten by the crew. He berated the pilgrims for fake bravery. He feared he would never hear the voice of Kurtz. All at once he saw the station on the south bank and, in a brown suit patched with coloured cloth, a figure like a harlequin yelling, "Come along. It's all right. I am glad."

Harlequin pointed out Kurtz's decaying house upon a hill. Marlow peered through his binoculars and was knocked back by the sight of a row of poles topped with human heads. On the north bank, after Yakusu Hospital, after the island almost plugging the Lindi River's mouth, after a wharf and a couple of factories, the forest begins to thin; between planted trees warping in the heat, I see visions of a "gothic" church and cloisters, of smart and run-down villas, high walls and gardens, of blackened houses blasted by grenades or shells. Salim drove in from the east to take over Nazruddin's store in V. S. Naipaul's rich and sombre novel *A Bend in the River*: "I found that Nazruddin hadn't lied. The place had had its troubles: the town at the bend in the river was more than half destroyed." Mostly the wounds of the 'Sixties have healed. Kisangani is now a city of almost half a million. We stagger past the Roman Catholic cathedral; we may yet dock today; Rebecca may catch tomorrow's flight to Kinshasa. Upriver a great mosque's towers gleam like confectionery and, beyond, I glimpse water boiling over rocks, the first of the Falls.

Here are cream ONATRA buildings with red tin roofs, and crowds pressing at the port gates. Here is a swarm of *pirogues* and frantic shouts at our skirts. Here is the end of a thousand-mile voyage, fifteen days and nights on the boats. At 2.55 pm *Major Mudimbi* berths with a crash. Bottles in the cabin go flying. People leap from the barges and climb iron rungs in the jetty wall. We make warm farewells: Jean-Pierre, the parrot-catcher, the haughty beauty, Prospère, the police-man's wife, her baby, her fish and her maggots. We vault over the rails.

No one to meet us, or Rebecca. A grinning official in an olive-green uniform plucks us into Immigration. Or tries to. While we wait for the office to be unlocked, the Revd Andrew Gandon, a young Anglican missionary, arrives carrying his small son. Our message, via good Dose Lebeke and Upoto, got through two hours ago. The official shepherds us. His boss, in a barred cell-like room, demands a currency declaration form we were never issued with. Peter, a young Englishman who boarded the barges at Bumba, hasn't got one either; he is fined five hundred zaïres. Rebecca's documents are in order. Three soldiers of the proud parachute regiment expostulate about their detention: their pet chimpanzee has no papers. At a second interview the boss returns our passports, waives the required form, and welcomes us. We all pile into Andrew's second-hand Izuzu pick-up, with a picture of Ayatollah Khomeimi in the cab, and take off along the town's potholed boulevards. We pause for bread at a *boulangerie*: ice-creams within, crippled beggars without. We drop Peter at Hôtel Olympia, reluctantly kiss Rebecca goodbye at the Peace Corps base. Soon we reach home — it feels like home at once — in the Quartier des Musiciens. Andrew and Margaret, and their colleague Clive Main, sit us down to chicken curry, *pai-pai*, nuts and rice followed by mango crumble and custard. It's a feast, and extra welcome after the *Mudimbi*'s final offering of dubious meat and weavilly beans hotly disguised with *pili-pili*.

The moon is full. A bird chimes with the regularity of a metronome. Bats sound the darkness. Drumbeats ebb and flow on the thick air. From ditches that drain the garden — the water-table is high in Kisangani — frogs raise their voices: inflated sacs of skin pulse like deep throats rasping, electronic bass at the ear-drum, contraltos throbbing; a whirring, thrumming, slowly shifting rhythm that thins and dies, then resumes in concert at full volume. Tucked under a mosquito net, after long talk and a late walk, this the lullaby that carries me off. The throbbing hardens, a human voice edges in. The watchman raps at the window, crying "*Mwizi!*" It is 4.45 am. *Mwizi* is Swahili for thief. The watchman woke from his watch-keeping to find one in at the back door. He has run off, swag-bag full of nothing.

I must run to the lavatory. High ceilings and tiled floors make the bungalow a resonant receptacle; it seems as if I fill it with the thunderous downpour of diarrhoea, explosive, torrential, as if my belly is heavy with equatorial wind and weather. Foul weather, and weakening. Thieves may not have touched passports, notebooks, money or cameras, but now, for a week or so, something drains me, steals energy, life-force, courage. I did not intend to follow Conrad so closely. He confessed his poor health to Marguerite Poradowska: "at the Falls (its native country) I had an attack of dysentery which lasted five days". As the little, loving, treacherous continent that is myself quakes repeatedly, I cannot help but sit and brood on Conrad's despair, or on Pliny's glossed proverb, "*Ex Africa Semper Aliquid Novi*", out of Africa always something new, a long tradition of novelty. I'm in it.

Was the school across the road of packed gravel the *lycée* that Ferdinand attended in *A Bend in the River*? Railings enclosed its grounds, but I couldn't see the iron archway surmounted by that ironically optimistic motto, *Semper Aliquid Novi*. When Andrew drove us to the Lindi River, it was as if we entered Naipaul's territory more fully. We passed the University, a part of that New Domain where Salim found love with Yvette; tarmac lasted until the military airport; a dirt road took us past SORGERI, a dockyard and factory for refined palm-oil, margarine and soap. There was a marvellously overgrown *lycée* with painted concrete gate-posts topped by balls and a weathered arch on which I seemed to distinguish *Novi*; wishful thinking abetted by equatorial amnesia, an early morning dream. Elegant residences thinned to strung-out palm-frond village. Chickens and goats prospered in a burnt-out school. The track fell to the Lindi. Noëlle and I joined a canoe laden with pedestrians and a Vespa. It was chilly on the water. The ferryman demanded a larger fare from us than from anyone else, but made do with a small tip. A Land Rover with a male nurse aboard met us and took us to Yakusu. Folk huddled round fires in the village, women pounded, a thick-tailed he-goat chased a she-goat, hoping to generate heat. The nurse fetched his bundle and said goodbye to all the villagers who clustered around us. He was off into the forest on a clinic trip with the English doctor and his wife. There was no room for us to travel with them, but we could have the doctor's house. I was disappointed, but my guts agreed emphatically with plan B.

   Yakusu, properly Yakoso, was the Baptist Mission's Inner Station, founded by Grenfell and Harry White in 1895 and built up at the cost of many speedy deaths. Harry White's first doorless bamboo hut, set in the forest fringe among anthills thirty and sixty yards in circumference, was succeeded by a wooden house on piles. Forest was cleared. Broad paths were carved out of the undergrowth. Now, between a two-storey hospital and a cavernous church adorned with brass plaques to brief white lives, a line of weathered brick houses stands on the high bank. On the verandahs we met nurses, the builder and maintenance man, bible school teachers, and white infants so acclimatized to life here that they cried at the sight of us strange *mindele*.

Gardens were lush, planted with mature trees: mulberry, guava, *pai-pai*, orange, lemon, *saffra* and *coeur de boeuf*. The verandah of the oldest house was roofed with *ndele*, palm-fronds; an *ndele* screen hid a newly-dug *wai-sai* in the back-garden. Fences of stakes, some rooted and sprouting, were woven together with *nkekele*, lianas that tighten as they dry out. The houses' outbuildings are not occupied by servants any more; cooks and gardeners live in the village; the river-path in front is no longer reserved for whites; the hospital, with all its clinics, serves a forest area the size of Wales; its quality attracts patients from the city. Drs Clement Chesterman and Stanley Browne pioneered leprosy work here. Colonel Blashford-Snell had been reading too much Stanley when he issued his men with guns on this "dangerous" stretch of river, and stated that there was no health care in these parts.

We surveyed the station from the top of the church tower, waded in the overgrown graveyard where the last young white martyr to blackwater fever was buried in the 1970s, crossed a schistosome-infested stream, saw the newly-protected spring and strolled among decaying, make-do-and-mend school buildings and hostels. There was new building and development, but too many victims of unpaid government grants and salaries, too much energy expended fighting elemental battles. The years 1895 and 1985 rubbed shoulders uneasily. Every working day was still punctuated by old Tata Tula's talking-drum: 6 am — rise and pray, 7 am — start work, noon — midday meal, 1 pm — resume work, 3 pm — finish work, 9 pm — old curfew time; for us he smiled a heavily cicatrized smile and beat from its lips a message of welcome to the "spirits from the forest", the drum phrase for whites.

That night we ate spam fritters and tinned peaches with Sue Evans, a Welsh nurse, by the light of Tilley and kerosene lamps. The station's small generator lit the hospital; the big one was out of action. It had last been repaired by travelling German students in return for VD treatment, but now it needed both skill and spare parts. The meal was a treat, a contrast to goat and beans; all the same, Sue apologized for flat bread made from weavilly flour. We talked of the Lokele people, of local tribal rivalries, of the power of the forest.

One Sunday, after preaching across the river, Sue fell sick with hepatitis. Catholics said that the Baptists had poisoned her. Women who collect medicinal plants gave her a cure: a root that village midwives used as an enema, inhalation, bath or, ground up with *pili-pili*, as hot medicine. They taught her signs of pregnancy: pallor, spitting and swallowing, a tell-tale pulse in the neck. She recalled a girl, on the run from the police, who had given birth in the hospital. She abandoned the baby, but its sixty-year-old grandmother was traced and treated with a stonecrop from the forest until her old breasts squirted milk. Sue knew of cases where men suckled motherless children after the same treatment. Many things were hard to credit, she said, on both sides. "A girl who knows me well once asked why I killed my babies. She was sure I returned to Britain on furlough for abortions." Back on our verandah, sheltering from the rain with a small flame flickering in its glass chimney, with a cockerel roosting on a chair beside us and fireflies like sparks in the grass, with the forest behind and the river in front, we thought on these things. We could have been at the Falls Station that Conrad knew, if not at Marlow's Inner Station.

I took a faecal sample to the path lab, nine days after the attack began. Amoebic dysentery? Giardia? They found nothing. Anyway it was now controllable, if not comfortable. Noëlle attended a delivery in maternity and was impressed by Zaïrian nurses who routinely perform Caesarean sections, as well as hernia or cataract operations. She was startled by the paleness of the newborn child; in a few days it would darken. I attended the piebald house-cat's production of black and tortoiseshell kittens in a cupboard. Kelekele Ofeka Kama, a man of the Lokele, took us to his kingdom, the *Imprimerie*, birthplace of books in a dilapidated courtyard. The smell of ink. An Albion. The sigh and thud of a treadle-press. A guillotine. Two sewing-machines for which thread was unobtainable. And a big press, the historic one from Lukolela via Bolobo, converted to electricity. Lack of power and a cracked roller rendered it useless.

Kelekele led us to his home in Yakoso. Each clan had its own talking-drum mounted on a tyre before its compound. The long drum-message we'd heard at 5 am told of the death of a woman in the hospital; three times the drum said, "With tears in your eyes and wailing in your mouth . . . the spirit has left her body that lies stretched out on the clods of earth. . . ." One leaf in the forest shook a different way to all the others. The drummer said, "When I beat my drum it is not only the ears of flesh will hear, but those of the people

under the ground." Here was the tomb of Tata Tchoko, master of the
drum language. Here, to greet us, was a descendant of Bolamba, the
first Christian at Yakoso. Bolamba descended from Bokanda, one of
chief Koso's sons. The Revd Kempton, who lived and died here
1901–8, was called Bokanda; each missionary was a reincarnated
ancestor, named accordingly. Thus the progeny of Koso — *Ya-Koso*
— claimed each "spirit from the forest with a bunch of leaves", white
man with a bible.

Big muscles rippled in an old woman's arms as, squatting on a low
stool before the bamboo screen of her hut, she worked clay, yellow-
grey like the cloths she wore. In a dished stone, she shaped it with
wooden tools into a round-bottomed cooking-pot. A semi-circle of
pots whitened in the sun. Dried ones were stacked under wood laid
ready for firing. They would emerge glistening black. Kelekele told
how the Lokele language spread because the people of the forest came
to the river for this pottery.

Folk gathered for the funeral. Behind Kelekele's house, his brother
was fashioning the coffin. Inside there was a fine table with
intertwined legs from Bas Zaïre, a piece of petrified wood from the
river, polished like bronze, and a painting of a white female nude.
After a meal of fish, maize and *makemba*, Noëlle returned to the
hospital and I set out with Kelekele for the forest. First, a grove of tall
trees planted by Dr Chesterman, with silvery bark and black fruits
used to treat leprosy in the early days. Scrub reclaimed old manioc
gardens. Wild pineapples ripe for the picking. Termite mounds like
pale grey mushrooms. We climbed to the top of a high conical anthill
and saw giant trunks erupting from the secondary forest's canopy.

A narrow path leads us in out of the brightness. Above black
wellington boots, Kelekele wears white: a foolish *mondele* might lose
him in the dark otherwise. My feet are cramped in tight borrowed
boots. The path becomes a stream with a bed of sand, gem-like gravel
and ironstone ledges. We clamber over a dam of logs with a basket-
work fish-trap set at its centre; we duck under branches and liana
nooses; we climb out on to dry paths. My eyes strain to take it in. My
brain is cramped in a tight skull. This is a dim world of wonders,
mirror and shadow of the village, supply-line into night, rich
resource, other world of lore. A day's march from primary forest, but
already it has the claustrophobia and freedom of a landscape for
another lifetime: the upholstered desert. On a small tree like coarse
elder, ceramic-blue fruits burst from red-green rinds. Kelekele offers
me a red *banane de la forêt*; it splits to reveal white interlocking

segments, like a puzzle except that you don't piece it together again, you eat its parts, moist sweet forest bon-bons. I learn from it as I chew. These buttressed trunks, these festoons, these subtle tints, these exuberant leaves, these riotous quilts of ferns and lichens, all this vegetable enigma is not to be understood; it is a place in which to luxuriate, to be alert and to relax. Let others have the mastery. I point out a squirrel-trap on a branch just above our heads, a creature of twigs and fibres sprung by a pliant stick. Kelekele leads me deep into darkness down an eroded path, but he is not a man of the forest; the people of the forest, the Turumbu, call the Lokele *Ba-Liande*, people of the river.

However, tradition demands that Lokele teenage boys undergo a rite of passage — *libeli* — in the forest; they live in a sacred enclosure for three months; scared and scarred by a dramatization of the ancestors' power, they submit to the elders and to circumcision; skins painted with chalk and ruddy clay, they wear parrots' feathers and cloths spotted like the leopard, leopards' teeth carved of white wood, and shells which fishermen love to catch: a rare mollusc called *lokele loa Ndiya*, "blessing of the water spirit". Initiates wear them round their knees to jangle in the dance. The word *lokele* means "oyster", "spoon", "peace" and "alliance"; elders mix powdered shell with water, sprinkle it on antagonists' heads and sing the song *Aliongo Lokele*, "Long live the alliance". In the *libeli*, the inwardness of river and forest meet: day and night, *lokele* and leopard, quick and dead. Initiates learn the language of the forest, men's power-words, such as the curse *lilwa*, of which H. Sutton Smith writes:

> Say it distinctly, with emphasis on the last syllable, and end up with a jerk. "Lee-lwah." Partially close your left fist and place your right palm over the aperture with a slam, pronouncing the magic word as you do so. Do this in front of a woman or a girl and she will quail before you and flee in terror.

In 1877, when they attacked Stanley's expedition, the ochre-and-white Lokele chanted their war-cry; Stanley noted down "*Ya-Mariwa!*", but what they shouted was "*Nyama li!wa!*"; *nyama* means "meat" and with the curse-word it signifies, "There's meat on the river, let's kill it." In 1910, after a three-cornered debate between village elders, Lokele Christians and missionaries, church members were required to renounce the *libeli* and *lilwa* ceremonies. But still, in village or market, no man will say the number "nine", *libwa*, to a woman because it is so close to *lilwa*. Instead they substitute a word that means "a little laugh".

Kelekele picks a tri-lobed fruit covered in stiff spines and demonstrates its use as a comb. He finds a tree, whose fruit has finer spines, whose fibres were used as thread for fishing-nets until *les blancs* brought nylon. Kelekele gives a little laugh and explains that a man must not speak when he harvests the thread; he must not even greet anyone on the path. After cutting the sticks he must wash, take water into his mouth and spit it out, praying to the ancestors to make his fishing fruitful. Then he can talk. Nylon has expunged this custom, but men still keep silent when they cut wood for floats. The silence of the forest. The darkness of the forest. The language of the forest. Unseen parakeets in the tree-tops. Everything speaks to me, but in unintelligible voices. Kelekele loses his bearings. We circle in the underworld, struggle beneath trunks slumped across a stream, cling to spiralling lianas, push between the caressing fronds of epiphytes that smother the forest's pillars, and blink at sudden sunlight off the water.

A great tree has fallen, a gash in the canopy, a mound of roots and poor soil thirty feet high like a hill in the forest. I pick spherical brown fruits and study the abstract pattern, an enigmatic script, etched into woody skins. I hear snuffling, rooting and grunting. What forest creature is this? Wild boar? Kelekele laughs, assures me it is a village pig. The stream flows out into light. The sun is miraculous, the burning sphere that holds the forest up, fixes the whole ecosystem's nutrients in leaf and timber suspended between exhausted soil and humid air. The pig follows us out into fallow gardens. Fraser's rusty thrush flies into darkness at our backs. A woodland kingfisher leads us riverwards. A female pin-tailed whydah swoops and hovers, trailing long evening dress. Everything out here is airy, sparse and spacious. Yakoso seems like home. Weaver-birds of gold and black, with green tails and orange eyes, chatter sharply and cluster around woven globes suspended from stripped fronds. The palms might be in my back yard. Thirteen hundred miles upriver is nothing. Kelekele did not take me so very far into the forest, but it is the longest journey I have made.

The birds speak, here. At the time of the 1964 rebellion, when the blood of twenty thousand flowed in Stanleyville, fearful folk ascribed to the pigeons a repetitive apocalyptic warning *Ntango ejali te*, there is no more time. Every day between eleven-thirty and noon the kuku dove starts to cry, *Mbele mbele kuku*, to tell the fishermen that it is time for canoes to go downriver. Much earlier, when mist still possessed the river, we started out with a Zaïrian health team in a dug-out with an outboard motor. We sat on stools and insulated vaccine boxes and pressed at the current between afforested banks breathing vapour. Where a path dropped down the bank we clung at branches while a sixth nurse climbed aboard; his T-shirt was emblazoned with *Santé Pour Tous*, his trousers were of Macleod tartan, a stethoscope hung around his neck and a transistor radio in his hand throbbed with the heartbeat of Kinshasa. We glided into the Lindi; past the island at its mouth the river opened out, the sun unravelled the mist, and black-and-white-tailed hornbills led each other a dipping dance on fan-shaped wings.

Lindi means "river". It is the Aruwimi's little sister; its source lies within a day's march of Lake Idi Amin and Uganda. Here, the Tshopo emptied into it, the banks grew higher, and stairways of logs climbed to the neat palisades and huts of small settlements. Huge spiders' webs glistened in dead branches. Dug-outs sheltered in the shadow of the bank's emerald flounces. Smoke filtered upwards from clay hearths. A man often takes his family on three-week fishing-trips, but not a wife during her period because crocodile and hippo scent blood. Nets, cottonwood floats, weights of burnt clay, fish-basket, curing-box, a pestle and mortar, a pot of palm-oil, paddles, punting-pole and people were partially sheltered by each pitched roof of bamboo bound with fibres and covered with drying laundry. We dropped two nurses to conduct a *kilo* at a small village on the west bank. There was treacherous water ahead which we would not attempt but, after ninety minutes on the river, we bucked across lesser rapids and landed on the east bank below Batiakoko. It was a hot steep climb up the cliff's stones and tree-roots.

At the top, an elderly chief in a white crocheted fez welcomed us. The nurses hung scales from the branch of a tree by a liana loop; children were weighed in a sling; this ceremony gives health visits the title *kilo*. Each mother and child had a record card for immunization against polio, tetantus, TB, and measles which is a cruel killer in Africa. Children screamed as the needle went in, and women buried their faces in each other's bosoms. They queued for anti-scabies ointment, a yellow paste which they folded in large leaves. They took monthly doses of daraprim to reduce the risk of cerebral malaria, gratefully received analgesics, and proffered wounds and thrush-infested gums for anointing with gentian violet. These people, the Bakumu of the Lindi valley, are small in stature with remarkably short toes; small people, but great forest-fellers, charcoal-burners and cultivators; despised by the Lokele for being slow, and uneasy in a canoe. But the village that the chief invited us to view, with domestic areas behind rather than before the huts, was immaculate compared with untidy Lokele settlements where, so long as canoes were tended, all was well. In the market, a man with a moustache and piercing eyes beckoned us to follow him between long, low houses to a framework of bamboo and lattice, roofed with shrivelled vines and populated by phallic images like miniature totem poles. The man, the *nganga*, vanished briefly and reappeared adorned with the skin of a civet cat on his shirt-front, a crocodile-skin hat and a staff. He stood proud before his shrine of circumcision fetishes and, after our cameras had clicked respectfully, allowed us to pass on.

A broad path led into the forest. Black and turquoise butterflies sunned themselves on the soil; flame-coloured ones flickered amongst the foliage; a large velvety one, marked like bark, perched on a trunk. A woman, with a baby bound on her back and clothes balanced on her head, came to a log bridge over a stagnant stream; she crouched to wash her laundry. I wanted to ask her about the tiny fenced enclosure nearby. And the bent stick, both ends planted in the ground? A bow-string of fibre, on which folded leaves were pinned with thorns, was stretched across it. Plants flanked it, and between them stood a bowl for libations. Was it a grave? We shared no words, just smiles in the half-world between village and wilderness.

Later, I stood alone by an ant-hill on the cliff, looking down through fan-like foliage upon a deep blue river and canoes like match-sticks. One world to another. I turned to find women in their compounds watching me. We smiled. I couldn't find words to ask the questions. I couldn't find the English. A boy begged me to examine his arm. It was blotched with a pale rash. His terror was leprosy. All I could say was, "*Je ne suis pas médecin.*" Litiliyo Wawelo, a French-speaking Baptist, asked me to come and see a sick woman. "*Je ne suis pas médecin,*" I said, but he led me past his chapel of poles and plank benches to the door of a low house. What about the health-team? No, no, it was me he wanted. We entered the shadows. I could see children, a grandmother, flaking mud walls, a swept dirt floor. Squatting on a stool was a woman in anguish, her eyes brimming with fear. I greeted her, "*Mbote na yo, mama,*" in Lingala; "*Mais, citoyenne, je ne suis pas médecin,*" I repeated. She peeled the cloth from her breasts. One was long and heavy; one a wound, crusted, palely exfoliating, above and below a great black nipple. The roof insisted I stoop, the people insisted I examine. I felt sick, fraudulent, a foolish white man. But it was a *mondele*'s judgment they wanted. The eyes above the

abscesses beseeched me. I knew she'd not want my verdict on her
cancer. In French I said she must go to the hospital at Yakusu, at once.
Litiliyo nodded, translated. He led me out into the heat of the sun. The
woman moaned in the darkness. The white man had spoken.

In the filigree of shade beneath a fan-palm, men mended a rent in a
hunting-net. Would that healing were so nimbly done. A wooden bell
with a wooden clapper hung silent at the trunk. On an old truck tyre
lay a talking-drum, its slit mouth dumb. Citoyen Litiliyo gave me his
address. The *nganga* begged for money. Back at the makeshift clinic,
the last expectant mother had had her blood-pressure taken and urine
tested by the female nurse. A man asked Noëlle about our children.
We have none. Who, he asked, has sinned?

We said goodbye to the crowd, to the chief, to Batiokoko, to the
Bakumu, and slithered back down the cliff to our dug-out. The
outboard motor failed and we drifted for ten minutes, but got back to
Yakusu in time for a meal of *fufu*, aubergines and high antelope
wreathed with flies. The night was full of stars, distant lightning and
fireflies.

When we crossed the Zaïre to Yalisombo, the old chief was bathing
naked at the landing-place. Why had not Yakoso's drums announced
us, he asked. We climbed to the Romanesque church of brick. Its
porch and bell-tower were half-gone. The bell and its beam stood on
the floor. Beyond a lush streamed a line of hollow palm-boles, like
lopped pillars of lost empire, led to the hospital of *The Nun's Story*. It
was a ghost. Notices, like *Consultation*, still clung to the inner doors.
Signs of a squat in a surgery: bedding, utensils, a mournful plant, a
broken window, a gaping roof. The nurse-in-charge had shown us the
roof blown off the corner of his own house, the falling walls, his wife
behind a curtain in a blue-painted room. He regarded the framework
of his new house just as mournfully. He ran a leprosy clinic here, but
the village was no longer a leprosarium.

Burnt-out cases squatted at the doors of ragged houses. Goats
butted each other off the summits of craggy ant-hills. Children saw
us and ran away to hide. Mamas tended pots over fires: three
hearthstones, and three long sticks nudged inwards as they burnt. A
man up a bamboo ladder sewed mats of *ndele* on to the roof of his
house, as we would lay tiles. Towards the centre, the compounds
became more orderly, with broad streets shaded by trees including
rough-skinned mango, *pomme rose* with pear-shaped red apples and
deckle-edged leaves, and saffra or *mosao*. We ate the latter's dark-

blue, almost black fruit, paled in hot water, peeled to lime-green dry flesh, rolled in salt and pepper, a subtle savoury I did not love, a date-like stone.

Through a compound where a friendly society was palavering about a funeral, we approached Yalisombo's heart: a magnificent round-house on an earth-plinth, half-walled with canes, which in the old days would have been adorned with skulls. A slatted door was opened for us; hoops supported the pointed roof above a great talking-drum and wild rubber beaters bound with raffia. It was very hot and quiet in the house's shade. I felt privileged and expectant. Nothing happened, until bolder children began to beat for us on an old cow-hide drum.

Two men plaited cord out of raw fibre. They offered me a tug-of-war; it was strong enough. A man squatted with a baby on his lap and wove a mat out of raffia. A woman dropped an aluminium kettle on a string through the narrow tin-drum mouth of a deep well; it slapped bottom and came up scattering droplets in the dust. A conical pit was lined with splayed poles stained red: a mortar for pounding palm-nuts. Oil was separated on a slide made from a diesel drum. Pulp was squeezed in a fibre net twisted between two sticks. A headless palm stood as a memorial to the oil plantations' technology. Palms grew tall amongst rubber trees; for congealed red rubber, whites drove a Lokele clan from Île Yaolimela; their cousins at Yakoso, where they made their home, still taunt them as strangers.

Scars notched on beige-and-green blotched trunks, V-shaped cicatrices, were healed. Breeze stirred the undergrowth. No tapping of trees or vines, no rubber-barons now, no nun's story. The aisle of the vegetable cathedral led us to the river. The sun was doused by cloud. Wind combed the water. Soon it would be too choppy to cross before nightfall. We called warnings to women at the bathing-place, and climbed down to our dug-out. Farewells launched us upriver with the counter-current, spray breaking over the gunwales, before we took on the mainstream and crossed obliquely to the beach below the Yakusu's market.

We said goodbye to Sue and Kelekele and the rest. Soon, with Andrew and Margaret, we waited for the barque at the bank of the Lindi. The pick-up was a *fula-fula* for hospital day-visitors. Guitar music trickled out of the officials' hut. A drunken *Chef du Quartier* demanded a lift, threatened reprisals. He it was, he boasted, who had authorized the ferry to collect us. *Wapi!* A man cradled tree-seedlings wrapped in leaves, for shade in the city, he said. Another wheeled a

squirming vine-trussed pig between splints on the back of his bicycle.
The ferry came. Its engine shuddered. Women with huge loads
swayed, leaning back to back on the deck. The troubled river was
purple and, above the island, flame-fringed clouds cruised in a blue-
green sky. Nine of us, including a malnourished boy fresh from
treatment, bounced in the back of the pick-up, with rucksacks and the
boy's mother's baggage: a back-pack of wood and vines, provisions
wrapped in leaves, a cloth bundle, a mat and two brand-new cooking
pots. I gripped one between my knees. In it a firefly shifted and shone.
More burned in the outer darkness. Somewhere we passed the *lycée*
arch where *Semper Aliquid Novi* should have blazed forth. Then there
were flame-lit stalls at the side of the track, then tarmac and
streetlamps, and then Kisangani's one set of unchanging traffic-lights,
lightless, saying nothing at all.

Always something new, some new problem. We walked about the
city on gravel, sand and tarmac. We rode on borrowed bicycles. We
got lifts. We tried to find a way to travel south. The Inner Station had
sprouted offices and stores, spread out suburban bungalows. Streets
of palms and pillared shop-fronts looked hollow as film-sets. The
Marché du 24 Octobre was a spacious refurbished square, a parade-
ground for empty concrete stalls, surrounded by shops or ghosts of
shops. Sparse, barely organized shelves looked sumptuous to us. We
searched for clothes-pegs for Margaret. We found sickly banana
sweets and bubble-gum called BUM. It was a hot walk to the makeshift
market. There was no bread there, or in the *boulangerie*, because the
city had run out of flour. Cars queued at a FINA sign because dry
garages had just been blessed with petrol. One day, the market had
been pushed wholesale from permanent to temporary site on scores of
charrettes. It was thick with colour and the smell of stagnant water,
sweat, fish, blood, smoke and aromatic stuffs. Roofs of mats or iron
shaded glowing cloth and women tailoring flounced blouses. There
were polythene sachets of tea, bunches of tobacco leaves, mounds of
garlic, onions, tomatoes, coriander and ginger, all piled and priced.
Pineapples and sugar-cane. Paraffin and palm-oil by the coke bottle.
Second-hand engine-parts. Bits of clocks and watches. Bicycle
repairs. Smoked monkeys and a sleeping baby lay among heaps of
blackened fish. Jewellery glittered against dark cloth, black skin. Blue
flies glistened on fresh meat. The close maze of stalls dilated into areas
where commodities impregnated the very dust; rice and manioc heaps
stood in a white ground, charcoal in black, maize in *el dorado*.

A make-do-and-mend military village occupied several acres of town beside a red-brick prison with castellated turrets; the skeleton of a car stood like sculpture before a small house from which Culture and Art were administered; soldiers and officials drank beer while their wives cooked on the ground. To limit our value as an involuntary source of beer-money, we tried to obtain permits to photograph throughout Zaïre. We got them, though it took five days. Fast. Early one morning I cycled to INZAL — British Leyland — to see the boss, the Honorary British Consul, François Seneque, a genial Seychellois married to a Belgian businesswoman. Two things surprised me: his uncanny likeness to Noëlle's father, who'd spent half his life in West Africa, and the heat in his office. The air-conditioning was off. He explained that he was chilly, malarial. He'd come to Zaïre for two years, fifteen years ago, and stayed. He was used to occupational hazards. He sent me with a note, and his Zaïrian fixer James, to the Hôtel de Ville. There, in what must once have been beautiful gardens, we greeted the sharp and sharply dressed *Commissaire du Région* before entering his pink palace. Its courtyard, corridors and offices were tatty. Between waits, we did the documents-and-passports-routine with four ascending officials.

At noon, James and I walked to Haut-Zaïre's Radio and TV Office. Vines festooned pylons and radio dishes; TV vans without wheels squatted in the rutted courtyard. Three men saw me. My project interested them. But I must return with one wife, two cameras and passport photos in triplicate. That afternoon Noëlle and I cycled in search of Photo-Rapide, negotiating hand-carts and dust-clouds raised by lorries. It was shut for stocktaking. We traversed Avenue Mobutu, a dual-carriageway with grass in the middle and monuments at either end. Before the Hôtel de Ville, where Stanley's statue had dominated old Stanleyville, stood an angular white structure which should have sprouted an eternal flame, black walls shading concrete benches, and a shallow pond, empty but for dust and leaves and litter. At the other end, where King Albert of the Belgians used to stand in what is now Place de l'Authenticité Zaïrois, a fairground-coloured monument reminded me, via V. S. Naipaul of more volatile times:

> The rubbish hills in the centre were being carted away. The corrugated streets were being levelled and graded. And paint! It was everywhere in the centre, slapped on to concrete and plaster and timber, dripping on the pavements. Someone had unloaded his stock — pink and lime and red and mauve and blue. The bush was at war; the town was in a state of

insurrection, with nightly incidents. But suddenly in the centre it seemed like carnival time.

We found a bare studio, a grinning photographer and, two days later, the mug-shots ready as promised. Back at the Radio Station they compiled the documents, affixed photos and discussed their pro-gramme schedule: news, light music, listeners' letters, what's on, women's programmes, and culture in Swahili, Lingala and French. My guts were still treacherous and they brought me a bucket of water to flush their stinking toilet. But the big man wasn't there to sign the papers. We drank sodas at Au Rendezvous Snak Bar — Service Impeccable, found one tin of pipe tobacco in a smart shop, bought a pot of jam from a fat Greek and climbed the great plinth of steps on which the post office stood. We passed bays of P.O. boxes — *circa* three thousand for a whole city and its environs — and queued to book a call to England, North Devon, our mothers. Then we waited for a free booth.

Here Patrice Lumumba had been a postal clerk, and chairman of Stanleyville Evolués Association, founder member of the Belgo-Congolese Union, founder-president of the Post-Office Workers' Friendly Society. Imprisoned for embezzlement, he worked on his credo, *Congo, My Country*. He moved to Leopoldville in 1958 and, after the supra-tribal Mouvement National Congolais was formed, flew to Accra for the first All-African People's Conference. He drew inspiration from Kwame Nkrumah. His Stanleyville speech of October 1959 was famous: riots and prison followed. In January 1960, he was released for a Round Table Conference and arrived in Brussels, with handcuff marks on his wrists, as Kasa-Vubu walked out. By 30th June he was Prime Minister. Senators in Stanleyville and chiefs throughout the Province were tortured. President Kasa-Vubu dismis-sed Lumumba on 5th September, denouncing him for this and for genocide in South Kasai. On 27th November, Lumumba fled for Stanleyville but never reached it. Next day, whites in the city were rounded up and beaten. Soon, Gizenga proclaimed Stanleyville the capital and himself Congo's leader. . . .

Our call was through. We entered a booth and shouted Happy Birthday to my mother. We heard nothing. We were hurried to the switchboard, all wood, brass and red bakelite. There, one word in ten, we gathered that only one letter had reached them. Five minutes for ten pounds. We hoped they'd understood we were fit and in Kisangani. Staging was being erected outside. We were about to begin to wait for a visit from a President who had just reshuffled nine ministers. Back at the Radio station the stamps and signatures were barely dry. Now, they said, the papers must be stamped and countersigned. We fled back to INZAL.

James drove us, in one of François Seneque's limousines, out of town to the old Governor's residence and the Centre Nationale de Recherche et Immigration. We added to the pile of Belgian, Greek and Portuguese passports on the big man's desk. A dossier on us must be compiled. For our protection. Come back tomorrow. I went to sleep for the afternoon. Noëlle worked on a health education display with Margaret, and persuaded her of the virtue of river fish. Rain fell like spears. The gardener came to ask Andrew for yet another advance on wages, for time off because the grass roof of his house had blown away. The fine jam we'd bought was black, seven years old. The cloudscapo waa luminouo. The lavatory wao loud. Chewing DUM wao no cure.

I took *Heart of Darkness* to bed with me. How much more vivid it was now, how much more desperate. I weighed the bleak humour it held. I sympathized with the dramatic irony based on Marlow's ignorance. I'd met the pilgrims. Here they were, stranded in warehouses and stores down-town; slouching Belgians, villainous-looking Portuguese guarding stocks of bicycle pedals, shoes, mattresses, radios, booze and padlocks. I'd met the manager, the helmsman, the crew, some of the gang of virtue. I'd stood on Kurtz's bones. Georges Klein was sick unto death. Dysentery wasted Ludwig Koch and Conrad Korzeniowski. When Conrad was a little recovered Camille Delcommune wrote him a formal letter, in September 1890, begging that he assume command of the *Roi des Belges* until Captain Koch's recovery. Arthur Hodister was away down the Lomami, making for the copper country. I wanted to go there. Put more unintelligible distance between me and home. Frogs' song bored into my sleep. I was baggage aboard a small plane flying in a storm between high buildings that erratically reflected the engines' panicky growl and whine.

All this time we'd been trying for a route south. Any sane tourist would aim for fishing and wildlife at Lake Mobutu, where the *African Queen* steamed before Bogart and Hepburn took command; or for pygmies and gorillas in the Ituri Forest, for volcanoes and Lake Kivu, for snow on Ruwenzori. We wanted to follow the Lualaba/Zaïre. Eighty miles of railway bypassed the Falls to Ubundu, two hundred

miles of river reached Kindu, and a thousand miles' more railway led to
Lubumbashi. But tales told by two Zaïrian students who'd attempted
the journey put us off for good; weeks of uncertain waiting for boats
and trains, breakdowns and near drowning, harassment by soldiers
and beatings by bandits. What looked adventurous from England
looked like madness from here. We hated the idea of flying back to
Kinshasa and on to Lubumbashi, the conventional route. N'djili
airport twice! And the jokes about internal flights: "*Quelle est la
différence entre Air Zaïre et l'Armée Zaïroise?*" Answer: "*Air Zaïre ne vole
pas.*" Instead, we thought of making for Goma and taking the boat
down Lake Kivu to Bukavu; there was a chance that a Methodist
mission plane might fly us from there to Lake Mweru.

Andrew and I jumped over excavations for a new episcopal cess-pit
and tried to make radio contact from the tiny squalid "phoney" room
in the bishop's house. Just fizz, hiss and burble. Bishop Tibafa Mugera
was a small, corpulent, charming man weighed down by money-
worries. We witnessed his joy when an English parish pledged him a
Land Rover, we heard his yearning for a cathedral. The Catholics had
one, down by the river, with *Mimi ndimi ufufuo na uzima* — "I am the
Resurrection and the Life" in Swahili — framed by a painted Fall, the
baptism of a black Jesus and a carved Christus Rex on the cross. They
had guest-rooms off a verdant cloister, and a sealed cell where Pope
John-Paul II had slept. They had shops which made money . . . and
Père Nicholas who, with spade-shaped white beard and dangling
cigarette, presided over a hoard of carved tusks — a cross between
Naipaul's Father Huismans and Conrad's Kurtz. Catholics had made
the Anglican bishop's crozier, a tall twist of ebony tipped and topped
with ivory. With this in hand, tricked out in a wine-coloured hat, red
and purple vestments, a rich stole and a big crucifix on a chain, he
looked imposing. But his *prie-dieu*, his pulpit, his choirs and his
congregation all fitted into his front-room. He picked his nose and
listened to the preaching of Citoyen Balensi, the tailor who had run up
a stylish wax-print blouse for Noëlle. Now she wore it, with a
matching *limputa*. The bishop's wife wore a T-shirt, her bust piously
emblazoned GOD'S GIFT TO MEN.

We tried the Baptist phoney too, in the riverside compound that, of
all Kisangani, must most resemble the old Falls Station. Pastor Mokili
sat before ordered bookshelves at a desk covered with paper, a mango,
a tiny teapot, a cup and saucer. I studied him as he fine-tuned his
transmitter. He was a fine man, called Mokili after a missionary whose
Lokele name it was. An old pastor, who had recently died, was

carrying half a human leg when missionaries first met him. Now, workmen were adding breeze-block aisles to the old brick church on the bank below us to accommodate Mokili's flock. He cajoled the phoney for us, but bad atmospherics scrambled our message.

At last Andrew heard that the Methodists would only fly essential missions in the region of Lake Tanganyika and Lake Mweru; not long ago, in the "war zone" around Moba, one of their 'planes had been burnt, and the pilot shot. We understood. We'd keep our ears open. At least we'd got out passports, papers and permits from the Agence National de Documentation, the security organization that had succeeded the Belgian secret police. The dossier they held on us had a number, inscribed on our visas. And it had only cost us three hundred zaïres. What's more, Danielle Seneque was flying with a freight-load of cloth to Lubumbashi on a SOTEXKI plane which made the trip perhaps three times a year. I sped, sweating and gasping, from INZAL to a white leather chair in her office. Andrew generously fetched our tickets, but even so Danielle insisted I accompany her out to the factory to check. I was chauffeur-driven into a different world. Black, brown and white together, we'd eaten at the old SOTEXKI club in town, swum in the pool to the throb of tennis, the thwack of squash balls ricocheting around roofless courts. But the factory complex was a little empire: its buildings were freshly painted, even its grass was green. Its two thousand workers produced nine hundred thousand metres of cloth a day. Men wielded axes over cotton bales from the firm's plantations. Sparks flew from welding, sawdust from carpentry shops. On ranks of looms shuttles sang like bullets. Great sheds exhaled cotton-warm breath. Our flight was confirmed. We visited John, an Indian from Kerala, in one of the houses where senior employees lived: marbled floors, air-conditioning, clipped lawns, roses. Tarmac roads. A plush club with jungle birds in cages and a swimming-pool. We reclined in the shade of a trim *paillotte* beside quivering blue water above the Tshopo valley. Dug-outs on a brown river, mud-and-grass houses on a bank below great forest trees. Short distance. Two Africas.

Only failure of imagination prevented one seeing this all the time. Like emissaries, two men came peddling pet monkeys and ivory trinkets. The life of forest and savanna furnished toys for the rich. Not far upriver we'd watched how the Tshopo Falls boiled and smoked down rocks beneath a narrow iron bridge with wheel-tracks of planks; just above it water spewed from the sluices of the hydro-electric dam which fed power to Kisangani. Factories and breweries cluttered the far bank, but one noise overlaid and underpinned the Falls' roar: the full-blooded pulse of Tshopo's drums. Below the white water a man spun out a net from his canoe. Two naked boys rushed into the river, then rolled and whitened themselves in the sand. We walked from the beach through tall grass that swallowed up the posts of a volley-ball court. There, I could not have imagined that SOTEXKI world was so close. Beside the Tshopo road, beneath trees and shack-roofs, craftsmen laboured over tusks clenched in vices, tapping, filing, polishing, gripped by an immense rhythm.

In town, men bent over sewing-machines in a row of booths. Across the road, a great bamboo tree shaded men being shaved: a crowd of stools, stands with mirrors, and buckets of pink shaving foam. Back at the *lycée*, students smart as Naipaul's Ferdinand poured out of class. Over the wall a man shinned down a palm-trunk with a calabash full of palm-wine. But one man haunts me: he fell about, raving, down by the river, wearing tatters of cloth, filthy multi-coloured bands on arms and legs, wide eyes staring through glassless welder's goggles, lost somewhere between initiation in the forest and twentieth-century Zaïre.

Part Three

TO THE GREAT WHITE WATER

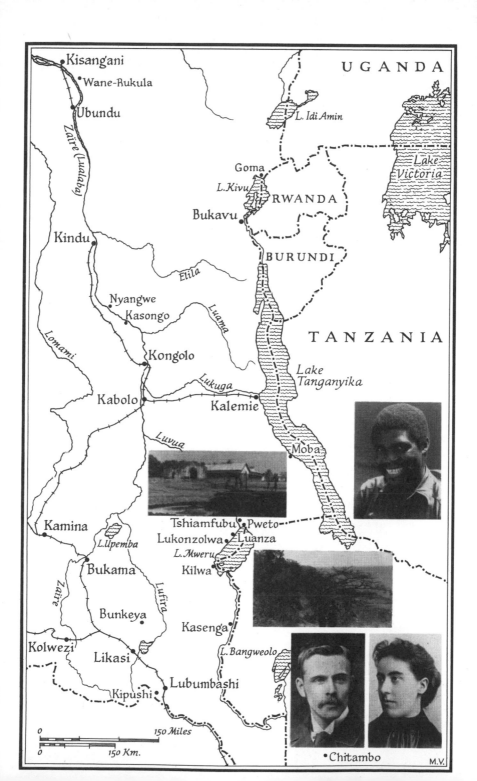

Kisangani
Wane-Rukula
Ubundu
Zaïre (Lualaba)

UGANDA

L. Idi Amin

Lake Victoria

Goma
L. Kivu
RWANDA
Bukavu
BURUNDI

Kindu

Etila

TANZANIA

Nyangwe
Kasongo
Luama
Lomami
Kongolo
Lukuga
Lake Tanganyika
Kabolo
Kalemie
Luvua
Moba

Kamina
L. Upemba
Tshiamfubu Pweto
Lukonzolwa Luanza
L. Mweru
Bukama
Kilwa
Lufira
Bunkeya
Zaïre
Kasenga
Kolwezi
Likasi
L. Bangweolo
Kipushi
Lubumbashi

0 _____ 150 Miles
0 _____ 150 Km.

Chitambo

M.V.

XI

LOW-LEVEL HISTORY

I do not think I was made for an African explorer, for I detest the land most heartily, and I doubt whether he [Livingstone] could have a worse companion. . . . The blacks give an immense amount of trouble; they are too ungrateful to suit my fancy.

H. M. STANLEY *Diary entry of 14th November 1871*

Dear Mr — , I have duly received your complaint against that old native in particular and all natives in general. You and I differ rather radically on this subject, but I again venture to hint (seeing you have been such a short time in the country) that my knowledge however limited cannot be controverted by your ignorance however extensive. Yours truly,

DAN CRAWFORD *A postcard c. 1920*

Hussein offered me a chair and a sickly-sweet cup of tea in the humble office from which he ran his trading-house. He agreed to transmit our arrival time to Lubumbashi in case the telegram didn't make it. He was large-framed, languid-looking; but he chain-smoked Ambassade cigarettes, his bald pate glistened, and his eyes continually played over the shelves, counters, staff beyond the glass. Air-conditioning chilled his little room. Wax-prints, Muslim texts and an Afro-girl calendar hung on the back wall. He was a Pakistani who'd never been to Pakistan. An East African drawn, like Salim, to the centre of the continent.

Hussein saw Gizenga attempt secession from his capital, old Stanleyville, saw him falter, fall out with his support, regroup, extend power to the east and south, falter again and make his last stand in town, with fourteen dead. In 1964, when the blood of thousands flowed here, Hussein fled to Tanzania for two months. The rebels took the city, and sixteen hundred foreign hostages, to bargain with Tshombe's Katanga gendarmes and white mercenaries. Then Belgian paratroopers dropped in. Hussein's business was looted, destroyed. He rebuilt it, and sat out the mutinies and revolts which shook Stanleyville in 1966 and 1967. With the Seventies came authenticity and nationalization. Zaïrians took over the business for a time. Hussein spent two years in Canada, then returned.

Why? With what courage? He shrugged. "It's what I know, the business, the place, the people. They are good workers if you pay them properly, help with medicine and education. Then they don't steal and are loyal. It's a good life: night-clubs, restaurants, discos, and the casino on Sunday." On my walk here I heard music belting from Bar-Restaurant Ekunde and saw a sign advertising Avocat Mbongo's services. "Oh yes, mbongo — money — talks! But I can work with people here." Coarse grass had been cut and spread like a carpet each side of open drains beside the dust road. A man was sweeping it up. Hussein never said, "I love the place," but he did. After the glass office, the store was hot, the street hotter. I passed a park of ruinous concrete benches and rife grass; it looked like a cemetery. A European eye could not help but see decay, amongst the once-immaculate bungalows. Kisangani's people had other priorities. There were deep wounds of dependency and Independence to heal. There was energy, and life to make out of history's leavings.

Dense mist is our perimeter as we wait on the runway in the clammy dawn to board an ancient DC4. Andrew drove us here through darkness made palpable. Past the port, the ferry, the Baptist compound, past the secretive Presidential residence and over a stream to where the mosque's mushroom-shaped lights lined the road with ethereal, swirling glimpses of fretted depths, pale pinnacles. Fire flared in roadside lopangos. Darkness wrapped the humble Bon Samaritain hotel, hid the turning to Wagenia Falls, and all but filled the grand new air terminal. One light, one watchman. The building leaked. Under a high roof the concourse was a pond. There was no water, or paper, in the lavatories. We burrowed through dark corridors and banged on the Immigration Officer's door. He paused in his sleep and, finding his ledger full, slowly inscribed our details on scraps of paper. The watchman asked six hundred zaïres for permission to drive to the

SOTEXKI hangar. We walked. Danielle Seneque had arrived with a Zaïrian and an Egyptian. We rub hands, stamp feet, study the shaky-looking ex-Air France plane and hope it needs nothing much more than paint. I stare into the mist. Three especially potent visions of Kisangani possess my inner eye.

Ten days before, Sunday morning, I'd stood amongst a great crowd on the riverside. Four soldiers watched from the car-ferry's green superstructure. A very black, very slender man of the Mangbetu, with an elongated skull bound in infancy to achieve the effect, climbed on to the roof of a pick-up to get a better view of the water. Two men from the roadside market jostled me gently in the crush. The zip on my bag was being eased open. I closed it, clasped it tightly. They sidled off. The air filled with Lingala hymn-singing. Kisangani is at the Lingala/Swahili boundary; the Anglicans, historically from the north-east, speak Swahili; the Baptists, who came upriver, use Lingala. A long procession of people clothed in white, in ranks of seven, snaked from the Baptist church to the beach. Seven pastors, led by Mokili, waded into the river. Assisted by their sponsors, the first rank descended. Pastor Mokili spoke the sentences. With praying hands, the seven affirmed their faith. The pastors ducked them. Seven by seven by seven they came. Each pastor in turn pronounced the words. The Christians were received out of the water and rubbed down by laughing women. It was joyful. The river that eats rivers declared itself a new creature: a grave for death, a womb from which the reborn stepped back on to the earth, more than four hundred men, women and children.

Saturday. A translucent red sun poised between palms. Then grey clouds, cool wind, hard rain. Towards evening the sun reappeared and we made for Kisangani's principal attraction, the Wagenia Falls. Boys at the car-park threatened to wash Andrew's pick-up. Men insisted on guiding us. Ignore them. Black-headed weavers shimmered in the trees and piles of stone quarried from the river-bank shone purple in the late night. Rugged plinths, stairways, stepping-stones of rock, and water sluicing, frothing and cascading, lay between the bank and the top end of the island on which Conrad saw "a solitary little light" and said to himself with awe, "This is the very spot of my boyish boast." I wanted a mythic place, not a tourist attraction. Conrad found the sordid reality of the Falls Station. "Still, the fact remains that I have smoked a pipe of peace at midnight in the very heart of the African continent, and felt very lonely there."

Kisanga-ni means "at the island". The narrow rapids that run down its near side calm as they reach the island's lower end and form Still Haven where the early steamers berthed. Stanley negotiated with the Bakumu and Wagenia, and established the first Stanley Falls station on the island in December 1883. The man appointed as its chief pleaded to return to the coast, so Stanley installed Mr Binnie, a diminutive Scots engineer of the *Royal*, with thirty-one armed natives, "and left this mite of a volunteer all alone in the very heart of Africa" with tears in his eyes. Binnie built up his station, and his stature among the people. "He rises to the top rank of proper men through sheer pluck and bravery of spirit." Back in 1877, Stanley had first met the Wagenia with force, he confessed to his diary: "Thirteen guns and a few successful well placed shots sent them flying to the village." But he admired their skill: "They are clever at wooden boxes, paddles, cord making. . . . They catch an enormous amount of fish by means of the poles and conical baskets attached to long canes."

I studied those poles: a structure rooted in the rapids, so says Wagenia tradition, ever since the day when their chief woke to hear the Falls' roar subside. He blessed the spirit of the Falls, sent his people to fell timber, set them to building on newly naked rocks, and cornered the market in the currency of the river: catfish, rhino-fish, electric eels, great barbels, tiger fish, Nile perch, Tanganyika perch and *capitaine du Zaïre*. White water flung itself at the poles, the Lualaba with all its wealth. Women pounded washing on the rocks, boys spun nets into shallow pools, men repaired conical fish-traps twice their height, and wove ropes of rattan. Ropes stretched like power-lines between one structure and the next. It would take a few zaïres to coax men to scale timbers, straddle horizontal poles and haul up reedy cornucopias. I paid, and felt they had cheapened a noble tradition, made a side-show of themselves; but I saw that their dignity, their mythology was as resilient as the frameworks that stretched to the island, and beyond, some way into the main stream that plunged down a great step between the island and the far bank. The river might roar, but this monument of sticks silhouetted against the setting sun would stand, pride of the Wagenia who rode it, nimble as acrobats, sharp as knives.

Two days before, we crossed to the left bank with Margaret in a long, laden dug-out. At the beach, as Noëlle stepped into a neighbouring canoe to get ashore, the two drifted apart. One foot in each, she'd have hit the mud or split like a wish-bone had not fellow-passengers dragged the canoes close once more. Her scream turned to giggling. It was to this bank that Marlow, and presumably Conrad, steered. The island station had long since been burnt down by the Arabs. The Falls Station of 1888 — with its plantations of rice, manioc, sweet potatoes, coffee, cocoa and bananas, its warehouses, prison, hospital, and powder magazine, its quarters for State officials, servants, workers, freed slaves and the *Force Publique* garrison — was growing up on the right bank: embryo Stanleyville. On the left bank, the Arab camp still stood above the Falls; just below them lived Binnie's successor; and, below the State residence, stood the premises of the Société Anonyme Belge. This was where Hodister's agent Klein languished. Left-bank Kisangani — Lubunga — was as near as I would get, in the real world, to Kurtz's Inner Station.

It is an undistinguished tin-roofed town thick with trees, as if the forest was already reclaiming it; beside dust roads there are moments of antique grandeur, columns and balconies, ruins and inhabited shells of colonial buildings, the "gothic" façade of a *Rizerie*, the stone wall of nothing at all. The brick tower of the Catholic church alone dominates the trees. Weed-lined tracks lead south out of the Great Lakes Railway station, presumptuous ribbons of iron running from the heart. We threaded between the railway workers' regimented houses, a concrete and corrugated camp where village-life survived; we crossed rough ground and passed beneath gnarled trees until we came to mud-and-wattle huts and the woman that Margaret had come to see. She rushed to get chairs, showed us her son treated at Yakusu for kwashiorkor, showed Margaret the soya she was feeding him, and the shallow latrine that had been dug. She fetched a wizened breast to the baby's mouth. I held the scales while Margaret weighed the pot-bellied boy. He was four, and the weight of a two-year-old. Children crowded round; the small ones smiled. The big ones resumed a serious game with a deflated football. The kitchen was a scatter of pots and charred sticks on the ground. Across the mud threshold was a swept dust floor and a plank covered with tattered books and clothes. Margaret wrote a note for the health worker. The woman knelt to receive it, then handed it to her eldest boy who could read, before accompanying us as far as the railway track. The earth smelt of blood.

Soon we entered an *hortus inclusus*: flowers, shrubs and a dovecote within cloisters. A Polish *père* welcomed us with beer. He summoned two Zaïrians who sat and talked about the *premier poste*, about Stanley's island, and about the slavers Tippu-Tib and his nephew Raschid in the nearby camp. We climbed the church tower in darkness, feeling our way up rough zig-zag ladders. I scrambled

around above the bells, peering through wind-holes. The river snaked
from the Falls, fattening as it went. The horizon, in every direction,
was forest. I saw where we were. Below, the tree-scape was peppered
with rusty roofs; there was no solitary house on the hill, no poles
topped with human heads, no single "wild and gorgeous apparition of
a woman". But the dark tower cast a long shadow; I took in shifting
figures, forest, river, voluptuous clouds. I forgot the Virgin in church,
the poor mama in a mud hut offering a slack teat to her child. I saw
sky, water, trees. I saw Kurtz's familiars and, with Marlow's eyes, the
woman, "savage and superb, wild-eyed and magnificent", bedecked
with fetishes, gleaming with ivory, aglow with brass, whose arms
flung skywards, whose shadow moved on earth and river and
gathered the tin-pot steamer into her embrace.

Forest materializes as mist evaporates. Sadly we part from Andrew,
thankful for all his help, and climb a ladder into the belly of the DC4.
My luggage is longing, my souvenirs visions of a river reborn, of
rapids spanned by proud poles, of the Inner Station's insubstantial
bones. The plane is stacked with bales of cloth, and twelve seats at the
rear give the five of us plenty of room. Everything rattles as the
engines roar. The propellers spin into invisibility. It's reassuring. We
taxi, quaking as if we struggled to escape a chrysalis. We stop. Then at
seven-thirty, an hour late because of the mist, we are launched, pent
and shuddering, down the runway. We clamber into the sky. The
Egyptian is pleased with himself. He hasn't thrown up. He demonstrates the patent thing he sticks behind his ear to prevent it. I walk
from side to side and look out of the windows. We've risen to meet the
sun and, below, the whole world is steaming forest bisected by a
glossy stream punctuated by torpedo-shaped islands and the cataracts
that Stanley battled past. We cross the Equator. Sometimes we lose
the stream, the mighty Lualaba, but for an hour or more we plough an
invisible furrow above the green sward from which the sun has risen
and into which it will sink. My mind skips back to the school
laboratory: the chemistry of chromium. That brilliant metal whose
hydroxide burns to a green oxide fuming and spreading like a
vegetable quilt. Plated, untarnished river. Precipitated forest. Effer-
vescent clouds.

   Conrad steamed north-westwards from the Falls in command of a
Roi des Belges replete with ivory, Camille Delcommune, a sick Captain
Koch, a dying Klein. Koch recovered by Bangala and Conrad's brief
captaincy ended. He watched Klein's burial at Tshumbiri on 22nd

September and reached Kinshasa two days later. After Kurtz died Marlow "wrestled with death". Conrad found strength in Marguerite Poradowska's love: "Indeed, while reading your dear letters I have forgotten Africa, the Congo, the black savages and the white slaves (of whom I am one) who inhabit it. For one hour I have been happy. . . ." The promise of a command on the Lomami expedition was broken. "Everything is repellent to me here . . . men above all. And I am repellent to them too. . . ." How he longed to be sacked, or for dysentery to send him to Europe "if not into the other world, which would at last solve finally all my troubles!" His wish came true. Two days after Alexandre Delcommune's expedition set off, Conrad wrote to his uncle, in a febrile hand, to say he was sick. Conrad made Matadi on 4th December, the day after this thirty-third birthday, and, "always with *Almayer's Folly* amongst my diminishing baggage, I arrived at that delectable capital Boma," he wrote in *A Personal Record*, "where before the departure of the steamer which was to take me home I had the time to wish myself dead over and over again with perfect sincerity." He was in Brussels by the end of January. In London by the beginning of February. In hospital before the month was out.

Hodister steamed south up the Lomami in 1890. Alexandre Delcommune followed with what Conrad satirized as the Eldorado Exploring Expedition. We fly south above a sinuous Lualaba towards its sources in the copper country; we buzz a noble and squalid history of exploration. Down there, mists finally clear. The world shifts into sharp focus. Chemistry becomes embroidery: the forest's needle-point, appliquéd clouds. Giant trees stand above the canopy like pale sticks or stitches. Threads of smoke hang above settlements hidden in green depths, above dun-coloured villages on the banks of a river grandly gathering its silken tributaries. Danielle has seen it all before. She talks of travellers she won't help with lifts, the Stewart Granger white-hunter types with designer stubble, safari-suits, and machetes in their back-packs. "I tell them, you get undressed before you come with me. I'm not travelling with understudy mercenaries." She suppresses a yawn. "Two of my uncles organized safaris until the troubles. They got out. Better than suicide. Now they run a haulage business between Matadi and Kinshasa. What a life. But you have to eat first, then you can dream." She's right but, as I tell her, I try to get paid for dreaming. She climbs on to her cloth-baes and arranges herself for sleep.

I can see the rusty roofs of Kindu, the chief town of the Maniema sub-region set out like a model village: the port, the ferry, the tree-lined streets and the track which resumes the rail-trek south. Kindu has succeeded its neighbour, old Riba-Riba, as the forward post of Islam. Forest thins to savanna. The fluidity of the river is reflected and amplified on land: contours made visible by swirling purples, reds and ochres, all the greens from viridian to lime, snakes and coils and bunches of trees. There is history down there: intricate tales of discovery and dispute entangled with the names Burton, Speke, Livingstone, Cameron, Stanley. Down there are the relics of Nyang-wé; there is Kasongo, and there, after a tortuous progress from its headwaters near Lake Tanganyika, the swift Luama unravels into the Lualaba. In October 1876 Stanley saw the meeting:

> A secret rapture filled my soul as I gazed upon the majestic stream. The great mystery that for all these centuries Nature had kept hidden . . . was waiting to be solved. For two hundred and twenty miles I had followed one of the sources of the Livingstone to the confluence, and now before me lay the superb river itself! My task was to follow it to the Ocean.

Not that it was simple. David Livingstone had spent two years in the Maniema region as the Arabs were expanding into it: "Many have found out that I am not one of their number. . . . I overhear the Manyema telling each other that I am the 'good one': I have no slaves!" In 1869 Mr Punch parodied his convictions:

> Father Nile presents his compliments . . . and begs leave to inform the world that the Father, at the suggestion of the Reverend David Living-stone, has removed his head-quarters to a delightful region about eleven degrees South of the Equator, or Equinoxious line, where for the present he is to be found by his friends. Carriages to set down at Cazembe, a couple of hundred miles or so South of Burton's Lake Tanganyika.
> N.B. You are heartily welcome to any refreshments which you may bring with you. Niggers about here don't need to be shot.

Theft of supplies forced Livingstone to depend on the Arabs until, at Nyangwé in July 1871, he was sickened by their massacre of Maniema and the burning of villages. He could get no canoes to solve for good the Nile/Congo problem, and so made back to Ujiji, that depôt for slaves and ivory, where Stanley "found" him in November. Lieutenant V. L. Cameron too failed to obtain canoes at Nyangwé. There in August 1874 he wrote:

> This great stream must be one of the head-waters of the Kongo, for where else could that giant amongst rivers, second only to the Amazon in its volume, obtain 2,000,000 cubic feet of water which it unceasingly pours each second into the Atlantic?

Cameron was forced to march south and west to meet the ocean at Benguela. Two years later, Arabs and Maniema alike told Stanley that the river flowed "north, and north, and north, and there is no end to it". Stanley and Frank Pocock tossed a rupee, "Heads for the north and the Lualaba; tails for the south and Katanga", and drew straws repeatedly. Always it was tails and short straws for the south. They resolved to go north regardless. Tippu-Tib and his force agreed to accompany them, for a huge consideration. Four days after they tramped out of Nyangwé, Stanley debated in his diary whether to follow the Lualaba north and west to the sea, assuming it was *not* the Nile, or to continue north and north. At Kampunzo, forty miles north of Nyangwé, the 550-strong expedition made camp, Stanley's breakfast was cooking, his mat was spread on grass "soft as an English lawn", and his men cut down the reeds that obstructed his view:

> Downwards it flows to the unknown! to night-black clouds of mystery and fable, mayhap past the land of the anthropoids, the pigmies, and the blanket-eared men. . . . Something strange must surely lie in the vast space occupied by total blankness on our maps, between Nyangwé and "Tuckey's Farthest"!

He at last set his heart on an epic voyage, and set his men to hollow out canoes, assemble the *Lady Alice,* and ride the river to the sea. Thus, with Stanley, the Arabs reached the Falls, the foothold from which they later advanced to Isangi and Basoko.

In 1887 Tippu-Tib was made Governor of Stanley Falls, so that he might police his people for the State, but early in 1890 he retired to Zanzibar, leaving Arab interests in the hands of his son Sefu as sultan of Maniema, Raschid at the Falls, and an old Arab, Mohara, on the Lomami. They had some residual loyalty to Stanley and the British, but despised the Belgians. Hodister pressed south down the Lomami. Like Kurtz, there was no end to what he might achieve. In 1891 he returned to Brussels, was appointed director of the Katanga Company, and voyaged back to Congo with the aim of founding trading stations and posts of the Belgian Anti-Slavery Society on the Lomami and Lualaba. Early in 1892 he sailed from the Falls in the *Roi des Belges*. He sent four men to establish posts at Riba-Riba and Kasongo. He and three others founded posts at Yanga, Bena Kamba and Lomo on the Lomami. But agents and officials were jealous of Hodister's success; they believed in confronting Arabs; the Arabs resented Hodister's stand against slavery; his own men did not like giving up their beds to his favourite local women. Hodister was caught in a web he could no longer control. Of Kurtz, Marlow says:

> Everything belonged to him — but that was a trifle. The thing was to know what he belonged to, how many powers of darkness claimed him for their own. That was the reflection that made you creepy all over. It was impossible — it was not good for one either — trying to imagine.

Maniema, Arabs and pilgrims all turned against the gang of virtue. Two of Hodister's agents at Riba-Riba were captured and their heads spiked on poles before the palace of the chief. Ignorant of this, Hodister approached from Bena Kamba. He was ambushed. He tried to palaver with the Arabs, but his party was seized, tortured, killed and eaten by Maniema troops. Their heads too were stuck on poles. It seems that, at the Inner Station of *Heart of Darkness*, Conrad allowed Marlow to glimpse Hodister's fate through his binoculars.

Marlow never confronts "the horror" in close-up. Conrad — "a Polish nobleman, cased in British tar! What a concoction!" — never wandered off blithely into the wilderness like Casement or Hodister. In them he met an indecipherable ambivalence: "Things I have tried to forget, things I never did know." In himself he found a fascinated revulsion for Africa's underbelly and for the white man's black heart. Hodister wrote against slavery. Kurtz wrote a paper on the Suppression of Savage Customs; scrawled at the foot of its "burning noble words" was the imperative, "Exterminate all the brutes!" Marlow describes Kurtz's paper as "vibrating with eloquence, but too high-strung, I think." *Heart of Darkness* is the same, though Conrad neither wanted, nor dared, to spell out the implications of his tale.

However problematic Hodister had proved in life, his death gave the State grounds for a campaign of conquest dressed up as an anti-slavery crusade. Mohara regretted Hodister's death and took care of his two half-caste children and their mother, but in October 1892 he enticed Emin Pasha to Kinena, east of Ubundu, and had him killed. In November Commandant Dhanis crossed the Lomami. Three thousand Arabs died. The Maniema Chief Ngongo Lutete had changed sides and reinforced Dhanis's forces with his irregulars. Next spring the Wagenia provided the army with canoes and Dhanis took Nyangwé; in a night attack on the Arab camp he captured Hodister's children. Emile Lémery, one of the force, wrote home:

> The ground is comparable to a cemetery of bones. At Nyangwé . . . a thousand people were killed in a few hours. Happily Gongo's men,

cannibals *par excellence*, ate them up at the same rate. It's horrible, but exceedingly useful and hygienic.

Sidney Hinde, an English medical officer attached to Dhanis, recounts how the Maniema Chief was later court-martialled on a trumped-up charge of conspiracy and shot after attempting to hang himself. The scandal fuelled mutinies for years. Dhanis knew what he owed the Chief and was inflamed with fury; he, after all, was made a Baron for his trouble. Hinde graphically describes the short-lived empire that was being destroyed; luxurious houses appointed with silver and crystal, granaries fat with rice, maize and coffee, plantations of grain, sugar-cane, guavas, pomegranates, pineapples and bananas, herds of three breeds of cattle. At Kasongo:

> Our whole force found new outfits, and even the common soldiers slept on silk and satin mattresses, in carved beds with silk mosquito curtains. The room I took possession of was eighty feet long and fifteen feet wide, with a door leading into an orange garden, beyond which was a view extending over five miles. . . .

Danielle sleeps on bales of cotton. The earth is lichen-covered bark, or a liquid batik of all the colours of corrosion, distinct but flowing together, cut clean through by the Lualaba. Tracks radiate from villages. Fields fan out like green and brown-backed playing-cards dealt down on a beige cloth. Single trees stand in their own pools of shadow. Ant-hills stud the terrain with beguiling near-regularity. It's easy to see patterns in landscape and history from up here, freed from the stimulus and anxiety of the immediate. Once, I observed myself like this; high with fever I hovered, cool and peaceful, above my own bed. I watched my sweats, the doctor, my mother, Noëlle gathered about me. I saw the tide of love, and threads of breath that tethered me, just, to life. Now, I watch Noëlle watching Africa. Like the explorers, we have to hack our way into the heart. We cannot overfly ourselves to see where we are. We are too close. The observer affects the observed, attracts and repels the spirit's elementary particles. The uncertainty principle. The past is easier than the present, and the future only lasts so long. Danielle's breathing is regular, but her eyes quiver under closed lids. What chaos is she ordering? What is she dreaming?

Near the Portes d'Enfer, whose gorges almost throttle the furious river, the town of Kongolo holds the memory of invasion, about 1500, by

Bantu from the north led by chief Kongolo, seed of the Luba empire. Maize and manioc from the Americas, brought up the Kasai, fed its expansion in the sixteenth century. Around 1600, a brother of the Luban king broke away to the south-west and laid the foundation of the Lunda empire. Royal messengers trimmed the power of conquered chiefs, co-ordinated the running of the centralized state and controlled the caravan traffic that traversed it, while the military captured slaves, manpower for the agricultural economy. The Lunda expanded in pursuit of Luban slaves, salt, copper and ivory.

In 1798 the Portuguese governor of Mozambique reported that the great chief Kazembe, to the south of Lake Mweru, was waging war against a chief whose ground yielded brass. Eight years later, two *pombeiros* (half-castes), who crossed from Angola to Mozambique, reported green rocks from which copper was extracted in the hills of a land called Katanga. In 1854, Livingstone first passed on Arab accounts of the land of the Lunda *Mwata yamvo*, "king of vipers". By 1870 an adventurer from east of Lake Tanganyika, called Ngelengwa, gained the favour of chief Katanga, allied himself and his muskets with the Sanga copper-king against the Luba and was acclaimed as ruler. He took the name M'Siri (Msidi or Mushidi) and made his capital at Nkulu, later called Bunkeya. When Livingstone, obsessed by the Nile sources, parted from Stanley, his plans were clear: "On crossing the Lualaba, I shall go direct south-west to the copper mines of Katanga. Eight days south of Katanga the natives declare the fountains to be." During his last journeys he learnt more and more about the country of malachite, copper and gold, but never quite reached it. He died in the marshes south of Lake Bangweolo on 1st May 1873, asking, "How many days to the Luapula?"

Joseph Thompson, whose explorations created British East Africa, got as far south as the Lualaba/Luvua confluence in 1878, but could not reach Bunkeya. A German explorer, Reichard, was the first European to penetrate Katanga in 1883. Capello and Ivens mapped its southern border two years later. A Scots missionary, Frederick Stanley Arnot, reached Bunkeya in 1886. In 1888 Dan Crawford met Arnot in England. "He told me of those far off lands beyond the Lualaba. He spoke of tribes unreached by him, but waiting for me. He told me how Livingstone, even in death, had dreamed of that Katanga." Crawford landed at Benguela in May 1889. Eighteen months later, despite fearful obstacles, the nineteen-year-old who had dedicated the rest of his life — whatever his tuberculosis allowed him — to Central Africa, walked into Katanga and M'Siri's bloody nemesis.

We fly low over that Katanga, now called Shaba, "copper". At last I see the Luvua flowing into the Lualaba, a confluence in whose elbow a lake glitters. The Luvua twists, tumbles and glides all the way from my destination, Lake Mweru. I look at the river for the first time, but with recognition, as if it's the road home. Forward, Noëlle checks with the navigator, but he hasn't been following the chart. However, ground and map soon confirm where we are: angular lakes like nerve cells, slime-green neurones threading interstitial tissues of marsh, great Lake Kabamba like shaken foil, a drum membrane vibrating in the heat, fishing villages clustered upon its promontories. The Lualaba slides away to the west, the earth corrugates, brown and black with tatters of scrub, the foothills of the Kibara mountains. The ancient plane bumps and jives over steep bleak valleys, then calms above fields, orange and lime intricacies of ox-bow streams, the tangled ribbon of the Lufira. The Katangan heartland lies within the triangle formed by the Lualaba, Lufira and the Zaïre/Zambezi watershed.

Can you run away home? Escape can feel like homecoming, love and success like death. Travel is gloriously promiscuous: the shifting destination, arrival again and again, the unknown possessed, the quest for an illusory home. So many have travelled light with a heavy heart. The quest for a cure. I'm in the air, unearthed like Antaeus, needing to make touch. The journey is a parable. The heart needs roots. I know it, though I've ignored the knowledge too often.

With Noëlle I peer down at savanna, fields and rumpled hills, trying to see Bunkeya: river, town, and the site of M'Siri's court to which Dan Crawford came, in November 1890. I can't; our flight-path must be just too far east for that. Our shadow speeds across the eastern edge of the lake that gathers the head-waters of the Lufira; its surface is crazed and clear, crazed and clear. Now there is smoke in the air, black and red dishevelled earth, mining townships, great plantations of trees, savanna's pelt and the turn, lurching and bucking through air-pockets, into Lubumbashi's Luano airport. The Egyptian vomits discreetly into a bag, but the touch-down is smooth.

The door swings back. Beyond the tarmac it is autumn on the savanna: straw-coloured scrub, golden and silver trees. The midday sun is brilliant, the wind is keen. Here, almost twelve degrees south of the Equator, it is a different climate. The Peruvian pilot and the Zaïrian co-pilot who brought us down bid us farewell. Hanging on to a knotted rope we descend a ladder into an instantaneous crowd hoping to carry baggage. A soldier asks if we've come from Zambia. No, I say, Kisangani. He looks unconvinced. We walk apprehensively towards the Neapolitan ice-cream-coloured terminal, neat pistachio green and strawberry pink, but officials hurry us through immigration and there are no customs at all. So quiet. Next time it was different. Military bands marched, counter-marched on the airport tarmac. Radios were loud with choirs and the voices of Cardinal Malula and the Pope: the mass celebrated in Kinshasa for the beatification of Nengapeta, the blessed Anuarite. Rather than submit to rape she had been beaten, bayoneted and shot by two Simba colonels on the night of 30th November 1964. As John-Paul II flew from Kinshasa we flew the other way, greeted at both ends by white and yellow banners, *Totus tuus*. Today, we wish Danielle and her companions well and pile into the only visible grass-green taxi. After agreeing what must be a silly price, we speed into town on the landscaped Route de l'Aéroport flanked by hoardings for Air Zaïre, Zambiair, Okapi cigarettes, Lubumbashi Round Table and Mobutu, "our only guide, our only chief, our only saviour".

The route smells of history. Boulevard M'Siri commemorates the old colonialist despot transfigured by myth into heroic freedom fighter. Avenue Lumumba is a road for pilgrims; off it a side-road leads through tall grass to an abandoned farmhouse where Okito, Mpolo and Lumumba, the first prime minister, were held after their flight from Moanda; savagely beaten by Baluba guards, they could hardly stand when they landed; they were clubbed between the DC4 and the jeep which drove them here; and it is alleged that, between 17th January and 13th February 1961, they were murdered here in Tshombe's presence by one of his Belgian mercenaries. Avenue Kimbangu honours the miracle-worker who died, ten years before Lumumba, after thirty years in prison.

White blossom, white villas, white Greek Orthodox church, clouds of metallic violet — jacaranda trees whose white-painted trunks stand in line along white-painted curbs. An old man urinates against one of them; loaded down with freight and loud with passengers, old trucks jostle one another; a closed lorry, all black but for a white cross, precedes us on the Rond-Point de la Révolution; it's the hospital death-wagon. We turn down under a red and yellow railway bridge advertising Gold Leaf and up to where soldiers, "white-hats", are stopping lorries and *fula-fulas*. Occupants who prove reluctant to contribute to their fund are given a hard time. They let us pass, though another day, after twelve hours of sweat and dust, we were stopped for driving into town during *salongo*. The white-hat, who confiscated the ignition key, exclaimed *"Discipline!"*

A row of shops including Pharmacie Luapula and the mud–brick Dancing Club Dallas 2; wire–netting stalls set into hedges, or walled with woven mats; a railway–workers' township. Then larger houses and gardens, some kept up, some run–down. Have Keith and Senga Lake, our contacts here, received our telegram or Hussein's radio message? We turn into a driveway between dark, feathery pines. I'd thought our destination was a private house, but it is a compound: home of seven missionaries, supply-base and guest-house for the Garanganze mission that grew out of Arnot and Crawford's work. It's called "Restawhile". We will, until we find transport to Lake Mweru. At least it's not "Dunroamin". Hussein's phoney message hasn't got through. The telegram has!

"But where exactly have you come from?" asks Senga.

"We've flown from Kisangani."

"Impossible," she says.

Everybody says that.

A MOST MALARIOUS MARSH

Yesterday the trail ran out on this large "tin town", and lo! there I see my first railway train in over 20 years. Also . . . my first motor-car. Then, beyond, the hum and hurry of 800 whites, with here and there a white baby's pram pushed gingerly by a young negro. Hundreds, too, of our natives . . . on scaffoldings and roof-tops working away. They pass the news along that I'm in town, and oh! what a heart-melting welcome I get . . . one is struck with the cosmopolitan look of the place. Above all, the ugly bars — 65 of them — kept by Greeks, Italians and others.

DAN CRAWFORD Letter of 14th March 1911

Congo continues, partly farce, partly tragedy.
    HAROLD MACMILLAN *At the End of the Day*

Dan Crawford walked to M'Siri's capital a year before the great chief's empire crumbled. After "twenty-two years in the long grass" he walked into Elizabethville when the copper-capital was barely a year old. For the first decade of this century, Katanga had been administered from Lukonzolwa on the cliffs above Lake Mweru, a site suggested by Crawford. In 1909 Elizabethville, now Lubumbashi, was a nothing, in Edwin Tilsley's words, "on the edge of a most malarious marsh abutting on the mining area". That year, a prospector shot a rhinoceros where the post office is now. In 1910 the Vice-Governor of Katanga made the pragmatic, if not salubrious, move. Tents and grass huts sprang up. Streets and squares were planned. As

Crawford walked into the embryo city he met a funeral cortège walking out:

> a hundred Britishers all solemnised, but without a minister. Four words in the ear of the chief mourner does it all, and with a look of pleasure he allows me to lead the way with open Bible, out past the railway line, out into the sweet, still African forest where the grave is.

Crawford had strong views about imposing urbanization and so-called civilization on Africa. In a long interview, published in the *New York Times* in 1913 during his one furlough from Congo, he said, "Do you realise what it means to think black for twenty-two years? Every word I utter I must first translate. Every word has become — shall I say, blackened, hoping that you get my meaning?" He talked of seeing his first Elizabethville shop: "I am fascinated as by a basilisk. I stand all eyes at the window, and gradually the money melts from out my pocket." He recalled Dr Johnson and Boswell making their progress down London's Oxford Street. "When it was all over, the silent old Sphinx remarked to the attentive poodle, with a classic grunt and a growl. 'Sir, I have discovered the many things we do not need.'" But, asked the *New York Times'* reporter, does Africa not need progress?

> "Progress? Query, progress!" explodes this amazing man, and jumps from his chair to pace the room. Dan Crawford is small, but there is strength in his square frame, in his knotty hands, while the eyes that look out under the close bushy brows are fiery and keen. He has a most startlingly abrupt manner; his sentences fairly bite themselves in two, and a flashing smile follows every fierce frown
>
> "Progress?" he repeats, and tugs at the confining linen collar quite unconsciously. "There is a going forward that is a going back. Too far east is west. New York will hit the recoil, I prophesy. . . . When I saw your skyscrapers, I saw all, I understood all, I forgave all . . . instead of sprawling out horizontally like John Bull over the face of the earth, Uncle Sam says: 'I'll try the clouds, thanks'. . . . Nevertheless, I must laugh because you are so mad."
>
> And he does laugh. And while he laughs . . . he looks you through and through. The cut of your coat, the turn of your apt phrasing, these count for very little underneath a searching gaze which has witnessed the first principles of civilisation at work and can place your little devices in the history of progress. You feel uncomfortably that you are dwindling.

Like many Scots, Crawford was a frontiersman at heart. "Underneath I have always been, in a sneaking way, an American, and always I shall have faith in you." He had high hopes for the United States. "Underneath all this absurd veneer, you are you, and are truly going forward and up," he said. "But always there is dragging you down this loathsome materialism that I see written on nine out of every ten faces which pass me by in the street." He talked of corruption, of the crudity of colonialism, of the subtlety of African manners and customs, of smallpox and sleeping sickness, of crooked sanitation and crooked morals — "I could talk for twenty years and not tell you half". Of America, he would carry what enriched his vision to Africa. The reporter asked, "Shall you never come back?" He shook his head and smiled; his voice became gentle, "I cannot tell you how much work there is to be done at home. And I am going home to do it."

Like Crawford, Edgar Sengier first came to Elizabethville in 1911, but by train from the south. Or from another planet. He could hardly have seen his place in the universe, his rôle in Africa, more differently. With fellow-Belgian and British mining interests, he planned not a "tin town" but a city of precious metals. Smallpox and famine blocked Joseph Thompson's survey of Katanga in late 1890, but Cecil Rhodes's partner Robert Williams oversaw systematic prospecting and, with King Leopold, founded the Union Minière du Haut Katanga in 1906. Edgar Sengier was to become its President, in control of the most powerful force in the Congo, with a concession more than half the size of Belgium inherited from the Katanga Company. He was Hodister's heir and, to quote John Gunther, "one of the great unknowns of our time".

Sengier came to the Belgian Congo. Casement's Congo Report had been published in 1904. The Commission of Enquiry, which Leopold set up to justify himself, found against the king. He was toppled from his Free State perch in 1908. The Belgian Parliament paid him for the privilege of taking the Congo over. He died in 1909 and his will was probated at $80,000,000, but records of dealings and concessions were destroyed before they could be audited. Mark Twain proposed a memorial for Leopold — forty avenues of skeletons leading to a pyramid of 15,000,000 skulls — and Vachel Lindsay's *The Congo* provided an epitaph:

> Listen to the yell of Leopold's ghost
> Burning in Hell for his hand-maimed host,
> Hear how the demons chuckle and yell
> Cutting his hands off, down in Hell.

In 1911, Sengier had to walk the hundred miles from shanty-town Elizabethville to the mine at Kambove, near Likasi. The railway had not yet pushed north-west to Likasi and Ilebo on the Kasai River, nor west via Kolwezi and Dilolo to Benguela on the Angolan coast: the great Benguela Railway, completed in 1927, which laid down an iron road where Crawford had left footprints in 1889–90. From almost nothing, if you ignore the long line of noble African "copper-eaters" dating back at least to the eighth century, Sengier and his colleagues built an exploitative, paternalistic industrial empire without parallel in tropical Africa, digging not graves, but vast holes in the "sweet, still African forest".

Whatever you think of this success story, the "progress" it embodied, the training of skilled Congolese, the hospitals, schools, housing, welfare services, clothing and food that were supposed to compensate for low wages and vestigial unionization, in Zaïrian minds it remains the Union Minière of dismal memory. It did not just gouge riches from African soil. It was parasitic upon the African soul. The wealth of the ancestors was stolen for quick gain. In the Depression of the 1930s, people flocked to railway stations to watch whites departing with the spirits of black men in their baggage, destined for slavery in Europe. In better days, fat whites in First Class were said to be on their way to a leave-long feast of butchered black flesh. It was an old story. In the Belgians' model black hospitals, people were killed, so it was said, and their souls exported to *Mpoto* to make "the many things we do not need" that were imported into Africa.

The Kitwala movement, that arose in the Stanleyville region and spread in the east, is an indigenous Watchtower/Kimbanguist cocktail, whose Jehovah's Witnesses preached that colonialism was the handiwork of Satan. God has three Sons: an Asiatic Jew, a European and an African. This last suffered hurt and mockery at his brothers' hands, but the apocalypse would soon bring justice for the black man, and theocracy instead of government. This, in the 1930s, was dynamite. Black prophets, come down from Heaven, were arrested and chained for proclaiming that, within months, *bantu* would gain white skins, though those who worked for *blancs* would stay black. Around safe white dinner-tables, these hopes and fears were a great joke; they made a change from guessing at the salaries of Sengier and the other directors of the Société Générale; bosses preferred their employees, and their mistresses, to keep their colour; and wives, who shared a *penchant* for Elizabethville's famed male prostitutes, exchanged winks and the knowledge that they liked their lovers black.

You may laugh too, and agree with M. Grévisse, *Commissaire District* of Elizabethville in the 'Forties, who qualified his considerable appreciation of African intelligence by adding that,

> in the mind of every African who has come into contact with the white man's way of life there is a clearing, larger or smaller according to circumstances; but round the edges of that clearing the primeval forest still stands, and very strange things sometimes come out of it.

Implicit in his liberal-minded opinion is the myth that the white man stands out in the open, under a bland and rational light. Conrad knew he did not. The passage from clearing to forest filled him with horror. Casement made the voyage blithely at first; then it became burdensome. Crawford enjoyed the forest's embrace for almost forty years. He knew that those black-and-white African myths of colonialism, with the hopes and fears they hold, are shockingly apt metaphors for the truth.

Lubumbashi's Kenya Market squats and sprawls in the tarnished orange dust of a brick and breeze-block township. A white man haggles over drums of black-market diesel. People crowd and shove us, importunate to the point of aggression. Our slow market Swahili, learnt in the civility of Kisangani, has no chance here. It's a rich city, with relatively high wages and higher expectations, sprung from a prospectors' town with an eye to the main chance. In Yoka Lye Mudaba's *Tshira*, a dance of masks and shadows, the cultivator mourns:

> Our lands have been violated for the sowing of coffee, cocoa, cobalt and copper. . . . Mother, look! your fields are shrinking like a troubled skin, and your sweat no longer fertilises them, but feeds the jackals of these civilised times.

There's a predatory spirit, an entrepreneurial edge. Amid the hustle, the white man is having a hard time exchanging drums of contaminated fuel: drums of water topped with a layer of diesel. He tells the dealer what his filthy oil will do to his vehicles. "They will die." *Kufa*, "to die" and "death" in Swahili and Lingala, applies to any breakdown, anything that's clapped out, finished. I speculate on the connection with the Kikongo *fuka*, which means roughly the same. *Kufa* is in the air here, but the white man gets what tests with dip-stick and hose promise is cleaner fuel. He's a good customer; the scarcity of legitimate supplies means he'll be back for the South African stuff. In the maze of stalls the press of people parts for rolling drums which young men heave up on to the back of his truck.

The air bites sharply at my nose and throat. I can taste the sulphurous tang of hell. The tall chimneys of the Lubumbashi smelter rise high above us, but heavy fumes drain earthwards. The city's greatest landmark is a black mountain of slag growing ever skywards. It is a reflection of the great pits, the city's reason and excuse. It is the negative of white villas, office-blocks and churches.

The mammoth spoil-heap is a mine waiting for more advanced technology. The slag contains two per cent copper. Inefficiency is not such a worry when your ore is ten or twelve per cent red metal. Eighty-year-old machinery, safety standards to match, budgets shot to hell, Zaïrian bosses consulting the old white bosses at four times the previous salary bill, debts of millions: these are set against the black mountain, investment for the future. The past has been treacherous. Between 1973's policy of Zaïrianization and 1975's radicalization, the world copper price crashed from £1400 a ton to £600; copper represents seventy or eighty per cent of Zaïre's foreign exchange. A fickle world market transformed the national economic dream to nightmare. Colonial capitalists were succeeded by black *nouveaux riches* unused to economic trauma. Soon the heavy footfall of the World Bank and International Monetary Fund resounded in the corridors of power. The zaïre was devalued again and again. The Mobutu Plan recognizes that the image of bronze has feet of clay; it aims to restore productivity, self-sufficiency and nobility to agriculture. Years of compulsory planting in Belgian times, education and the flight to the city made the young despise the soil and the hoe, but growth and harvest must complement the country's mineral spoils. The story continues.

At night we wait outside the Gecamines refinery gates. This morning a tour was booked for us. I look forward to treading the catwalk above molten metal, to witnessing ruddy torrents in breath-stealing, skin-searing heat, to watching cool alchemy in the electro-lysis shops. A man comes to the gates to announce that the tour is cancelled. At three o'clock this afternoon the furnaces were shut down. For a month. So it goes.

Edgar Sengier and his successors have been concerned with more than copper. Kasai-Oriental is number one in the world for industrial diamonds, but most of the country's metal ores are mined in the Shaba. Zaïre is now only seventh in the league of copper producers, but it supplies sixty per cent of the world's cobalt, as well as tin, zinc, germanium, cadmium, manganese, tungsten, columbium, platinum, silver, gold, radium and uranium. There used to be a large block of pitchblende, from Chinkolobwe, standing at the entrance to Elizabethville's old museum. It was black and gold, and blotched with a greenish encrustation. It had a sinister celebrity and a label, *Attention. Bloc radioactif!*

At the beginning of the First World War a Belgian prospector brought a lump of *blende noire* to the local manager of Union Minière, an American interested in nothing but copper. The bankrupt prospector later sold his pitchblende to a mineral dealer in London. A Belgian professor of geology bought it; he'd never analysed such rich radium ore. In 1922 the Chinkolobwe mine opened. It closed before the Second World War, because the market for radium — hospitals and laboratories — was saturated. The mine was flooded, but only to be reopened secretly and with great difficulty. Sengier made sure of it. In 1943 it began producing uranium ore for the United States: 3,650 tons in 1946, for instance, at a cost of $5,332,000.

It is a brilliant, clear, autumnal day. For autumn read dry season. Golden and bronze leaves lie crisp in the gutters. Half-naked trees scour a sky blue and blue and blue as the salts of cobalt; tall plump cacti, green as malachite, stand up to the sun. It is forty minutes' hot walking to the museum. Noëlle is dressed in her wax-print outfit, black and brown on turquoise. In the bustle of Avenue Kasenga and in the tree-lined residential streets she receives compliments from Zaïrian men, smiles from women. The stylish new museum building was finished in time for Independence. That is, for the secession of Katanga under Moïse Tshombe. It became a barracks, and then a brand-new ruin. On the paving outside, a man is assembling shards of pottery from an archaeological dig. Curved and finned roofs, sheer concrete and stone-faced walls shelter well-ordered exhibits. We buy tickets, a guide-book, and a guide for a whistle-stop tour of Central African history and pre-history. We are the only visitors.

Stone Age tools, weapons and cave engravings, seem as far removed from us here as they do in museums at home. The Bronze and Iron Ages are not distinct; the Iron/Copper Age saw the rise of agriculture, metallurgy and ceramics. Skeletons in graves of the eighth to sixteenth centuries are accompanied by knives, spades, copper bracelets, ivory beads, shell currency and richly decorated pots with elaborate rims, lips and handles. A notice spells out the message: "Beyond death and beyond forgetting may our exhumed treasures bring hope and pride."

We have seen humbler versions of these pots in villages, and the potters moulding them. Their tools are set out on the first floor, in one of the dioramas that celebrate traditional crafts: spatulas, stones, maize spears, string, toothed wheels, with which women shape and decorate vessels great and small, crude and intricate, for water and oil, pigments and tobacco, liquor and glowing charcoal. The museum's thick walls keep us and the exhibits cool. We could be in Europe,, looking at dead things.

We have watched men hollowing *pirogues* and mortars, carving rods and floats, hafts and spears, masks and figures; we have heard drums and gongs, stringed instruments and xylophones like these; felt the forest from which timber is chosen for lightness or weight, resilience or resonance; wood worked with iron, and finished with the abrasive leaves of *Ficus capreaefolia*.

We have seen plaiting and weaving: split bamboo, reeds, palm ribs, lianas and fibres made into ropes and mats, sieves and winnowing frames, granaries and baskets, fish-traps and filters. We have bought raffia velours like these, dyed black and red and gold, woven in zig-zag and triangular patterns, prized as barter currency or dowry money. Such fabrics reached the west coast in the fourteenth century; about 1500, Duarte Pacheco Fereira praised Congo's "cloths of palm leaf soft as velvet, some embroidered with velvet satin, beautiful as any made in Italy".

Though the finest craftsmanship is seldom seen in the real world, and too much belongs to history, many of these things are hardly museum-pieces. Everyday artistry is on the street: a fish-joint placed, so, on a waxy leaf, the swing of a market mama's hip, her elaborate coiffure. But in here, there are things beyond our recognition: copper *croisettes*, currency cast in the form of a cross. A Kongo crucifix of the fifteenth century, with the patina of pain. Glass beads, perhaps Venetian, imported by Arabs. Photographs of late nineteenth-century village life: the intricate riches of tribal cultures on the brink of being tamed, vandalized and reorganized by force.

Here, reconstructed, are furnaces for smelting copper and iron that were built against termite-mounds in the dry season; remains of many have been found around Lubumbashi and in the forest towards Bunkaya. Iron ore or malachite is reduced in a charcoal furnace fed with air by ceramic pipes and bellows of leather and bamboo. Iron is worked on the anvil, *Nyundo*. Copper is re-smelted and poured into *croisette* moulds. The smiths here, like Kongo's blacksmith-king, held great power to themselves. Crawford gives us a newcomer's glimpse of the mythscape:

the ground begins to echo a metallic sound . . . the great Miambo copper mines, a huge mass of mineral rock, riddled all over with marks of excavation, and all oxidised into green. Exactly like a great old fortress shaken by war and riddled with shell.

We emerge into Lubumbashi of the black mountain. But on this side of town the sun shines clear down upon Belgian and Dutch-colonial-style houses, upon men in *abacost* suits, women in chic European clothes, and cars cruising broad boulevards towards the theatre. Youths are playing football in the park and, beyond it, the grand Hôtel de Ville bears the slogan, *"Le M.P.R. Avant Tout — La Reste Après"*. Elizabethville's bones have been reclothed in black flesh. The photographs in the museum still bear the stamp "Musée Belge de l'Afrique Centrale", but most things have been reclaimed. The Katanga Company's 1891–1990 lease on concessions was annulled in 1967, and the Union Minière dismantled. Belgium and its works stand all about us, but post-colonial amnesia has done for it. In 1975, V. S. Naipaul observed,

> how surprising it is already that so little of Belgium remains in the minds of the people. . . . Most of those under thirty had heard nothing about the Belgians from their parents or grandparents.

But, set in a white arcade of boutiques, shoe-shops and jewellers, is the jewel of Belgian enterprise, Chez Monique. The white *patronne* gives us a nod and we climb upstairs to a table bathed in the aroma of coffee; soothed by the bland piano-playing of Richard Clayderman, we are served by waiters offering gâteaux, tarts, fresh fruit, pastries, sumptuous ices. Other tables are filled with businessmen, officials and, across the room, a lively group of office-girls. I order strawberries, an *abricotine coupe* and two coffees. There are a few whites in here too and, at a table together, a sleek Pakistani, a fat Greek and an obese Belgian glare caressingly at the black secretaries. In their eyes blouse buttons pop, skirt zips sing, breasts swell, thighs glisten. The tray is unloaded. We sip at novel delights. A sad-eyed, elegant young man sits alone by the window. Chez Monique imposes its own manners. The young man's face takes fire; up the stairs sweeps a black goddess in flowing skirts and a cowl top, as if she's alighted from a fashion-house catwalk; she and her fabrics settle at his table. They kiss, in public like white lovers. On our menu, beside a request not to deface it, is the inscribed equation, "Doris + Jonas = $\heartsuit$".

In the heat and dust down among Renaults, Mercedes and pick-ups, I took out my camera to snap the streetscape. Instantly a beggar on crutches vaulted across the road crying, "*Interdit!*" The mere mention of my official permit made him cringe, ask pardon and creep back to his pitch. Cameras stayed in our bags, though, when we walked in the main square. The Post Office was a strategic target — like an airstrip, a bridge, a dam, a port, a frontier, a soldier — and its portrait was not worth prison. Everything stayed firmly in our bags or pockets, for we were besieged by men and boys selling gold jewellery, carved wooden figures, elephants in polished malachite, reliefs of village life in beaten copper, boxes of geological samples, ivory, apples and strawberries. In the Park Hotel, the tariff for a room with a sink, running cockroaches and no water was 2,000 zaïres (£28 or $40) a night. Postcards there were fifty each, the same price as the copy of Placide Tempels' classic study, *Philosophie Bantoue*, that I bought in the St Paul bookshop across the square.

We squatted on the pavement, beside a shoe-shine boy, and watched whites supervising road-works — preparations for the Pope's visit — in front of the Post Office. I thought of Moïse Tshombe's reliance on *blancs* and wondered if much had changed. When he recruited Belgian paratroopers, Italian soldiers and German stormtroopers for his mercenary force in January 1961, he said, "In these matters I trust only whites." He held on to Belgian advisers and wooed Union Minière for their taxes. He kept his British and American friends sweet with anti-communist rhetoric. After the Coquilhatville summit of April, he was charged with high treason and the murder of Lumumba, but gained his freedom by agreeing to end Katanga's secession. He reneged as soon as he was back in Elizabethville. This was a routine he performed again and again. June, and the first anniversary of Independence, was rife with rumours of bribes, double-crosses and coups. The balance of power was impossible. Kasa-Vubu with Ileo and Adoula, Kalonji in his Diamond State of Kasai, Gizenga in Stanleyville, and Tshombe all clambering on a see-saw, trying to get off the ground; Kennedy and Khrushchev, poised between the Bay of Pigs and the Cuban missile crises, had a hand at either end; the fulcrum was the United Nations, set off-centre, to the right; the CIA was both discreetly and crudely throwing its weight about. Gizenga was named deputy prime minister and temporarily threw in his lot with the régime. UN troops arrested many of Tshombe's mercenaries and occupied Elizabethville's Post Office and Radio Station. Tshombe seemed to capitulate, but not all his mercenaries were repatriated. In mid-September UN troops had to resume a fierce fight at the Post Office and other key positions.

Conor Cruise O'Brien, who had demanded the removal of Belgian agents from the Katangan secret police, prematurely pronounced Katangan secession at an end. Tshombe fled to the British Consul's house and then to Rhodesia while the fighting went on. Katanga had the one jet fighter in the Congo and used it to strafe UN positions. Dag Hammarskjöld flew by an indirect route to meet Tshombe; his pilot announced his descent to Ndola airport just after midnight on 18th September, and then there was silence. Daylight revealed the wreckage nine miles away. The fighting went on: atrocities, UN blunders, strategic cease-fires, air attacks upon Elizabethville, Kolwezi and Likasi. Macmillan supplied British bombs for Indian Canberras. UN mortar fire hit a hospital. The USA, opposed by Britain and Belgium, pressed Union Minière to pay taxes to Leopoldville. Talks were, in Edmund Gullion's words, "endless, labyrinthine, Byzantine, Bantu," and Tshombe drained Adoula's whisky dry. "I have signed nothing." He ducked and dived, allied himself with the pro-Marxist Gizengists, went on and on. Finally, in January 1963, Tshombe renounced his secession. Elizabethville was no capital. The furies were free to find a new focus in Stanleyville.

The Post Office looked safe and solid now. Suddenly, Noëlle jumped up and grabbed her bag from the hands of a man, shouting, "You bugger! *Voleur! Mwizi!*" I hadn't felt a thing, as he slid it from between us. He walked off unconcerned. No point in chasing, or calling the police. People smiled and shook their heads, but where did their sympathies lie?

Kids hawked model cars and trucks intricately made of wire. We checked passport, papers, money, camera and went to Pharmacie de la Santé to buy pipe tobacco of a sort. A man pushed a very nice carved box of mineral specimens under my nose.

"*Combien, citoyen?*"

"*Six mille, monsieur, un bon prix.*"

"*Wapi!*" I said and took a hard look, "*Deux mille.*"

So we bargained. At last he led me off the street into the marble hall of a shop, where I dealt 2,500 zaïres into his hand. Back at "Restawhile", our host, Keith, reckoned I'd got a good deal. He knew about these things. He talked of artists and craftsmen he valued, and of the Chengi brothers, famous sons of a Catholic priest, who carved wood, worked copper and painted for prices higher than we could afford. We bought two canvases by Kahilu, atmospheric scenes of forest and savanna, framed in semi-precious *Tchikalakala* wood.

Keith and his colleague John knew about thieves too. While they filtered drums of precious diesel in the compound, they described how the back walls of their locked store-houses had been removed brick by brick at night. And they knew about white men: such as the Belgian officials brought in to sort out corruption in the Customs here; they were sacked for creaming off so much loot; "We knew we'd get caught," they said, "but if we'd known how quickly we'd have taken a bigger percentage."

We are waiting for a lift. There seem to be no traders or missionaries driving to Bunkeya just now. We could try for a lift on a lorry going to Kolwezi; drop off at Mulungwishi and hope for a ride north. It could take days or weeks and I don't feel strong enough yet. One of the women missionaries here has been waiting three weeks for a lift south. Our priority is Luanza and, after only a few days, Bev Turner arrives from Ndola with Kabula at the wheel of a white Landcruiser that serves as Luanza's ambulance. They have to gather supplies in Lubumbashi, and get first-aid for the Landcruiser's pan-caked suspension, before driving north-east to Lake Mweru. There may be room for us. Then two more New Zealanders, Murray and Joy Stephenson, arrive, on the way south from Luanza, in a Chevrolet truck with a leaky fuel-tank. That, and numerous road-blocks, have held them up badly. They and their children are red with dust and exhausted. Their companion, Mukunto, the Zaïrian *prefet* of the secondary school at Luanza, seems fresh enough. He talks to me of his home town, Bunkeya, and of his people, the Basanga. The Bemba people of Luanza have accepted him more easily than they do people from Kasai. He is pleased that seven of his pupils passed their secondary exams last year; they cannot afford to come to University here, but have to be happy earning money fishing. At school in Bunkeya he was taught about the great M'Siri. The present chief is his descendant, and on 20th December every year M'Siri's story, as told by his son, Mwenda II, is rehearsed by the elders. The story told at Luanza is that of *Konga Vantu*, "Gatherer of the People", Dan Crawford. "You will hear it," Mukunto says, "when you reach home." And to make sure of it he helps Kabula re-tension and re-bolt the Landcruiser's offside rear spring.

Crawford's memory lives. Murray says that after celebrating his spirit, his strength and his wisdom the people unfailingly recall how, if he lost his temper or wronged them in any way, Konga Vantu would go down on his knees and ask forgiveness. "There are not many white men, even now, who'll do that!" So I may meet him more fully than I dared to hope. I walk down Avenue Kasenga a little way and turn off on dust roads that run between small houses set in hedged *lopangas*; it is a twilight zone, this urban village, semi-deserted, quiet, with smoke from fires stealing upwards into the last lustrous light. Beyond is the savanna: a vista of scrub trees, ant-hills, spoil-heaps, indigo mountains. A booming and a thudding shake my thoughts: two lads kick big oil-drums expertly down the path. My greeting, *"Jambo, habari?"* is sucked into dry ground, stony faces. The vast indifference, the shifts in perspective, the time-warps this trip presents, they make me shiver. I walk back in the dark. I'm kufa'd.

There was beef on the table. John had taken us to an abattoir. A crowd bought and sold bloody bones outside the gate. Inside *commerçants* queued for coils of orange-skinned sausages which they cut up and sold in chunks in the market. The big man was a young blond Belgian who dispensed fine ranch-grown meat off immaculate white counters to fashionably dressed colonials. His staff staggered out to waiting cars with crates of choice cuts. So we sat down to roast beef, Yorkshire pudding, cauliflower cheese, carrots, tomato and onion salad, boiled potatoes, rolls and butter, followed by baked Alaska and coffee. We hadn't seen a meal on that scale for months. It was wonderful. The novel tastes assuaged the guilt. This was a guest-house, after all. It would have seemed ungrateful to consider what Crawford said about missionaries who lived in style: "Shut up in their cosy comfy mission stations they were far, yes a million metaphoric miles, far away from the natives." So many South African imports too, and I knew what Crawford thought about South Africa.

The talk was down to earth though. Rosemary and Sandy, a doctor from Jamaica and a nurse from New Zealand, were doing a statutory *stage* at the Sendwe Hospital before going into the interior. The politician, Jason Sendwe, was a medical student whom the Belgian system had barred from qualifying as a doctor. At the hospital named for him, there was a new grass-roofed extension to the morgue. Respiratory diseases were rife, thanks to Gecamines. AIDS too. Sandy was horrified by the rats and cockroaches. A woman had been brought in on Saturday with a miscarriage, haemorrhaging badly; she was told to wait until Monday and would have bled to death had not missionaries come to her rescue. There was no plastic surgery, and Rosemary described a woman with thirty per cent burns on legs, abdomen and breasts, under general anaesthetic for the fourth time in a month; her wounds were scrubbed with Savlon and a hard brush.

One day we met them from work. A colourful queue of people carrying bowls of food waited quietly for visiting-time. A woman burst from the hospital gates with her arms flung high, walking in a trance, wailing an extraordinary tune, strong and plaintive, an exalted dirge, her spirit straining after the spirit of the dead. Sometimes I can almost recall the fierce quality of that sound. Sometimes it seems like the anthem of Africa.

In the mission compound I felt detached from the world. Noëlle looked and felt good. Her hair was glossy, not frizzy. Her skin tanned. Her metabolism agreed with the climate and the vitamins. She read Greene's *The Heart of the Matter* and recognized it. I thought of Scobie asking himself why he loved the place so much. "Is it because here human nature hasn't had time to disguise itself? Nobody here could even talk about a heaven on earth. . . . Here you could love human beings nearly as God loved them, knowing the worst. . . ." I drew water for washing from an oil-drum in the compound and we went to bed with blankets and a hot-water bottle. Went to sleep with wild drumming in our ears. I dreamed I was playing light-hearted tag with a crowd of Africans, hawkers perhaps, the lads with oil-drums, Kahilu's hunters coming between the ant-hills, the thief, the white-hats; I was chased, chased, chased and suddenly, in my dream, weapons appeared; I grasped a knife and woke wanting to use it. I lay there chilled, appalled. Had Lubumbashi's edge cut me that deep? Had it summoned up the spectre of racism in me? Nightmare Kurtz? Or a simple anxiety dream, the cumulative effect of dealing with endless obstacles, uncertainties and officials? The drumming was oddly comforting. It lulled me back to sleep.

Keith drove us sixteen miles out of town on the Likasi road. We passed a windowless, almost roofless secondary school and the run-down University whose library, a black professor told us, had not been able to buy books for years. Bush, brick kilns, termite mounds, leopard-skin hills and the flooded mine-workings of Lukuni. We wound around the lakes to the spot that Keith, Senga and the children liked best. A crowd of boys on the cliff above us were watching a white priest and a black girl swimming and cooking food on a camp fire. Now we too would entertain them. We unpacked chairs, a cool-box, a cold-drink dispenser, a picnic-set and an inflatable rubber dinghy with oars. We rowed after ducklings on the lake; skeletal branches poked above the surface, bleached by the searing sun; we swam in blue water under cliffs of ochre and green. Copper sulphate guaranteed the water bilharzia-free. You could pick up malachite everywhere.

What was it like before it was dishevelled, before Sengier and Elizabethville were names here, when Crawford met Captain Bia and Lieutenant Francqui at Ntenke, a little to the west, in 1892? Francqui made astronomical observations, plotted their position on the map and told Crawford, with mock seriousness, "We are now in the middle of Lake Bangweolo!" The Lake, and the swamps that killed Livingstone, were a fortnight's march to the east. So much for the map. The swamps killed Bia too. He carried the fever with him to Ntenke. Blackwater overtook him. For two days the bouts horrified Crawford, who bathed his body and shared the vigil. Lucien Bia, who had discovered the famous copper mine at Kambove only months before, died in Dan Crawford's arms.

We swam, and ate, and walked around the open-cast terraces that stepped down to still, sapphire waters. The parched grasses were like blades. The near hills shone with green ores, the distant ones were blue. Sengier walked this way to Kambove in 1911. I had Kambove and Lukuni's minerals in the box I'd bought. I had samples of uranium ores too: Kasolite, Cuprosklodowskite and Pitchblende. Before Sengier reopened Chinkolobwe mine for the Americans in 1943, he was able to supply them from a New York warehouse where, on his own initiative, he'd stockpiled Congolese uranium ore in 1940. Despite the fact that Belgium was occupied by the Germans, the Belgian Congo provided all the uranium for the United States' war effort: Enrico Fermi's first chain reaction in Chicago in December 1942, the first atomic bomb test of July 1945, the bombs themselves. Sengier was in New York. Early on the morning of 6th August 1945 the phone rang in his hotel room and a voice told him to stay by the radio all day. They thought he had a right to hear. Hiroshima. That was forty years ago and far away and closer than you think. We drove back to Lubumbashi in marvellous ruddy light, the grass like fire, the green leaves luminous, the tarmac a blue sheen, the sky deep, the cloud above the city violet.

XIII

EXODUS

Oh! hearts that meet, and hearts that part!
  The world is full of sorrow:
Men love and die — th'almighty mart
  Puts up new hearts to-morrow.

Was this Creation's scheme at start?
  Oh! then I little wonder
That Lucifer's proud human heart
  Preferred to God His thunder.
ROGER CASEMENT The Heart's Verdict

Born as I was by the seashore, now it is the curtain of memory rises, and this
wide waste of waters welcoming us as we emerge from the long choking grass
makes us feel as though we had escaped from a tropical trap.
DAN CRAWFORD Thinking Black

There was room in the ambulance, just. We'd packed it tight. Soon
after 5 on that Sunday morning we took our film from the fridge,
stuffed the last things into our rucksacks, and took off. Dark, cold,
misty. Empty streets with no soldiers to stop us. Kabula drove fast,
even after we left the tarmac. Bev, the pathologist from New Zealand,
and Noëlle were in front; I was neatly packed amongst boxes, bags,
water-bidons, diesel-cans, an oil-drum, and a vaccine-fridge, when all
at once potholes and ridges made everything lurch, judder, shove,
abhorring the vacuum that was me and my air-space. All the lashings

of cord that held the load relaxed; I fended it off with knees and elbows, holding on tight. If I relaxed it encroached, and my head beat a tattoo on the roof. Through the side windows I could just see the purple sky. The back windows showed glowing, swirling red dust. This, I'm told, is what you pay for on trans-African safaris: a view of miles and days of dust-cloud from the back of a truck. I wore all my clothes but was frozen. Clenched hands, tensed limbs were numb.

Then, mercy! we stopped. We'd timed it right and reached the first military barrier 6.05 when it was supposed to open. It was closed. I tightened knots, repacked what was toppling, extracted Noëlle's anorak and put it on over mine. Opposite a small mud fort, there were huts and a *paillotte* where soldiers with greatcoats and automatic weapons huddled by a fire. A very tall soldier and a short one stirred. They looked at the red cross, said "*Mission du Luanza?*", grunted and wandered off. The barrier was lifted. We rattled across the first of many noisy bridges over shrunken, dry-season streams and rivers, leaving a queue of lorries waiting to enter Lubumbashi and soldiers free to extract "tolls" unobserved by missionaries. That's what we were, for this trip. *Missionaires*, prudently pronounced, not to be confused, please God, with *mercenaires*.

An iced pond, speared by reeds. We were above four thousand feet, but I hadn't expected it to be this cold. I hung on with blue fingers and let my nose run. On this same day — Sunday 21st July — in 1889, Crawford's small caravan left a plain studded with stately trees between wooded mountains, penetrated a tangled mass of forest and forded four streams; he mounted his donkey for the crossings but, at the second, was tipped in head-first. It was the fifth day of his march from the Angolan coast to Katanga, and already he had remarked to his diary, "Oh! the raw coldness of the morning. It is difficult to believe oneself in the Torrid Zone." He had landed at Benguela, with Arnot's party, in early May. The first whites he met were a widow of a few days and a mother mourning her first baby. Languid Portuguese traded calico, rum and gunpowder for rubber and slaves. Malaria put him to bed for ten days. Arnot found no carriers at the coast and went inland to raise a caravan of 160 men.

Crawford grew restless, hired six bearers and, independently of the other missionaries, bade farewell to the Atlantic. The nineteen-year-old ex-lawyer's clerk with TB started for the heart of Africa with one personal bundle: bedding, spare coat and underclothes, an ulster, a pair of slippers, a cake of soap, as much tea as he could hold in two hands, a small copper kettle and a cheap rifle. Slave yokes and shackles by the trail. His first hippo. Great baobabs and cacti. His Lunda carriers redeemed one of their own women from slavers. First mountain ridge. First negotiations with King Ekwikwi. First big river crossing in a leaky bark boat. He met the Arnots at Bailundu but marched on without them, after drawing one bale of barter cloth, a medicine chest, books, utensils, and a box of goods for the Portuguese veteran explorer and ex-slave-trader, Senhor Silva Porto whose house was on his route.

With his six loyal carriers, he crossed soft black bogs, deep streams, creaky bridges, through herds of game and a bush fire. To his fresh eye ant-hills were domes and minarets, "as though some sculptor had been let loose to turn this long tract of country into a miniature Moslem city". On 6th August he suffered from the cold wind, "biting, because my thick jacket was stolen at Bailundu by some poor black, who doubtless thought he deserved at least one of my 'many' belongings". The wind's dirge and all the noises of nature were in the minor key: "Old earth's sighs for what? 'To wit — the redemption'." Four days later he reached Belmonte, Silva Porto's house set amongst tall sycamores in the kingdom of Bié, and found it reduced to charred ruins. The septuagenarian Porto was living in an outhouse. His first landfall in Africa had been marked by guns saluting Queen Victoria's coronation. He had met Livingstone in 1853. His influence had helped Arnot escape Barotseland in 1884 and set him on the road to M'Siri. Silva Porto congratulated Crawford on his small baggage: "That's the only way for Africa."

With forced marches Crawford tried to join one of two caravans leaving Chisambo, but just missed both. He stayed in a mud hut with Mr Currie, the American Mission's vanguard. Both Portuguese and Biheans were edgy. The new king Chindundumuna was "the terror who makes earth tremble". Crawford's route was blocked by warring and politics for the next ten months.

He redeemed the time by learning Umbundu and observing village life. On his own he could melt into the background. "You only hear what you *over*hear," was his motto. When Arnot's party, less three who had died and three who had turned back, caught up with him at the end of the year, they built a station, cultivated and sat out the rainy season. Crawford felt the contrast keenly; he saw that living with seven whites was an obstacle; linguistic mistakes were reinforced; the people adapted their ways to the whites; rich musical idiom degenerated into kindergarten talk. Crawford took himself off to a village as the chief's guest. His windowless, chimneyless hut had a stool, a narrow bed and a grass mat. He absorbed habits and customs, joined men around the evening fire and, after snuff-snorting had catalysed palaver, learnt tales and proverbs. He, for his part, began to "lisp the sweet tale of Calvary". When a villager lost his prized gun in the river, Crawford dived for it, not a little encouraged by the reward of a pig. He didn't find it. "I wanted that pig badly; I had eaten no meat for a long time." Intuition became policy: to be free among the people by forgoing the luggage of European life. He was gloriously contented, if always disturbed by his colour's fake prestige. "One thing I often wish I had not, and that is a white skin."

The sun red and huge, the sky silver-gilt, the dry earth bronze-pink, grass like fresh wood-shavings. People moving between dawn fires wrapped in pale, flowing cloths. Thickening bush. Termite mounds in successive styles, pillars, mushrooms, volcanic cones; successive colours, white, buff, orange. Charcol-burners' huts like bee-skeps, stumps of trees, smouldering trunks. Oases of palms and banana trees marking villages; houses increasingly painted with stripes, zig-zags, chequerboards, stylized plants and figures in white, black and ochre; grass roofs increasingly shaggy like punk thatch. I was acclimatized to claustrophobia now. Bridges took us over watercourses where people washed between shocking green growths of grass and reeds. We turned left, off the road which leads to the Luapula River, and drove straight through the hunters' checkpoint where, on the return journey three weeks later, we were inspected for game smuggled from the Kundelungu National Park. We halted in the village of Kabiasha. My lurching, shivering world settled.

   I got out into pacific sunlight, silky air. Long before the state set up rest-houses in large villages, Crawford established them around Lake Mweru, simply furnished and supplied with eggs, fowls and flour by arrangement with the chiefs. The mission still has a simple two-roomed hut in Kabiasha, and the use of a tiny, exquisitely thatched latrine in a grass enclosure. The caretaker and his wife welcomed us effusively with water for washing and a gift of oranges. I warmed up, we were refreshed. I saw what had been at my back, the swell of the Kundelungu mountains rising to six thousand feet. In a high cleft, falls sparkled off the plateau. At the far side of the mountains I knew that the Lofoi River plummeted down vertical falls of over a thousand feet, the highest in Africa, and rushed on into the Lufira valley, Crawford's first destination.

At the end of 1889, his route was still blocked far off in Angola. Chief Chindundumuna, the "terror", ordered the party out of his territory and sent a war-band to enforce his will. Silva Porto walked twelve miles to warn them. But the leading warrior recognized Arnot, and all was well. Next, a Portuguese military expedition tried to pass through with herds and hangers-on. Chindundumuna's forces repelled them and feasted on the spoils. Silva Porto had determined upon peace, but his overtures were rebuffed. He retired to his ruin, advised his people to find safety with the missionaries and dragged ten barrels of gunpowder into his private chapel. He spread the Portuguese flag over them and lay down on the bizarre couch. "Above a sinister trail of black powder that snakes its deadly way into one broached cask," wrote Edwin Tilsley, "the wrinkled old fingers fumble with their last match . . . *Boom!* go the ten barrels. And the soul of Silva Porto goes out upon the crash to meet its God."

At last, in May 1890, Chindundumuna allowed the standard to be raised for a caravan. The Arnots and three others remained, but Hugh Thompson, Frederick Lane and Dan Crawford pushed on for Katanga. Crawford was the youngest, now twenty, but he had grown a full beard, a sign of maturity in Africa; he recruited the keenest carriers; he spoke their language. All acknowledged his leadership. They started on 3rd June and were steadily marching eastwards throughout the time of Conrad's stay with Casement, his trek to Kinshasa and his Congo voyage. Always delays, always one more river to cross, always hard bargaining with ferrymen, wily Charons who tipped loads in if mid-river terms were not met. Crawford's apprenticeship in palaver was rewarded with generous compensation and respect: "then it was that I learned the cash value of proverbs".

In mid-August, with relief, they crossed the Kwanza River and entered the territory of the Loimbe, who went almost naked, but wore fantastic head-dresses and wove beautiful cloth. They saw the spiral-roofed huts of the Chokwe; the hungry, sandy land from which Livingstone had once feared he would never escape, and "a sad, heart-revolting sight": a monster slave-caravan of perhaps eight hundred from the Luba country, months on the march, aged men and women near death, girls with burdens of rubber, mothers with new babies, crawling children. Crawford sprang with a stick at a black master who was clubbing a girl, his *olombongo* — "moving money", on the head. The man ran, but so did the slave children when Crawford smiled at them, for was it not white men who would buy

them. Crawford wrote up his journal at sunset. "An hour ago I
could not have trusted myself to write of the harrowing sights."
The Spectator seized upon his account, in *Thinking Black*, as evidence
of Portuguese complicity in the "suppressed" trade. My brother-in-
law vividly remembers seeing yoked slaves in Angola in the late
1930s.

Though food was scarce, Crawford did not touch a tin of white
man's rations. Tea was his indulgence. Wild honey was prized.
Scrawny chicken, which Casement suffered too frequently on the
river, was an occasional luxury. Fortunately Crawford liked manioc-
bread. "Some cannot bear the smell of it, much less the taste. To me
it has the far-off taste of bread and cheese." Crawford brought up the
rear through forest where stragglers were often captured from
caravans. By the time Conrad arrived at the Falls Station,
Crawford's party faced starvation, but thanked God for a little
manioc bought from a trading-party that had just been reduced and
robbed. In the next few weeks provisions grew more plentiful, the
land more populous, the politics — rights of passage — more
devious and dangerous. They saw blacksmiths at work and received
demands for gunpowder. They dispensed tribute of cloth and salt
and beads. They buried a dead carrier secretly to avoid fines and
delays. Here was their first African lake — Kalundu; here were the
salt flats of Kifumadzi; here was Kangombe, the Luvale chief who
had decapitated Mwata Yamvo of the Lunda; here, at Lake Dilolo,
they crossed Livingstone's old route to Loanda; here they entered the
Congo State. Dynasties in flux and the words of Ezekiel recurring in
young Crawford's head:

> Thus saith the Lord God . . . exalt him that is low, and abase him that is
> high. I will overturn, overturn, overturn it: and it shall be no more, until
> he come whose right it is; and I will give it him.

They saw Queen Nakandundu, her limbs covered in bangles of
copper and brass. After a week at her town, crossroads of scores of
trails, they began the last month of their march. Crawford redeemed
slaves, including Sombo, a baby girl. He and Lane made a detour to
the headwaters of the Zambesi. They passed Mirambo copper mines
near Kolwezi and entered the Lualaba valley. Renewed hunger,
tricky negotiations and the river-crossing were "dreary, and, if one
had let it be so, soul-withering". A note from the remarkable Charles
Swan, whom Arnot had left at Nkulu with the saintly W. L.
Faulknor, bade Crawford come on alone.

At last, on 11th November, he saw Arnot's village on the hill and was blinded by tears. He climbed, and Swan came down to meet the blue-eyed, brown-bearded boy in ragged kit. They clasped one another. Swan asked, "Where did you get those boots?" They laughed at the yellow boots with curling pointed toes, once the property of a Portuguese convict, that Crawford had bought in mid-march after his boots, and his slippers, had fallen apart. "Do they fit?" "God's provision always fits," said Crawford. At the hill-top he met the Canadian, Faulknor, looking ghastly pale, disabled from long illness; and turning he saw, sooner than he had expected, the great M'Siri, swathed in calico, sitting in state in a little green tent, "really he! He received me most graciously and kindly, and after handshakes asked me to sit on his right hand." M'Siri enquired after his companions; then turned to a retainer, "Son of the dust, go, bring them."

Formal audience and presentation of gifts took place at M'Siri's favourite wife's village. M'Siri ruled through his wives. Each of them, six hundred or so, had a village within reach of the capital. This one was extensive, palisaded by stout poles topped with white balls. Like Marlow at the Inner Station, Crawford had the sudden sickening realization that each ball was a human skull. Crude tables at the gates were piled high with skulls. "The very branches of the trees are festooned with the same mortal fruit." As they approached the king — *mfumu* or "death-man" — flies rose and resettled on a fresh head.

Three executioners squatted with axes before the waiting crowd. On the queen's verandah, two Arab secretaries took notes. At the apex, M'Siri sat enthroned, his ridged and lumpy scalp, a head of which he was inordinately proud, frosted with white hair. He was pleased with the blue cloth, the printed handkerchiefs, the robe and turban of Indian silk. Pleased too with Crawford's grasp of Umbundu; he was no stranger to it. Had he not sent his nephew west to open up the trade route? Had he not linked the Indian and Atlantic Oceans with a road of blood and gunpowder? He, not the white man, had pushed the Zanzibar trail through to Benguela. M'Siri was the empire.

On the trail Crawford had repeatedly heard, "He is very great: he slays much." Was he not one with Kara ya Rova, Chief of All Peoples? Kara had led humanity up from the south. Some, seeing the riches of Katanga, stopped to enjoy them; their penalty was blackness. The rest followed Kara north to wealth and wisdom; they kept their whiteness. Kara had left great footprints in the Kayomba mountains. M'Siri had stood there too and had masons carve his prints in the rock. Now the whites were returning. The Swahili had prophesied that a white man would come from the east to steal M'Siri's copper and gold. Within his skull-topped stockade, outside the many-roomed palace of Nkulu, M'Siri kept a sharpened stake ready for him.

Arnot had come, but from the west, in 1886. Faulknor and Swan, likewise, the following year. Two days before Crawford arrived, Alfred Sharpe had come from the dreaded east for the British South Africa Company; he left treaty documents with Swan in case M'Siri should change his mind and sign: Arnot had warned him not to put his name to bits of paper. Sharpe complained, "These missionaries do a great deal of harm when they take it upon themselves to advise native chiefs." He little knew how hard the missionaries worked to prevent M'Siri putting an "accident" in his way.

Crawford suffered recurrent fevers, headaches, bone pains; his "examination for residence" he called it. Swan looked after him in his mud house at "Mountain View"; Crawford wrote, "Mr Swan is the dearest fellow I have met for a long time, and we are so happy." In the lion's den, between bouts of malaria, his twenty-first birthday came on 7th December. M'Siri had little more than a year left. Crawford looked out across the Lufira flats to the sheer red ramparts of Kundelungu.

Our road ran between the Kundelungu mountains and the Luapula River. I was in front now, enjoying the heat; Noëlle in the back with the dust. Mile upon mile of autumnal woodland. Curled bunches of bamboo leaves looked like giant cream blossoms. It was dry, but not as dry as on our return. Then it was parched, but clumps and drapes of bindweed shone with lilac flowers; one village was full of white chickens, charcoal and white-blossomed trees; the forest trees had sprung lush, glossy, bright green leaves: foolhardy flourishes, miraculously forecasting the rains. Now, charcoal-burners' smoke seeped through the brush, and huge black birds with white wing-tips took off for the swamps. Kabula drove fast and expertly through sand-slides and over potholes, missing the occasional lorry on tight corners. It was exhilarating, this ambulance-ride, enhanced by the thought of the great white water ahead.

Crawford and Lane began to visit M'Siri every Thursday at his court: "We are seeking systematically to attack the citadel of his soul — that old black heart of his so long garrisoned by him whose name is legion." M'Siri was proud of his "white slaves". Proud too of his half-caste "white wives", especially of the three-parts white Maria del

Fonseca who called white men "brother". Crawford she called "uncle" since her real uncle, a slaver, entrusted her to him by deed of guardianship. White slaves might preach, but Maria, a Lady Macbeth in voluptuous velvets, was the only one who could shout "Pig!" at M'Siri, for she allowed him his title of *Telwatelwatelwanekumwinemputu*— "the-always-ever-spoken-of-one-yea-even-in-Europe-itself". For her he sent a caravan of ivory to the coast to be bartered for English china; the return load chinked for a thousand miles; all was smashed. Later, as a sick woman, she made for Crawford's lakeside town but died at the foot of the Kundelungus; her last wish, that her uncle should bury her in a white coffin.

By April 1891, Thompson and Faulknor had gone. Swan, Lane and Crawford moved down from "Mountain View" to be nearer the people, and M'Siri's palace. As they built, Paul Le Marinel arrived from Kinshasa, via the Kasai and Sankuru Rivers, with a three-hundred strong force. Conrad had helped to equip it. He had expected a place on it, or on Delcommune's Lomami expedition. King Leopold had despatched both, and Bia and Stair's Katanga Company expeditions, to prevent the British annexing the copper country. At Nkulu, Le Marinel's store of gunpowder exploded, killing twelve. M'Siri dreamt bad dreams about Belgians. Short of gunpowder, he abused Kalawfwa (Crawford) for utterly refusing to help him renew supplies; five times in 1891 Crawford outfaced his fury and still did not join the accelerating death-roll.

The kingdom's tribes rebelled, disrupting trade, and the Sanga began night-attacks on Nkulu. Crawford started preaching in Luba, astonishing Swan with his fluency. Swan left with Le Marinel, while two officers remained to set up a fort across the Lufira, on the north bank of the Lofoi. In July, M'Siri sent his last white slaves after them to fix the site of a new capital on the Lofoi's south bank. He never followed them. Crawford and Lane found good water, better health. Crawford wrote, "I have built my little mud hut in the most bewitching spot imaginable," amongst wily monkeys' chatter, hyenas' guffaws, lions' rumbling, but out of earshot of the terrible crescendo "Die, son of the dust!" He was joined by Mushimishi, one of the executioners, sick of his trade. He worked on language-study — Luba, Sanga, Lunda, Ushi, Lomotwa, Swahili and Yeke — scribbling with one nib and home-made ink in the light of a sesame-oil wick, a strip of shirt in the spout of his coffee-pot. When that last nib broke, how jealously he guarded his two pencils.

Alone, or with Lane, Crawford walked from village to village preaching peace and reconciliation in the middle of Luba/Sanga warfare. When cloth ran out, they were reduced to accepting food from the new State fort, and to hippo and buffalo hunting. M'Siri sat tight in half-deserted Nkulu. In October, Alexandre Delcommune's expedition arrived via the Lomami and Lualaba. M'Siri took secretary Crawford into his confidence and dictated a letter to Sharpe, recalling him to make a treaty with Britain.

In the November rains, Crawford began, with one man, to clear the forest for a garden to support his five adopted boys and the little girl, Sombo. In December he went to meet Thompson's returning party, and dared to refuse a warrior escort. "I am your friend," he told M'Siri, "but I am also the friend of the Sanga, and of your meanest slave." Crawford had accompanied Delcommune southwards a little way; the expedition's geologist had later been ambushed by Sanga who mistook him for "Kalawfwa". Crawford survived his twenty-second birthday and, though Thompson brought no personal baggage or reinforcements, he was glad of trade-cloth and mail from Britain. M'Siri expected great gifts, and flew into a terrifying passion at the Britishers' poverty. Crawford never lost his awe of these outbursts, though he knew M'Siri was just as likely to bellow to his court, as he did many times, "Sons of the dust! When I die this land is Kalawfwa's."

A messenger appeared before M'Siri and Kalawfwa to announce the imminent arrival of Captain Stairs, "Englishman Lord of Artillery": he who had demonstrated the brand-new Maxim machine-gun in Matadi. Crawford was sent to meet him. The force came from the east flying the Congo Free State flag. A Belgian, not a British, embassy. M'Siri panicked, consulted his overworked *féticheurs*, offered Stairs blood-brotherhood. Stairs declined. M'Siri refused the flag. Stairs planted it anyway, next to Nkulu on the sugar-loaf hill where M'Siri had long planned to build a stockade of elephant tusks. Then he ordered M'Siri not to kill again. All power, all prestige gone! At night, M'Siri slipped away to his first wife's village. Next morning, Stairs' men found him. Captain Bodson, a Belgian, took Zanzibari troops to fetch him to Stairs' camp. M'Siri challenged him and spat on the ground. Bodson advanced to the verandah, drew his revolver and shot M'Siri in the heart. Musaka, a bodyguard, shot Bodson and two Zanzibaris before he was killed. The dying Bodson, white man from the east, cried, "I have killed a tiger! *Vive le roi!*"

Stairs built Fort Bunkeya out of Nkulu's stockade. He ate his Christmas dinner off the door of M'Siri's palace. Crawford went to visit: unchallenged, ungreeted, he tapped the sentry on the shoulder and the man fell down. More than sixty of the garrison died from dysentery and stealthy shootings. Stairs evacuated the fort, carrying M'Siri's head away in a kerosene tin. He died before reaching the east coast. The people ascribed his death to great M'Siri's magic.

In the heat of the day we drove into Kilwa on the shore of Lake Mweru. The man at the barrier waved us on with a lordly glance. Bev had business to discuss with a Belgian doctor. We found him in his living-room, with his wife, three children, five *pères* and two *soeurs*, gathered around a map of Belgium stuck with flags marking all their birthplaces. They toasted the anniversary of Belgian Independence. Unexpectedly, and gratefully, we shared an Independence Day meal of carrot soup, roasted marsh antelope, and almond gâteau. The nuns twinkled and chuckled as the doctor gallantly topped their coffees with whipped cream and whisky.

Later, a Zaïrian woman welcomed us beside her much humbler home. Beyond an upturned boat the lake's skin glittered like scales and Kilwa Island's tawny pelt stood proud; westwards, dim intimations of the Zambian hills; southwards, the mouth and marshes of the Luapula; northwards, water unfurling beneath headlands: Lake *Mwerumukatamuvundanshe*, "the great white water that drowns locusts". Our hostess brought us water to wash hands. Corrugated roof, thin rafters, mud walls, black vinyl sofas, a meat-safe, table and chairs. We ate sandwiches, drank tea. A rat ran round the swept mud floor. The woman lovingly presented us with lemons and, desolate that she had nothing else, knelt to give me a ten zaïre note. I could not refuse it. I thanked her as effusively as my small Cibemba allowed. We left what pathetic, precious gifts we could: sugar, aspirins, elastoplast.

It was not until May 1893 that Crawford had his first sight of Lake Mweru shining "like a mass of liquid gold", and not until two years after M'Siri's death that he found a site on its shores. Those two years were rich and strange. Their inwardness is described in *Thinking Black* and their chronological fullness in Tilsley's biography of Crawford. Early in 1892, Lane left. Crawford felt the parting sorely. As he and Thompson travelled in the ex-kingdom's chaos, people begged them to stay and be their protectors. "We find the stupid and mischievous notion has got currency that since Mushidi's death we are the chiefs of the country." They made reconnaissance to the north where whites had never been. They saw the havoc wreaked from Kilwa Island by Simba and his Congo Arabs. A chief summed it up: "There was a great lion in the land devouring the people; now the lion is dead the people devour one another."

Back at base Thompson fell sick, so Crawford reconnoitred south with his five adopted youths, including seven-year-old Sankuru; no tent or food, just cooking-pots, a square of cloth, writing materials, quinine and a bible. Between sunstroke and fever he preached, hunted, escaped lions, met great hospitality. At Ntenke, Captain Bia died in his arms. Over the Luapula Chief Chinama cried out, "Come, come, I am old, but Konga Vantu is our father and our mother; the country is yours and we are your children." Konga Vantu, "gatherer of the people", was Crawford's name until he died. He was realistic: "they over-estimate our importance and influence."

At Lofoi once more, he suffered pleurisy. A flood swept everything, manuscripts, vocabularies, house, garden and all, away. Thompson rebuilt. Crawford climbed across the Kundelungu mountains and linked up with Livingstone's trail beyond the Luapula. Chief Kazembe had not allowed the Belgian Bia, to cross, but welcomed the brother of Ingeresa (Livingstone). Young Sankuru was reunited with his mother, but chose to march on. Crawford battled against severe neuralgia, septic grass-cuts and rashes. They returned home to a great welcome, after a terrible climb down by the Lofoi's gorge. Crawford discarded his boots for it. "I don't care just now to write or think about that descent, for some of the awful giddiness . . . still clings to me."

For three months, July–October 1893, he lived in extreme poverty, immobilized by lack of barter goods, dependent upon the generosity of those who flocked across the Lufira to live near him. Thompson waited to enter Luba territory but, as soon as he could, Crawford began his reconnaissance around Lake Mweru. In November, as he drew near Kalungwishi on the eastern shore, he saw the Union Jack flying above a British post. He fought with nostalgia. Bainbridge, an official whose colleague had just died, fed him, clothed him, gave him medicine and a letter from his sister addressed "Dan Crawford, Central Africa". It held a few grains of cocoa which they shared. Crawford was shy of his revived feelings. He wrote pleading with his dear mother to "cease the plaintive queries about coming home". He tried to nourish Bainbridge's fearful spirit. After five days he moved on northwards. "I have set my face like a flint to break up the virgin soil about here for years to come." Soon Bainbridge was dead. The rains beat the lake to a frenzy. Crawford staggered with malaria; there was bright blood in his urine; it darkened as blackwater fever took hold; he fell into a coma.

★

Our road became rough, sandy, hot, exquisite: we bumped up stony gradients, gazed down steps of land to the lake and Kilwa Island lapped with blue; we plunged into ravines, crossed rivers where women washed clothes and children fished. Silver, sapphire, emerald, gold. Freshly harvested reed-grass. Bush punctuated by trees, mountainous termite-mounds, black slopes of burnt-off scrub. Richly decorated houses, simple grass ones. Stalls empty but for one or two *paipai*. At Mukuba I met a man keen to greet Konga Vantu's great-nephew. He brandished Tilsley's biography, coverless but complete; he couldn't read English, but cherished the photographs and coloured them with memories. He gave us his blessing and a leg of antelope. Kabula sped us onwards.

Crawford surfaced from his fever at Pweto, the northernmost point of the lake. His young men had carried him many miles. Chief Mpweto's people danced tirelessly, singing a praise-song to Konga Vantu, full of hope that he would settle near them. Mpweto told him of a gathering of people at Chipungu on the western shore. By canoe, Crawford's party crossed the narrows where the Luvua flows out of the lake and twists through wooded mountains. By foot and water Crawford came south to Chipungu, where the Muntemune stream spills down. Chief, elders and people made much of him. They agreed a site, on a shelf of land above the lake, below the hills. The chief carved a square of bark from a tree. Crawford aimed and planted a rifle-bullet in the trunk. With his flintlock gun, the chief buried a copper ball beside it. So, Crawford's lease was sealed. He made off into Luba-land and back to Lofoi, promising to return.

We rattled bruisingly over rock-ledges and forded the Luanza stream at last. We coasted down through the small mud-brick and thatch town, past the market and into the hospital compound. Esther Sinclair, all in pink, welcomed us by the dispensary. We were all in red, covered in dust. People cheered and waved. As the light mellowed, I put the Cibemba greetings Bev had taught me to good use. Kabula edged on through the compound and around in front of an old mission house. Then my heart filled. We stopped before a still older house that I had studied many times in family photographs and books: the same weighty grass roof, no longer black-and-white but silver-gilt, the same mud walls, but warm red-ochre, the same shady verandah, its branching pillars clad with woven reed and bark-rope, golden and dark brown. Inside I walked, stood, peered at everything, and wept. Night fell swiftly. We ate in Esther's new bungalow, and talked and laughed and talked. I don't know what we

said. My journal is a blank. I know I woke up in Dan Crawford's
house.

Dan Crawford woke, on Christmas morning 1893, back at Lofoi.
What tears, what cooings, what dances, what songs, had greeted him
on Christmas Eve. On the trek, blackwater fever had again led him
down into the valley of the shadow of death for three insensible days.
His party had debated how to bury him. Sankuru had come down
with yaws. A lion had fallen to its death, trying to pluck one of the
men from Kundelungu's sheer face. But no one was lost, and
Crawford had gained seven more "sons" from chiefs around the lake.
He sent ten men back, under Mushimishi, to prepare the site. He
translated, concentrating on Luba-Sanga. His farewell tour of the old
kingdom was joyous and sad. The old tubercular cough revisited him.
Malaria too. But slowly he regained strength and the Lofoi fort's
lieutenants officially commissioned him temporary commandant
while they attempted, fruitlessly, to dislodge Simba from Kilwa
Island. "To mix myself up with the government . . . is the last thing I
would choose for myself," Crawford wrote. "If I were connected
with a missionary society I should probably be scored off the books."
   In mid-July 1894, he set off with his "daughter" Sombo, and thirty
"sons", including Sankuru. At their first camp a man loomed out of
the darkness, then many armed men, laden women, children. "We
have taken our hoes from their sockets and thrown away the handles.
You are our father. We are your children. Wherever you go, we will
go. We will not leave you." Crawford faced members of ten tribes,
and two Arabs. He told them that the old Lofoi life was dead, that they
were one people. Old disputes must die. Ahead was a new life. "And
as for me I shall teach you the words of God." "*Mo monka*," they
answered, "So be it." Next day, two hundred continued the exodus,
and every day more joined them. Kalawfwa, whose land it was, had
become Konga Vantu, gatherer of the people. By the second week of
August they joined Mushimishi and the builders at Chipungu. Soon
Crawford noted, "I am now snug inside my stockade. . . . There is
something like ozone in the air which reminds me of the days of my
boyhood by the shore."
   We woke in Crawford's house, and smelt that breeze. Not at
Muntemune, because the site there grew too small for the people
flooding into it, or for their fields. An advance guard moved three
miles or so south, and Crawford lived in a hollow ant-hill while they
cleared bush, burnt off the ground, broke the soil, planted maize,

beans and manioc, and planned the town's lay-out. Indigenous skills and raw materials were all they needed, all Crawford wanted. Ruth Slade spelt out his attitude:

> It seemed to him that material poverty and a direct dependence upon God for supplies, without any reliance on human agency, were both an essential mark of the missionary, and also a means of living closer to the people among whom he settled.

In April 1895, the whole community moved to Luanza.

In the shade of great mango trees between Esther's bungalow and Dan's house, chairs are set out for us and for the elders. It is our second afternoon. Five hundred people gather round, creating an arena. The light is golden. The air throbs with cries of welcome, clapping, choir-songs, everybody's songs. Kasongo, son of Chansase the eldest elder, orchestrates the ceremony with style and humour. He leads us forward. We circle, greeting, clapping hands in Bemba-fashion and stepping to the rhythm. Mitonga speaks of Konga Vantu, tells everyone that I have come from England to see what he began, exhorts all to continue in his path. I make my greetings in Cibemba to great laughter and applause, then, through our new friend Kalomo, explain that I have come to see Luanza and to visit Konga Vantu's grave, not because he ended there, but because his work lives on here. Noëlle, nervous and glowing in her wax-print outfit, thanks everyone through Esther. Chansase lifts his quavering voice in fervent prayer. A dense dust-cloud rises as the crowd charges us, ebbs, surges forward once more, touching, shaking hands, almost crushing a crippled child at our feet. Some stay to talk. "Eeh Bwana, Bibi, you have come home. This is your village."

XIV

KONGA VANTU

An enthusiastic, impulsive and single-hearted missionary, [Crawford] was careless of his own life and health. His one aim was to endeavour to experience African life from the inside, to live with the people to whom he had come, sharing their thoughts, their hopes, their fears. His life in Africa was one long essay in "thinking black".

RUTH SLADE *King Leopold's Congo*

I went beautifully to pieces and got my first dose of fever, Africa, my jealous first love, refusing to smile on me after such a desertion of her beauty. Temperature shoots up, nasty taste in mouth, tongue as rough as a nutmeg grater. Then my legs begin to wobble . . . so this decides me to get into a native canoe, a one-logger, and make a dash for home. . . .

DAN CRAWFORD *Back to the Long Grass*

After his one and only furlough, spent spreading the "thinking black" message in Britain, USA, South Africa and Australia, Dan Crawford came home to Luanza in mid-1915. Malaria assailed him on the long march from Elizabethville, and his canoe-trip on Lake Mweru put him two days ahead of the rest of the party. Luanza was taken by surprise. At nightfall he fired two rifle-shots into the cliff. "After a tense two or three moments of dawning silence, down comes the yell — wild, welcoming yell from the hills. Now for the point when the curtain must be drawn. It is all too sacred to tell." He does tell a little, though, of "all that follows in quick delirious succession". His beloved "black mob" rushed down the cliff as he jumped out on the sandy shore to greet them, feverish but with a joyful heart. He saluted the "glorious missionaries" who had held the fort for him. Hand grasped hand, "all of us in a dream, eyes dancing with delight and glad we ever lived for such a moment".

I hadn't dared to hope that Crawford's moments and years here would still be so vivid. I had no idea that the house would be so full of him. Esther always called it Dan's house, despite the number of people who had lived in it since his death. In truth it was his wife Grace's. Theirs is an extraordinary love story. Late in 1897, after their wedding and the celebrated trek to the grave of Livingstone's heart, Dan began to build a home. Lightning struck, charred its framework. It stood firm. God's imprimatur, the people said. White men urged Dan to use brick, but he didn't want to distance himself from local custom. He built substantially in mud and wattle thatched with grass.

Harry Brown recalls its impact: the gateway, the avenue of palms, the building "truly African in material and design":

> Entering the house we marvelled even more because we could easily imagine that we had got into the African section of some museum. The fireplace and mantelpiece, and the pelmets over the windows and doors, were all of black wood crudely carved by Africans. All kinds of drums, carved out of solid pieces of trees, were here and there in the room; the walls were hung with all kinds of carvings, and pictures painted on reed matting; the ceiling was also made of the same yellow reeds interlaced with black bark-rope. . . . There was a snuggery leading off from the big room, and through its windows we obtained a wonderful view of the lake . . .

That's just how it is. Like the Browns, we took tea off chiefly stools: seats supported by the upraised arms of squatting female figures with cruciform Luban hairstyles, vigorous breasts and protruding navels surrounded by elaborate erotic scarifications. Hidden amongst china, in the corner cupboard above our heads, was a half-empty bottle of strychnine once used to anoint goats' heads, lion and leopard bait.

Now and then Dan reinforced termite-damaged walls and extended the house, adding a new room for study and translation when its predecessor was full of papers. Following his death it was as if the house died too, for almost at once, thirty years after it was built, it began to lean and sag. Grace called Harry Brown down from Pweto. They stored the furniture and fittings. The house was demolished, rebuilt in sun-baked brick to the old pattern, and finished with identical details. Everything was re-installed and "no one was any the wiser". Grace named her new old home the Dan Crawford Memorial House.

Noëlle and I have it to ourselves, almost. The watchman has left his spears in the room where he sleeps and is taking a holiday while we are here; but Kola the dog begs entry every night and often howls at nothing in the early hours. We make a nest for the heavily pregnant house-cat in a wardrobe, where she gives birth to five kittens. All day Daniel, named after Konga Vantu, bustles around at the kitchen end of the house, cleaning, cooking, washing, ironing, his eye on the men who garden, do odd jobs and chop wood. The iron stove where he creates his dishes squats in the half-darkness of a detached cook-house shaded by a mango tree; the boiler-house, set against the bathroom, is a mudbrick oven in which an oil-drum sings over a fire.

Daniel is the chief steward, our guardian angel in a green apron. He speaks a very little French. His hair is greying, but his face is luminous, his eyes youthful. Efficient, day-long busyness never seems to defuse his good nature. For the first time in our journey I can relax deeply. I have reached my destination. And what a place it is. If it were on the shores of the Mediterranean you'd pay the earth to stay here. It must have been dull, that day in 1908, when Prince Albert of Belgium, relaxing on the verandah, turned to Dan and said, "Oh, here I sit imagining myself at Folkestone looking over at Calais."

Every morning I get up with the sun and let Kola out. The passage that divides the house is lined with hunting trophies, axes, a chief's staff, a bow carved with figures adorned with amulets, arrows, and an ancient floppy-brimmed straw hat hanging from a row of pegs. Doors at either end lead to stone-flagged verandahs, one facing the palm-flanked path to the village, the other dropping to the garden by deep steps between rose-trees planted in green oil-drums. Behind, beyond the village, is the steep backdrop of the Bukongolo hills. In front, across the garden, is a gate in a hedge of golden shower blossom, a path to the top of a precipitous cliff, and the lake. Sometimes, through haze, there is a hint of the Zambian hills. On our first night there was wailing; mostly it is very quiet; but by 7 o'clock every morning the butterflies and birds are busy. The sun grows hot. Cool breeze blows off the lake. A brilliant English summer day, except that the buzzards wheeling and mewing are not English hawks but sharp-winged *pumgwa*, the crows are pied, the doves laugh, and a pair of black-and-white *kimbo-kimbo* birds arch necks and duck mechanically one above another in a small tree, chiming an antiphonal electronic song again and again.

Clink of buckets, splash of water. A lad tours the garden whistling one tune, the same one every morning. Pausing only to return my greeting "*Mwashabukeni mukwai*", he sluices the roots of fruit trees, *pai-pai*, lemon, orange, tangerine. Their fruits are fragrant new moons in the early light. Tall, feathery trees with brown pouch-like fruits look after themselves, but the borders get doused: snapdragons, petunias and salvias, like Grace's

> poor little home flowers, the stocks and mignonette and wallflowers! They struggle so gallantly (like the Mission lady and the Mission baby) to persuade you that this is not so very far from England, and they fail so piteously.

I sit and write my journal or browse books plucked from Dan's library: Lord and Baines' *Shifts and Expedients of Camp Life, Travel & Exploration* of 1876; first editions of 1890s' travel books by Rudolf Slatin Pasha, Mary Kingsley, Henry Savage Landor, Richard Burton, Alice Balfour and many others; theology and missionary biography; tropical and homeopathic medicine; novels and poetry, including the Harvard Classics in fifty volumes and an 1890 selection of Browning's *Poetical Works*. There is remarkably little mildew or termite damage.

On the summit of loaded shelves is the *Times World Atlas* of 1896, inscribed "The African Prayer Book". Its celestial map has been re-oriented: Dan's pencilled radii centre on Crux at the galactic equator; a rough triangle links Sirius in Canis Major, Canopus in Argo, and Alphard — "The Heart" — in Hydra. Dan was not immune to sentiment, and laid out a family tree on the back of the map of Scotland, tracing the first Earl of Crawford back to the eleventh century and forward to the nineteenth, though he tries no explicit link with his own father, Archie Crawford, the Arran-born master of a schooner. In Dan's atlas, southern sky — cross, dog-star, ship's rudder, serpent's heart — and northern roots come into eccentric collision.

The books weave spells; in my head the first and last lines of Browning's *Home-Thoughts, from the Sea* seem to link Diogo Cão's charts, gnawing at blankness, with this annotated atlas:

> Nobly, nobly Cape St Vincent to the North-west died away . . .
> While Jove's planet rises yonder, silent over Africa.

Last night at dusk, springy loads of elephant grass floated along the path beyond the hedge, borne by invisible women. Giant sheaves are stacked in town, ready for thatching houses against the coming rains. Then, Zambia will be visible across the lake between violent storms, winds will lean against Luanza, waterspouts will be sucked up. Night-fishermen are safe this morning. Men set off for the shore with paddles and gear. I abandon books and give way to the lure of the lake. When I get back, Daniel's breakfast of toast, lemon marmalade, bananas, peanut butter, tangerines, apples, *pai-pai* and passion-fruit will be waiting.

Kola tacked across the path, prospecting tree-boles, thorn bushes, vetches, crimson cornflowers. *Pumgwa* with wings curved like bows rode the updraught, exuberant and baroque. Mukeya had shown me the mud-brick ruins of "Konga Vantu's first house", actually a writing-hut he built much later, hidden in tall grass. It was hard to find again, but at last I laid hands on the old quoins, before jumping overgrown gullies back to the path. Kola greeted me at the brink of the cliff. Two small boys sat on a massive ledge of polished rock, guarding a large aluminium pot at the top of the zig-zag descent. The pot gleamed, dark rocks glowed, boys' faces glistened; their red shirts, the ochre dust, the golden grasses were luminous; far below, green reeds and rice-fields, marsh and maize crops shimmered, and the blue lake creamed in. A small girl climbed, clutching a bunch of silvery *pali* fish; her brother wore the bottom of a blue plastic *bidon* on his head and carried a paddle and a reed basket of small *makobo* fish. They greeted me wonderingly. Older folk knew who I was. They clapped hands gently, bowing from afar, or shook hands, the double clasp, left hand on right forearm as a mark of respect. If only one hand was free they patted themselves on the heart, returned my greeting and asked after Bwana Konga's health. Humbled by that name, I replied that I was very well.

Sometimes I took off to the right, an overgrown path, a dry watercourse, rock-step to rock-step. Once, I trod on something that slithered away under matted grass; I jumped, but it did not raise its head to strike. A vast cantilevered rock overhung the Luanza valley. Falls that glimmered in the shade had eaten their way back, cutting cliffs whose vegetable cladding muffled the cascade's roar. Below, the stream disappeared. A hut and fish-drying racks stood in the sun, small figures clustered around a clinker-built boat and its catch, women mended a basket-work fish-trap beside the beached dug-outs. Distant headlands succeeded one another, leopard hills, tables of rock. On the nearest stood Lukonzolwa, Dan's site for Katanga's first capital. Sometimes I made off left on a narrow path, winding side to side and up and down across streams with which the shelf of land was riven. Blue and bronze dragonflies glittered. At one washing-place, a pool by the track, children waited their turn while their mother, a slim beauty, lathered her arms and back; suds dripped like milk from her full breasts as she raised her soapy head to greet me. Large insects with trailing legs flew clicking like castanets.

With faithful Kola I climbed down to a dramatic rock-plinth above a sheer drop. A broad waterfall stepped down its gorge, a naked cliff fell to gardens and banana trees, a house beneath palms, reefs of reeds and trees rocked by gentle breakers. I climbed to the top of the falls. Hot limbs of ironstone and a chill pool were overhung by trees and snaking lianas brimming with the charm of birds. I sweated back through manioc fields and the north end of the village. Every other man mended nets. Women pounded in shared rhythm. By a pile of mud-bricks, a rough pole was ambitiously labelled *Église Méthodiste*. A house, with high-crowned thatch and wind-holes, and humble huts were richly decorated by Mondrian or Klee limited to a palette of chalk, charcoal and ochrous soils. Straggly hedges, narrow ditches. On the bridge over a stream a young man sneezed. "Many of us have colds," he said. "We suffer. We suffer from the weather."

We didn't. Noëlle was in her element. She caught up on a little of the sleep she'd lost. She ate well, recovered some strength. She cooked with the women, shared jokes in pidgin French and Cibemba, and laughed with them a lot. She wanted to help in the hospital, but feared she'd be in the way. She enjoyed a holiday, though we both fretted over our lack of energy and initiative, and wished we'd come fresh to Luanza. It's hard to remember the strangeness of it all, the edge, the confrontations — friendly or threatening — every expedition implied, the crowd that followed, the rabid dog that terrified the village, the snake that lay in the long grass. Together we clambered down the cliff: steep slopes, deep rock-steps, roots and fallen boulders, angular overhanging trees and strata. Bottle-green sunbirds, a flash of yellow, blue butterflies. A path of peaty soil beaten across the marsh flanked by spiny gorse and red lilies playing host to gorgeous red-and-black insects. Clinker-built canoes, dug-outs and a red boat in the rushes. Two men bound a massive papyrus root-ball with fibres. They tried to explain with gestures. Later I learnt that the balls were bait, full of grubs and insects, dropped like depth-charges and ringed by nets. From a thrust-stage of black earth the men launched out into breakers and brilliant light.

Across the ruddy ridges of a manioc field we found a house pierced by a great pole. A notice on it, and another posted by gardens beside a stagnant pool below the falls, bore a skull and cross-bones, "*Danger de mort*" and a message in Cibemba which Esther translated: "Keep off tomatoes, don't strip sugar-cane or bananas, and don't hawk them to my door afterwards . . . He that hath ears to hear let him hear." The woman rightfully picking her tomatoes assured us it was an effective curse, though monkeys still came down the cliff for maize. Coucals brushed yellow and crimson broom blossom. Pygmy kingfishers made forays to and from the lake. A boy who drowned some months ago was interred here among banana trees. His mother never saw his body. He could not be buried up in the village. The spirit of the lake had claimed him. *Kimbo-kimbo* birds chimed their unearthly chime.

Livingstone discovered the Chambezi River in January 1867 and reached the south end of Lake Mweru by November. He hoped that their waters, with those of Lake Bangweolo that he found the next year, fed the Nile. "I asked about the waters, questioned and cross-questioned until I was almost afraid of being set down as afflicted with hydrocephalus." Even around Luanza, where the good doctor never set his booted foot, Crawford heard the song:

> Ingeresa who sleeps on the waves,
> Welcome him, for he has no toes,
> Welcome him, for he has no toes!

"One of my waking dreams," Livingstone wrote, "is that the legendary tales about Moses coming up into Lower Ethiopia, with Merr his foster-mother, and founding a city which he called in her honour 'Meroe', may have a substratum of fact." He found no monumental relics, and his source was Congo's, not Nile's. Crawford — Kalawfwa, Konga Vantu — dug humbler foundations and had other dreams on the shores of Mweru. Dugald Campbell joined him from the west in November 1894, and at the end of December Arnot brought the Ulsterman Benjamin Cobbe in from the east. Arnot had to leave within the month because of the pain in his spleen, but not before Crawford had spoken, beside Muntemune's sparkling falls, of his feelings for the girl he loved.

He had forgotten her christian name, but he knew she was George Tilsley's daughter, the one who felt a call to Africa, the one he'd yearned for at Bath in the spring of 1889, who might be married now, because he'd not spoken, restrained by the death-sentences hanging over him: tuberculosis and Africa. He had believed that "a missionary married was a missionary marred". He changed his mind. He did not know how she devoured the news he sent back to the missionary paper *Echoes of Service*. He could not know that she had learned catering in Bath, that she had trained as a nurse for two years in Glasgow, that her exceptional will was rewarded with permission to attend classes for student doctors. He did not know that she had moved to Barnstaple, North Devon, to care for the aged Brethren pioneer Robert Cleaver Chapman. But he sensed that this Tilsley girl was vital and forceful enough to be his companion, the first white woman to penetrate the interior. After his community had moved from Chipungu to Luanza, he wrote her father a letter. Many letters, all torn up. Then one was sent.

The British took Kilwa Island on paper, and asked Dan to negotiate with Simba. Dan's spy got there in time to see Simba shoot himself by accident. The myth is current that Konga Vantu's bullet, buried in Chipungu's tree of treaty, sped onwards, a spiritual trajectory of more than fifty miles, and killed the tyrant. Cobbe died of blackwater fever, Dan was devastated. He heard that three young missionaries were coming in from the east. Nothing from the Tilsley girl: "I am all impatient and nigh exasperated. 'Hope deferred maketh the heart sick'." In June 1896 he prepared to meet them. One barrel of a gun that Arnot had given him burst and almost killed him. The next day, the second barrel saved him from a leopard at ten yards. He preached his way to the south end of Lake Tanganyika. At Cameron Bay he heard that the party was already on African soil, together with the parts of an iron schooner for Lake Mweru, and yes, Grace Tilsley. He called together the elders of his caravan. He told the news. Juma, the Arab, broke the delighted silence. "*Mzuri*," he said, "At last our country is settled." Seven weeks later Dan wrote home:

> I met her at last, not here in civilised Blantyre, but out from its brick houses about 12 miles. First a wide road; then the ordinary African path; a hillside at a good gradient; then a runnel of water; a hamlet further on; and then a longish clump of grass, and — oh! . . . It was sundown when we met, but it might have been Sunrise in the Millenium!

On 14th September 1896 they were married by the British Consul at Blantyre in present-day Malawi. Lufi laughed when she told me how her father — who had escaped M'siri's slavery, prospected Muntem-une and founded Luanza with Dan — was made to dress up fine for the wedding. But back home, what a native feast they'd had. "Ah yes, they did it our way." Grace was tough, resourceful, loved and admired by the people, and by Dan. She made a home, which was also a guest-house. She cultivated the most glorious garden in Katanga, ancestor of Esther's plot from which we eat sweet potatoes, carrots, beans, spinach, cabbage, peas, aubergines, peppers, limes, lemons, tangerines, passion-fruit, *pai-pai*, strawberries, and much more. Starting with a bull and a cow Chief Kazembe had given Dan in 1895, Grace bred a magnificent herd; lightning struck the byres in 1924 and all but five died in the fire. But she did not stay at home. She undertook strenuous journeys, talking, teaching, negotiating, treating the sick. She delivered babies, while Dan treated dental patients, uprooting "the lion in the mouth that roars" with his forceps.

Lufi said they knew she was good when she patched up a man with crocodile wounds. Her test was a powerful hunter whose crude elephant-gun had burst and torn his right arm to pieces. For two years healers had only worsened it. Grace persuaded the relatives that she could end his agony with chloroform and a sharp saw. At last they agreed to the "death-sleep". Dan wrote: "In the coming years, no doubt, when Africa is a gridiron of railways, smart brick hospitals will grace these latitudes, but no surgeon will ever boast of such fame as this 'death-sleep' lady and her pioneer operation." Another of her amputees, a young lad with one arm, later proved his prowess by killing an elephant with a spear-trap. He, the meat, and the tusks were celebrated. The feast was bloody. "But Leopold's long arm reaches out for all the ivory, the resultant revenue to be nobly devoted to charity — the charity that begins at home."

Dan took women seriously. He understood the *budindu*, a female freemasonry which won notable legal battles against the men of the territory. He bemoaned the tardiness of English law on women's rights. He knew Grace's strength, and despised the view Conrad put in Marlow's mouth: "They — the women I mean — are out of it — should be out of it. We must help them to stay in that beautiful world of their own, lest ours gets worse." Out of it? Karen Blixen was a child when Grace was learning what *Out of Africa* means. "Long before others, here she is pioneering this Far Interior, the first of her sex." Village people thought that Dan had bought her for a pair of oxen, that soap whitened her, that she coifed her hair by twining it round her toes; "she is a huge ? mark, one everlasting 'why?' They look her through as if a human being were only an animal with a toilet." Her genius for planning tempered Dan's impulsiveness. "Africa is so essentially a domestic land," he writes with luminous irony, adding honestly, "that its pioneer ladies easily and evidently surpass mere men. . . . (Do not dare 'Poor ladies!' them; their smile of serenity freezes any such adjective on your lips.)"

Dan and Grace are renowned for goodness, strength and love. Our welcome is founded on that memory. Dan said, "The toughest thing on the planet is virtue. Take it logically or philologically, 'virtue' is only spelling 'virility' in six letters instead of eight." Women, like Lufi, came to see me because my grandfather had freed them or their parents from slavery. I say "grandfather" rather than "great-uncle" because it better conveys the potency of the uncle-nephew relationship in this society. Dan had liberated them and set them up in this city of refuge, a village that many, white and black, described as the best in the Congo. In it, Dan's notions of planning, spaciousness and sanitation were expressed in utterly African materials and building methods. He welcomed whole communities trekking from war; his memory is bright because he kept soldiers, Belgian officials, and Catholics — who purveyed what he regarded as spiritual colonialism and white fetishism — out of the town. He abhorred the idea of the de-tribalized "station-negro" and aimed to make Luanza the best that Africa, not Europe, could offer. Dugald Campbell wrote:

> Murderers, too, made it a city of refuge; Arabs, fleeing for their lives from avenging Belgians, halted or hid in Luanza's rabbit warrens; and slavers, escaping from State prisons where they were undergoing terms of imprisonment for their misdeeds, headed for Luanza. . . . It was difficult to know whether to give up a murderer, hand over a slaver, or deliver up an escaped slave.

In those days the town was surrounded by a stockade, with a fortified gateway, but it was a sanctuary in the fullest sense; the fence was no *cordon sanitaire*. Dan was not so heavenly minded as to be no earthly use. If the gospel meant anything, he knew that Luanza must encompass and transform the conflicts and contradictions of the real world. It was a magnet, a centripetal force; Dan's temperament was centrifugal. When workers began to join him from Britain, Germany, the West Indies and New Zealand, they were not holed up in an evangelical ghetto, but sent out to catalyse life in the region. It is no surprise that the church is now run by Zaïrians, but scandalous to some that that was Dan's purpose from the start: to work through, and only through the people. They were the key missionaries. Martha Dickie, an elderly woman of Luanza, gave me her handwritten account of his strategy, beginning "*U bwikablo bwa kwa bwana Konga* . . .":

> The character of bwana Konga. He loved all people and more than this he loved very much indeed the Word of God. That is why he chose some of the elders of the church sending them to different places to spread the gospel message everywhere, beginning at Nswiba with Difuwa . . . [she lists twenty more places and the men sent to them] . . . Luanza that is the mother of them all.

Mushimishi, once executioner at M'Siri's court, was Dan's first convert in 1895; baptized in the lake two years later, he became a pioneer elder. Before he died of smallpox, he urged his brother and his friend Kapenda to turn to God. Kapenda did, and is named in Martha's list as missionary to Kashyobwe. Mushimishi was blind but he saw two angels, *va malaika*, come for him. "Praise," he said, and to Dan, "Goodnight". The evangelist Bwana Nseko had been a *nganga* who had never seen a white skin, but he dreamt of a shining figure who commanded him to cease preying on people's fears. When the dream re-visited him he burnt all his fetishes. The vision told him to journey to a certain place. He went, and there met Dan on safari.

Two elders came before breakfast, with a younger evangelist whose son was distended by kwashiorkor, and young Mwema to translate into French. We arranged a meeting. They returned with a larger group, four of whom had known Konga Vantu. The sanctity of his memory and stilted translation made it hard for them to reminisce freely. They sat on the settle in Dan's room, eyes glowing in the gloom like the eyes of old men anywhere caught in the effort of recollection. Their thin ankles made ancient shoes look vast. Their welcome was heartfelt, their memories platitudes.

I was feeling shaky and troubled by pains in my spleen when three chiefs came to call. I greeted them with all the words and gestures of respect I knew. Noëlle, Esther and I faced them in the verandah's shade: Kapoposhi, from near Lukonzolwa, with a peaked cap and a buffalo tail "fly-whisk", and the Luban chiefs Kyona Mabimbi and Kyona Ngoi, one with a buffalo-tail and one with a dark brown scalp-hugging fez. "We regret not coming sooner, but we have only just heard of your coming, when we met at Lombe for the *madilo*." A very old man had died in a village to the south, and his wake had been celebrated over three days. "We are glad that you have come to your inheritance, and wish you to remain here." Kapoposhi flicked the air before his astute eyes, "My grandfather was chief when your grandfather came. I am his grandson and you are his grandson and I wish to greet you." These sentiments severally repeated. I expressed my gratitude for the honour they did me, but could not give them the assurance they seem to seek, that I would lay my bones here.

Later that day, the elders are more relaxed, more talkative. We sit in a back-room of the new brick church, beside the old one's ruinous arches. Outside in the burning sun, in holy ground, is a watery pit: mud packed into wooden moulds, ranks of separate wet bricks, drying bricks leaning like lines of toppled dominoes, stacks of dried bricks from which barrow-loads are wheeled away, rattling, for new building. Inside, the elders dig back to the foundations. "Konga Vantu is our father. No child of his has come here since Dr Tilsley," Dan's nephew, my uncle, who lived here 1920–1933, "so it is a great joy and honour that we can welcome you, child of Bwana Konga, to your village." They want to forge new links with England, with Dan's Scottish church. They want prayer, and help for poor evangelists. They fear that I won't stay, and request sixteen photographs of me. I talk very little. Much too little. I cannot find the English words I need, let alone French or Cibemba ones. I am profoundly moved, sick that I cannot fill our Bwana Konga's monumental memory.

A madman, dressed in brilliant yellow and green with a white sash swinging from his waist, follows me back down the palm avenue. I recognize him from his performance in church. That Sunday the *chef du terre*, husband of three wives, sat behind the preacher. He had greeted me twice, in hospital for VD treatment, and expansively drunk in his village. Tough, shifty-eyed, in a blue-green *abacost* suit, he listened to the choirs and a sermon about the fall of the proud. The local preacher waxed eloquent: how Herod was eaten by worms, how Nebuchadnezzar ate grass, how the Son of Man walked free in the punishing fire, how Daniel's wisdom triumphed over lions and powerful men. "Who here is wiser than Daniel?" Thunderous question. The chief surveyed the congregation and did not flinch. "Who here is wiser than Daniel?" The madman, head full of bible, waved his hand in the air twice. Now, with his texts and his songs and his seeing eye, he is following Bwana Konga down the avenue of palms. Before Luanza, I was a traveller, taken at face value. Here, I am an impossible creature, nostalgia incarnate, victim of unexpected homecoming.

Here I am, as far from home as I have been, in the house of my great-uncle. I, the youngest of thirty-six cousins, part of a tribe tight-knit by its sense of itself, scattered across the world — Australia, Tasmania,

New Zealand, India, America, England — but no longer on African soil. Here, where a man willingly, wilfullv, broke from his roots most decisively and dug himself in most deeply until some say only his skin was white, familial ghosts claim me, clasp me most closely. But Dan is not here. I suffer that loss. His heirs spread my inheritance before me. I am here with that obligation. They offer me a new life, a new name. I might earn their love. I speak against fear, fear that possesses Africa, and me. I am afraid. Not of Africa, but of what Africa is said to cure, the sick heart.

In Luanza, the promised land, the city of refuge, loss and death parade themselves with wailing and drums. I grasp at Ezekiel's parable: the dry bones, articulated, fleshed by God's breath. Paul's metaphor: foot and hand, eye and ear, members of one body, working together, suffering and rejoicing together. "If I speak in the tongues of men and of angels, but have not love, I am a noisy gong or a clanging cymbal." In Luanza, for a week of long nights and days, I fall apart.

How can I tell you about Luanza, what it meant? It was landfall in paradise, it was the bittersweet world, the valley of dry bones, purgatory, the beginning of a longer journey. Bit by bit we discovered the village. The poor market's rich kaleidoscope of vegetables and cloths. Kolmoni's store where we bought tea and candles in half-darkness. The tailor's house labelled *"Haut Couture"*. Avenue Mobutu, eighteen yards wide and tree-lined, as laid out and planted by Dan. Uphill past shock-headed houses, one decorated with an ochre, black and white motor-cycle and rider, one with a mermaid, spirit of the lake. The track hugged the hillside; above us was the tank which fed the town with good piped water; below, the schistosome-infested Luanza roared in its ravine. We walked up with Kalomo or, with Bev, rattled up in the ambulance to a *kilo* in the next village, Kazimuzuri, which means "good work". Loud welcome for Konga. We strode on to Kabulembe, walked back at African pace. Familiar mauve gentian, blue cornflower, yellow and purple vetches in a dry rocky landscape, tender bamboo shoots, manioc fields. Put up partridges. *Kimbo-kimbo* birds gyrated, giggling girls kept step with us, a man with a pair of huge yellow-green gourds curtseyed and smiled. Air to get drunk on. Luanza's web of streets, pointillist grass roofs spread out below in magical light which turned ochres ruddy, whites yellow, and the yellow road to Lombe golden. The lake deep, headlands hazy, cloud high and pink, half-moon climbing.

Kalomo showed me photographs of his friends in Lubumbashi, of the girl-friend whose family had jilted him, of a white girl cut from a magazine. His heart was bruised. We met often. He led us through the pillared, tree-shaded compound of the primary school, past piles of mud-bricks for Luanza's first "hotel", past a substantial café, The Lipton Kettle, to a well-founded, tin-roofed general store with a long counter and the usual range of goods. Its owner, "Tommy", took us through to the back room to meet his wife. We sat on red plastic upholstered chairs with crocheted arm-rests and antimacassars in a room painted citron yellow, turquoise and French navy. "My father looked after Bwana Konga's cattle," Tommy said proudly. But the framed photograph by his chair was of later missionaries, a conventional "Big Bwana" and his wife. The staid photo consorted oddly with erotic wood-carvings, and with the angry paintings by Kyungu, a naïf artist of Lubumbashi, that hung on the walls.

One of the canvases showed a monkey in a palm-tree throwing nuts at a man; in the others, a fleeing hunter was mauled by a lion; a mermaid was unsubtly entwined with a snake; a fat *Belge*, in baggy shorts and pith helmet, smoked a pipe and supervised a black lackey whipping the bloody buttocks of chained and crawling convicts; on parachutes like knotted handkerchiefs, UN troops descended upon the smelters and black slag of Elizabethville. These are the dark myths of Shaba. They go with the continuing burning of "rebel" villages, the 1970s' invasions from Angola by Katangan loyalists, the trauma of independence and secession; public works performed by chained convicts; the brutal *chicotte*, or hide whip; the power of the lake, the fear of witchcraft; Dan's friends eaten by lions, his own narrow escapes; the last monkey he shot, that clutched its heart and appealed to him with all too human eyes. He vowed to shoot no more.

The day the Scouts planned to escort us to Konga Vantu's grave started at 6 o'clock with wailing. It sounded oddly like a party or a football crowd; folk swayed beneath the arches of the TB ward. The dead girl was the sister of one of the troop. The day was for digging and mourning. Twenty-four hours later we made our pilgrimage into the hills. The night after that there was no wailing; cicadas strummed and picked, geckoes ran up the walls, a frog croaked in the lavatory; I woke in the night, dizzy, with a thudding headache, fists behind the eyes, bruised guts. In the cold sweaty darkness I leafed through a mental lexicon of dread diseases, blackwater fever or worse. Then I grew calm, knowing that nowhere was there a better place to die. I longed, until I dozed, to be packed tight in Luanza's soil. I woke shaky, pale, liverish, with shot bowels.

I tried to put away misery and steel myself for the day. At least I didn't fall over. Esther thought it might be malaria, or half-suppressed hepatitis. I relapsed into bed, slept and read. I couldn't open Conrad, but found a copy of Rider Haggard's *King Solomon's Mines* of 1885; flash-backs in my own dreams; twin mountains like earth's breasts, an inland sea like prehistoric Lac Zaïre, a high priestess: that archetypal *anima* which Jung identified in Haggard's *She*. And King Ignosi speaking:

> I will see no traders with their guns and rum. My people shall fight with the spear, and drink water, like their forefathers before them. I will have no praying-men to put a fear of death into men's hearts, to stir them up against the law of the king . . .

Sweet Ignosi, who had not heard of palm wine, nor of fear that possessed the continent before Arab or Portuguese or Englishman set foot on it. Poor Ignosi, noble savage that never was. I got up for supper, refilled the lamp and renewed candles before the generator shut down at eight-thirty. By early morning I slept easily. Next day I tried to carry on. I was distant, absent, manic, momentarily energetic, then almost catatonic. I escaped into Agatha Christie's *Endless Night*. Noëlle feared for me.

We looked at things, if not into them. Kalomo brought a man, from a fishing-camp seven miles off, to look at Bwana Konga. Past Dr Tilsley's old thatched surgery was the tin-roofed Dan Crawford Memorial Hospital he built. In its makeshift marvellous path lab Bev's white-coated students centrifuged samples, checked sedimentation rates and peered down microscopes at blood, sputum, urine, faeces. We stared at pneumococci, gonococci, TB bacilli, sickle-cells, schistosomes and ankylosomes. My blood looked good: haemoglobin slightly down, but far higher than the African average. We pressed our eyes to lenses; people pressed faces at the windows to observe us.

Esther showed us round the best and brightest wards we'd seen in a village hospital: red paint, white sheets, orange blankets, flowers, babies' cribs, mothers in grass-green cloths. A ticket booth for three dispensaries: for liquid medicine, pills, and injections. A child critical from a snake bite, daughter of a teacher who applied the black stone to the wound, then brought her in twenty-four hours late. Men chipping stones for the footings of a new TB ward. TB spines in traction —

wooden pulleys, leg cradles, weights made of paint-tins filled with sand — paralysis, bed-sores, wonderful cures. Beautiful Ngoi, lovingly looked after by her young husband.

Esther told of a man who walked 250 miles with his son in his arms to avoid the pain of a truck journey. Children struck by lightning: sorcery or punishment. Fear. Maternity ward struck, seared lengthwise between the beds, no mother or baby touched. Oil-palm struck, fierce bonfire on a pole. Madness drummed out of women. Poisonings in villages and in high places. Diviners who point at sorcerers. A boy, down the lake, sacrificed a few months ago so that his heart could be excised. Fear. The old cults of the Leopard to the north, of the Lion to the west. A lion-man can shrink ant-sized to get under doors, and re-form as a big cat. Fear of the white man too, pale-eyed as the big cats.

Respect for Bwana Konga. This fearful Bwana Konga. I was part of it. The observer observed, involved. A mere poet was no fit heir. Dan had written on the flyleaf of the book Esther gave me, "Poor Browning, he was better than a poet, but he lived for word jugglery and often for the trick of a turn of speech he let the words make a thought instead of the thought, the words!" Both were difficult then, for me. No better than a poet, I walked from hospital across the blank site of the last cholera village: built of grass and razed by fire according to custom at the outbreak's end. I crossed the Luanza by a plank bridge and entered the leprosy village. Oh Querry! I looked at the lepers looking at me. Huts with geometric patterns, a ship, a mermaid. Hen-houses on stilts. A woven fish-trap casting a fine net of shadow. Tiny mud church with mud benches like tombs in a vault. Importunate greetings. One man, a father of eight lying on the ground, could only breathe a welcome because the disease had taken his vocal cords. A hollow whisper, so full.

Then my face fell. I saw it in the morning mirror. The left side gone, paralyzed as if by a stroke, eye, cheek, mouth dropped. Bell's Palsy. I didn't care. I walked up the lake to the falls; returned to find Noëlle making bread, the dough in her hands lithe and live, her body too. After a week I woke with my whole face working again. All my joints were sore, my abdomen was sensitive and my head was raw, but there was less pain in my spleen, some light in my heart. It was 3rd August when I recovered, the anniversary of Casement and Conrad's deaths.

I could smile that afternoon, when Monty — May Montgomery, a Scots nurse with Africa in her blood — arrived from the north end of the lake. With her, an old woman on the way to see her daughter, one of three nursing orderlies accused, by divination, of witchcraft. Their houses at Tshiamfubu had been burnt down. They escaped, but were later beaten by the *nganga* and the people because they had "murdered" the first Zaïrian doctor at the hospital there, had sent the cancer that killed him. Monty brought news that a month ago the nearby town of Moba, on Lake Tanganyika, had been all but destroyed by soldiers flushing out "rebels". Esther showed me her photo of Tshombe's bodyguard — in cavalry boots, blue jodhpurs, scarlet tunics frogged with gold, tall black plumed hats — and told how recently bandits came here. They hit her, sweated when she prayed, ran to their deaths in another village. In the face of ancient long-running battles out there in the world, in scarred Shaba, how indulgent my sickness, my heart seemed.

Daniel presented us with a glossy grey cock, a present from the elders. Chansase brought us tomatoes from his garden. Young people hung garlands and welcome signs on Murray and Joy Stephenson's house for their return from Lubumbashi. There, I had taken to Murray's down-to-earth humour and now I enjoyed his company as he worked with his builders. He unearthed mission records for me, and we got an antique hand-cranked generator going. We talked of my great-uncle, of my uncle's fondness for local women, of life and death, spirituality and sexuality. "Don't blame your uncle too much," he said. I didn't.

Murray drove us north to Pweto and Tshiamfubu. We saw the orderlies' burnt-out houses, and my uncle's surgical instruments, still used in the hospital's operating theatre. There was no surgeon at Luanza, so urgent cases were driven here where Odilo, a skilled nurse, performed all kinds of elegant surgery. For vital X-rays, patients trekked to Zambia. From the mission's heights we looked east to Zambia's savannah: south to Lake Mweru, all seventy-five miles of it. A venerable tree spread branches wide. "Under that tree Bwana Konga made camp." We walked to Kamina, a leprosy settlement, and down through rocky, blistering scrub land to a cool tree-lined stream. There Murray checked the twin ram pumps that shoved water, by stream-power, up the hill to Tshiamfubu. Joyce from South Shields fed us well and told us how the army had protected the missionaries during the witch-hunt. We picked up a woman whose child by Caesarean section had just died, and drove back through Pweto, a frontier-town like an abandoned film-set with colonnaded shops and deep verandahs where Belgians used to sit and drink in the cool of the evening.

At the Zone the road was marked out with white-painted stones. We stopped for a permit to re-cross the Luvua. Soldiers smoked fish over a fire and tied it up with green reeds to send to Lubumbashi. Their officer asked me for our papers and our permits for the "operational zone". We had none. Didn't we know there was a war on? Flashing eyes. The smell of bad trouble. Murray blustered. In fluent French Noëlle asked about the fish, using their local names. The atmosphere changed. Everyone smiled. Did we have any news about Moba? No, we didn't. Communications are not too hot. Not long before, the Pope had asked President Mobutu about the Methodist pilot shot at Moba. Mobutu knew nothing, and sacked the Governor of Shaba for his embarrassing silence.

On a sweep of silvery beach we gathered sacks of sand for building, in sight of the hill round which the Luvua snaked out of the lake. The Arab fort's ruins on the summit overlooked a crossing point once rife with crocodiles. A soldier, who boasted he was Hitler's man, "USA" and a swastika on his belt, let us on to the German ferry. We watched the Luvua begin its dangerous descent to the Lualaba, the Zaïre. Murray dropped the ferryman a good tip. As we disembarked a boy was beating a tree for moths that swarmed from the branches like petals, bait in his butterfly net. We climbed through wooded hills in glorious light and stopped at village after village, scattering chickens. "The randiest lot of chicks I've ever seen," said Murray. He asked about population and water-supply, data for an international clean-water project. At Nzwiba, mango blossom glowed massively in the sunset. With an escort of children we searched for a tipsy chief, who gave us doubtful information, while the bereft mother waited in the Landcruiser. Murray explained the fate of a woman who dies without progeny; how her spirit is chased away, with none to influence or care for, into oblivion. And the fate of the husband whose wife dies in childbirth; how Esther had refused a Catholic priest who asked her to cut the foetus out of a corpse so that the dead could be displayed and the man accused: "How many did you kill?" How gentle were the shadowy shapes of Luanza beneath us on the fertile plinth above Mweru.

It was almost time to leave it, to drive back to Lubumbashi with Monty and Kaputa. The farewells were heartbreaking, and the exchange of gifts. Ngoi held Noëlle's hand for a long time. Kalomo's cousin Joyce, who was mortally sick, begged me with tears to stay. On our last night, four girls and the boys' choir came to sing to us. Oh, the raw freshness of the girls' voices, the range and sophistication of the boys' rhythms, multi-stranded lyricism, leading and trailing harmonies, their power. Dan and Grace's house, museum of love and gifts, pulsed as it should. In the moonlit dawn I would leave home.

XV

BLACK THOUGHTS

Tell me, oh truly tell me
Where will you emigrate to?
Charms are gone, our country is rotten
For Livingstone is dead.
An elephant is dead from a spear wound,
Oh, the lovely one is gone.
DAN CRAWFORD (trans.) *Chitambo's Lament*

Three days after my face had regained its rough symmetry, I had gone
out on Lake Mweru. It was choppy that afternoon; Noëlle stuck to the
shore and watched otters swimming in the reeds. Bev and I, with
Murray and Joy's small daughter Roz, were launched in a clinker-built
canoe. Sapi, the boatman, and his boy paddled through the breakers
until it was safe to tug the outboard motor into life. The canoe leaked
quietly at the stern and like a fountain at the bow. We sat on the
gunwales and got soaked. The boy stuffed rag into the hole. Lines of
nets were marked by papyrus flags. We greeted crews who hauled up
small catches, or sank bundles of papyrus bait overboard. Bev said
she'd seen a hippo last time out. Off Lukonzolwa we ran out of fuel
and tossed in the swell. I thought of Gustave-Marie Rabinek, cured
and given hospitality by Grace, and of the deed Dan witnessed, by
which the Governor granted Rabinek sole right to Katangan rubber.
He was arrested on this lake, aboard the British steamer *Scotia*; he died

in doubtful circumstances on his way to the appeal court at Boma, and
was buried on the river-bank just before Kinshasa.

Sapi filled the tank and re-started the motor. The wind freshened,
the waves hit us broadside. For a while, on that frail leaky perch I
envied Noëlle on dry land, and the sorcerers who swam mythical air-
tunnels for miles under Mweru's surface. Roz sang bravely and held
on to us. The date was 6th August; forty years before, Edgar Sengier
waited by his phone for news of what Katanga's fissile ores did for
Hiroshima. We rode the waves back past Luanza, beyond the next
headland, and saw the falls of Muntemune where Dan shot into a
tree, where he dreamed of the Tilsley girl. We returned, hugging the
shore of the great white water. Tawny cliffs, riven by slighter falls,
slopes planted with manioc, walled caves for drying fish. Two fish
eagles, *cembe*, opposed on a branch. Dare-devil swallows, *kamimbi*,
harvesting the evening air. A tribe of green monkeys jumping and
climbing, tree to rock-ledge, rock-ledge to tree. The shadows were
alive. The sun had gone down over the cliff. Our prow nudged black
peat at the landing-place. Roz was proud. Sapi smiled broadly. His
boy shivered. We climbed rock-steps and emerged from dusk into
the last light.

Dan's diary entry for 27th May 1897: "We are going to plunge — may
never come back or be heard of again, but it will be glorious!" He left
his colleagues busy assembling the schooner sent from Greenock and,
with Grace, Mushimishi and a handful of faithful men, marched down
the lake to fulfil a wish. Wish and obligation: to visit the "grave of the
heart" and prepare the ground for work in the bend of the Luapula, the
river that had possessed Livingstone's dying thoughts. Travelled
light, but for the luxury of a little tea and cocoa, dependent upon game
and hospitality. On a stormy lake crossed to Kilwa Island, Simba's
mausoleum. Southwards met chiefs, wary of Belgians and British,
who welcomed Konga Vantu with acclaim. Dangerous excitement
with elephant, lion, leopard, crocodile, tribal feuds. Across the
Luapula, in present-day Zambia, Chief Kazembe "declared that he
had come of age by looking upon a white lady". Corruption and
slavery under the flag of the British South African Chartered
Company. South, south, and west around and through the swamps of
Lake Bangweolo until on the last day of July they came, with Chief
Chitambo, to the *mupundu* tree. Found that Bia and Francqui had
never reached it, not planted the memorial tablet entrusted to them
by Arnot. Dan and his men cleared the bush, built fires, and by their

flickering light held a memorial service with the chief and his people. The very singer who had wept Livingstone dead now sang his death-song again. Dan wrote, "surely this is mighty Homer in sable skin".

The following February, Hugo Genthe found the site tended and informed the *British Central African Gazette*:

> There is quite a nice and strong circular fence round the tree apparently not many months old . . . I was told that a white man and his donna who had come from the north-west of the Luapula had visited the grave and caused the fence to be made. I went over to the two trees where visitors leave their card. . . . The one tree shows in one square the letters D.L. and underneath E.J.G. (the late Mr Glave, but who is D.L.?) The other tree P.W., 8.10.96 (Mr Paulett Weatherley), and neatly carved in big letters D. and G.C., 31.7.97 (the mysterious couple from the other side of the Luapula); and further F.S., 1.8.97 (Mr Frank Smitheman).

Grace had been surprised to find the barrel of Smitheman's rifle levelled at her. She was not the lion he was stalking. He, who had trekked from the south, was astonished that she and Dan had come from further in! Ted Glave, Casement's friend, was the first white man at the tree, but the story spread in South Africa, via F.S. and any number of bar-stool trekkers, that up around Livingstone's grave, deep in the heart, a white woman rode through the forest on a noble lion, queen of a barbarous tribe.

The pioneer lady stood on the spot where Susi and Chuma had buried Ingeresa's vital organs in a tin box, preserved his body in salt. She read the name and date of burial, 4th May 1873, which Jacob Wainwright, one of the slaves Livingstone freed, had carved. Reverent Africans had carried, and smuggled at great risk, the Doctor's body to the coast; Arabs had fired volleys of precious powder to salute "Dawid", the anti-slaver; Jacob Wainwright was a pall-bearer with H. M. Stanley; together they watched the glossy coffin sink beneath Westminster Abbey's slabs. Dan said, "The Abbey got him", but not his heart. Chitambo's people say, "He sleeps". In the dust beneath a *mupundu* tree.

The Dean of Westminster refused Stanley burial in the Abbey. He, who had traced Livingstone's river to Congo's mouth, was barely outlived by his creation, the Congo Free State. Leopold II had often "desired me to go back to the Congo," he wrote privately, "but to go back would be to see mistakes consummated, to be tortured daily by seeing the effects of an erring and ignorant policy". He suffered recurrent fevers which he called "Africa in me". A house in Surrey was enough; the Stanleys called its lake "Stanley Pool", its stream "the Congo", and its woods "the Aruwimi Forest". Like a *padrão*, a six-ton monolith of Dartmoor granite stands in Pirbright churchyard, inscribed with a cross and "Henry Morton Stanley — Bula Matari — 1841–1904 — Africa".

The British refused Ireland Roger Casement's remains until 1965, his State Funeral in Dublin. There had been honours: Commander of the Order of St Michael and St George and, after his South American campaign for the Putumayo Indians, a knighthood. He had written home, "Send me news of Ireland, and also what the papers say about the Congo, but chiefly Ireland; Ireland first, last, and forever." In Germany in 1916, he attempted to recruit prisoners-of-war for an Irish Brigade, to fight the British in Ireland. He was repatriated on a U-boat and arrested on the Kerry coast just prior to the Easter Rising. "I made awful mistakes and did heaps of things wrong, confused much and failed at much," he wrote from Pentonville Prison, "but I *very near* came to doing some big things . . . on the Congo and elsewhere. It was only a shadow they tried on June 26; the real man was gone. The best thing was the Congo. . . ." His first Catholic communion was his viaticum. He went to the scaffold fasting so that, he said, his God might be the last food he took on earth. He was hanged on 3rd August 1916, aged fifty-one.

Conrad revised his opinion of Casement: "already in Africa I judged that he was a man, properly speaking, of no mind at all. By emotional force . . . he made his way, and sheer temperament — a truly tragic personality: all but the greatness of which he had not a trace. Only vanity." Less than six months in Africa had done for Conrad's vanity. In May 1891, he wrote to Marguerite: "I am still plunged in deepest night and my dreams are only nightmares." He suffered swollen limbs, rheumatism, neuralgia, disturbed digestion, palpitations, suffocative attacks, fever, raw nerves. The shadow of Congo fell across *Almayer's Folly*. Almayer sinks under the weight of memory, of failure; he slumps like a broken man-doll. "Could I be a Punch?" Conrad asked Marguerite, ". . . legs and arms rigidly spread in that attitude of profound despair, so pathetically droll, of toys tossed in a corner . . . Would you kindly scrape together the poor devil, put him tenderly in your apron. . . ."

He sailed from London for a brief taste of the sea in his friend G. F. W. Hope's yawl *Nellie*. Did he imagine then that Marlow would

Nothing speaks to a summer on the Chesapeake Bay like sailing its waters and reveling in the beautiful landscape. With countless waterways to explore and hundreds of species to see, it's no wonder residents and visitors spend hours enjoying all the Bay has to offer out on the water.

Chesapeake Bay Foundation (CBF) wants to ensure that all of the Bay's rivers and streams are here for future generations to enjoy. That's why we are working with local businesses, farmers, and government officials to limit pollution and development around the Bay. By ensuring that its shores and waterways are protected and preserved, we can continue to enjoy this national treasure for years to come.

CBF is the Bay's only advocate dedicated to restoring not only the Bay and its rivers and streams but also the wildlife within its 64,000-square-mile reach. You can help save the Bay by making simple changes such as purchasing local foods to minimize transportation-related emissions and making your lawn Bay friendly with native plants. To learn more about how you can help CBF protect and restore this national treasure, visit cbf.org.

CHESAPEAKE BAY FOUNDATION
Saving a National Treasure

PHILIP MERRILL ENVIRONMENTAL CENTER
6 HERNDON AVENUE | ANNAPOLIS, MD 21403

Photo Credit: Kathrine Lloyd

exorcize his African experience, eight years later, on board the *Nellie*, at anchor on the Thames, awaiting the ebb? In November he enlisted as first mate on the *Torrens*. "I was then recovering slowly from a bad breakdown," he recalled in *Last Essays*, "after a most unpleasant and persistent tropical disease which I had caught in Africa while commanding a steamer on the River Congo." Ted Sanderson, to whom Conrad dedicated his second book, and John Galsworthy joined the ship in Australia.

I visited Ted Sanderson's daughter, Mrs Kit Taylor, before we left for Zaïre. She remembered Conrad's strong avuncular hugs, showed me a sweet letter he'd sent her. We spoke of his hard, distinguished life as a writer; of the honorary degrees and the knighthood he'd turned down. Then she wrote:

> I forgot to mention his voice . . . his speaking voice was in complete contrast to his writing of such perfect English. He had the strongest foreign accent — deep and vehement (the Rs almost a growl), and such warm amusement in his deep voice. When he burst into delighted spontaneous laughter it was irresistible. I think I value having *heard* him even more than having read him.

Marlow said of Kurtz, "A voice! A voice! It rang deep to the very last." Then, "The voice was gone. What else had been there? But I am of course aware that next day the pilgrims buried something in a muddy hole. And then they very nearly buried me." Joseph Conrad died at home in Kent on 3rd August 1924, aged sixty-six. His pilgrimage ended in a grave at Canterbury.

Dan Crawford died at Luanza, aged fifty-six, thirty-seven years after he landed at Benguela. He had known the pilgrims, the harlequins and the Kurtz's, and been intimate with the horrors and glories of Africa. On his one furlough, 1911–15, he praised Africans around the world. "He has a boundless admiration for the subtlety of the Bantu language as an instrument of thought," reported the *Glasgow Herald*. "He dotes on its 32 tenses, its 19 genders. The pure philosophy and keen poetic feelings of the cannibals of Central Africa inspire him with reverential awe." The *Western Daily Mercury* described his address to "a large number of journalists, authors, ministers, actors, actresses, and society people at the Bechstein Hall" in London. According to the *British Weekly*, "this large and representative company was held as under a wizard's spell by Mr Crawford's eloquence." The *Westminster Gazette* maintained: "His descriptions had the Kipling touch, his appreciation of the cannibals reminded one of Stevenson at Samoa, while his humour was always bubbling over — sometimes quite irrepressibly so." The *Methodist Recorder* quoted him: "You people in this boom of London, you do not hear the voices out of the forest . . . I could tell you such stories as would make you run out of the doors."

Crawford knew that the Thames, like the Congo, flowed out of the heart of darkness. Like Conrad and Stanley, he understood the parallels William Pitt had drawn between white attitudes to Africa and the Roman view of Britain. Crawford quoted Cicero: "The stupidest and ugliest slaves come from Britain."

The Crawfords went home to Africa in 1915. Dan finished his translation of the bible into Luba-Sanga in January 1926, and began to prepare the typescript for the press with Grace and Miss Bryde. He worked nights in his new mosquito-netted cubby-hole on the verandah facing the lake. On 29th May, his coffee-pot was empty and his oil-lamp was doused. Somehow he knocked the back of his left hand on a shelf above the bed. Deep sleep "made me forget the iodine which is the panacea of my life." Lufi told me that the next day, Sunday, Dan sang his farewell song. On Tuesday Grace sent a runner to Harry Brown at Pweto, but there was little that anyone could do:

> My left arm is poisoned and this poison is knifing me very hard, so we are in God's hand and all is well. It is harrowing and might have been avoided. . . . To say that it is *harrowing* is only to remind you that it is the *harrow* that produces the smiling lands of corn . . . Goodbye, dear friends; we will meet at The Appearing in excellent glory.

Most of Thursday he slept, or rather fell into a coma. Harry Brown arrived in the dark. Grace decided to amputate and went to fetch instruments. While she was away, Dan choked; Brown lifted him a little; Dan struggled briefly in his arms, and died. It was 6.30 pm on 3rd June 1926. Grace stared, "He has gone! Dan has gone!" The elders cried out, "No! No! It cannot be true." They touched his body and groaned. Konga Vantu was dead.

Noëlle and I flew from Lubumbashi to Kinshasa. Months before, I'd asked when the rains were due: 15th September. Everyone said that, precisely. It stuck in my mind because it is my birthday. As I stood on the verandah of the British Ambassador's residence, the sky thickened and the rains came, as predicted. Stair-rods, cats and dogs, buckets, all the clichés, but warm, thwacking and rocking trees and shrubs, a translucent blind drawn down upon the vision of Pool Malebo. I ran out and swam, in and out of the swimming-pool. That night, to crown their hospitality, the ambassador and his wife cracked a birthday bottle of champagne.

At the *marché des voleurs* beery solicitations were breathed in my face; I was beckoned and pushed and grabbed among stalls of ivory and malachite, masks and tourist fetishes. African grey parrots, a pennant-winged nightjar and an eagle fretted in cages beside the roundabout. Monkeys slumped in sacks or pranced, spitting, behind bars. At the Intercontinental Hotel, where coffee and cakes cost more than a teacher earns in a month, black mamas trailed little white charges who, under their influence, were composed, calm like African children; Noëlle relaxed. I couldn't. I walked miles through the city. Met a boy begging, with his handless, footless brother pick-a-back; thought of the mutilations Casement catalogued in Equateur, that my uncle Arthur Wright still used to see there in the 'Fifties.

With Citoyen Wakilongo's help we applied for export licences for our few souvenirs. Two days of walking and taxis between offices brought us at last to a decrepit block surrounded by a market: at the building's foot people slept in crevices, cooked fish, breast-fed babies; the lift-shaft was a dark maw full of rubbish; the office had broken windows, two girls and three men, one ledger, one typewriter and several chairs upon which our fellow applicants seemed to live; after form-filling and an hour we saw the imperious *chef*; after two hours he emerged with documents to be typed in septuplicate, stamped and signed; we paid 500 zaïres and got a receipt; not an official one though. Thanks to Wakilongo, at least the process was fast.

We survived the ordeal of N'Djili for the third time, the search for diamonds and Zaïrian currency. Then the attendant at the toilet asked Noëlle for a tip. Good try. We flew into Lisbon and on to Heathrow. Everyone there looked repulsive, drab, overweight, pale. Cicero was right. But the officials were in uniform and didn't demand money. Buses and trains ran roughly on time. Water came out of taps ready for drinking. I sifted through my notes, photos, souvenirs. I played tapes of songs; I summoned up the sounds of the river, the markets, the forest, the night. I missed the smell of *kwanga*, *bangi*, beer, corruption. And I did feel lost.

In my dream I emerged from night into blinding light, chased by three men. A waking pilgrimage must take you home, whole. I am getting there slowly. News filters through from the Light Continent: Zaïrian exiles stirring the pot from Paris, Gadafi's threats, Francois Lumumba's ambitions, friction with Angola, armed robbery at

Kimpese. Grenfell's old house at Bolobo has been pulled down. Dr Kurz flew home to Belgium and married his intended. Kalomo wrote to say that his cousin Joyce died, three weeks after we left Luanza.

I flew to Inverness to see Dan and Grace's granddaughter, Mairi Hedderwick. She searched out documents, books, the Luba-Sanga New Testament and Bible, albums of newspaper cuttings, and old photographs including a very faded one of the grave of Captain Bodson, M'Siri's assassin, at Bunkeya. There was a Luban mask and fetish figure, the ivory key to the mission presented to Dan by Prince Albert, a blue ribbon with gold star and the medal of Leopold II, 1875–1908. Mairi had grown up at "Luanza", Tower Drive, Gourock, with Konga Vantu's photograph on her bedroom wall: a homburg hat, trimmed grey beard, moustache and, beneath bristling grey brows, eyes that bored into her childhood.

Dan and Grace's firstborn boy had died in 1899, just one year old. Mairi's father, Douglas Lyndesay Crawford, was born at Luanza the next year. Regretfully, Dan and Grace decided he must be raised in Scotland. Grace confessed to a friend, "I would never do it again. I lost my child." Douglas felt that Africa had orphaned him. His mother returned to England in 1933 and died three years later at Weston-super-Mare. In 1953 Douglas died of an acute illness that some attributed to his African birth. As a girl, Mairi felt that Africa had stolen her grandparents and, mysteriously, her father too. I pointed out what Dan said to my aunt Audrey as he wistfully contemplated her children growing up at Luanza: "Look at me! A man of my age ought to have his children grouped around him."

I told Mairi about the elders who recalled her grandparents with such love: Chansase, Mitonga, Katanga and the old cook Kilombo. I told her about the women and their words. Lufi, in her smart cloth, her blue plimsolls, her rounded face with its kind lines and air of knowledge: she told me how Grace gave meat and oil for her marriage feast. Mary Yumba, in a pink cardigan, grey skirt and ancient shoes, with limbs like ebony sticks and skew eyes in a birdlike face: she showed me Dan's photograph of her amongst a group of schoolgirls, and said that Grace had saved her sight. Sisi, gaunt and large in a *limputa* celebrating 1980, twenty-five years of revolution: she chuckled at how, when she and her husband wanted to marry, they came to Konga for a piece of paper. Konga asked him whether he loved her, asked her whether she'd care for him; then told them to go away for a week and, if they tired of each other, not to come back; they returned for the paper. Sisi showed me the palm-tree planted on a small mound beneath which Mairi's father's birth-cord had been buried according to local custom. I showed Mairi my photograph of it. "Thank you," she said. "You've given me back my history."

Trees hold history. The tree of the bullets at Muntemune. The *mupapa* tree outside the Stephensons' house, the sort from which pirogues were shaped. The *mukunyu*, wild fig, in front of the Crawfords' house, that Dan cut down against Grace's advice. It sprang again, and was a perpetual reminder of his wife's wisdom. He wished to be buried in its shade. The carpenter Mubanga showed me that it is six trees now: *mukunyu* the venerable and fruitful, *mutaba* the inexhaustible source — a second fig whose bark may be beaten into cloth, *kapungupungu, kitombetombe, sitampa,* and a lemon tree; branches and roots woven together, thriving like the members of disparate tribes who gathered around Konga Vantu in the city of refuge. A promised land is not Eden, or perhaps it is, for out of that tree of knowledge slithered a venomous snake. We heard a commotion and ran to see what the lads were up to; they beat the greige-and-black creature to death and respectfully paraded it at the end of a very long stick.

The Belgian authorities tried to evacuate Luanza more than once. Officers, in full regalia, first came in 1894 to persuade Konga Vantu's community to shift away from the shores of the lake, out of Simba's reach. Captains Deschamps and Verdickt took their place beneath the State flag at Muntemune. Dan, in grass hat, patched jacket and trade-cloth shorts, sat on a stool beneath them. Deschamps made his speech. There was silence. Dan held his peace. Then one of the chiefs stood and told a tale. How, by a great river, *kimpinde* the musk-rat lived. He lived and he aged and, dying, he lay down to die beside the great river. The women found him when they came to draw water from the great river. The women told the chief, and the chief called his musicians, and the women and the men danced. And they sang:

> Little musk-rat, he has died right here,
> By the side of the river has musk-rat died.
> And the name of the river shall be this:
> Where-the-little-musk-rat-died River.

On his verandah in 1908 Dan told this tale to Prince Albert. To his credit, the Crown Prince was delighted with its dénouement: a trumpeting ramping elephant came from the forest to the great river and was angry to hear this song. And he trampled the grass by the side of the great river, and he tore up the trees with his trunk, and vowed to change the river's name, to give it his name. So on the bank of the great river he lay himself down to die, and he died. And the women came, and the chief, and the musicians, and the men. And they danced. And they sang a new song:

> The great big elephant died right here,
> The great big elephant's dead.
> He died on the bank of the big broad river,
> The Where-the-little-musk-rat-died River,
> The Where-the-little-musk-rat-died River.

Luanza is Konga Vantu's town. It is 8.30 am. Two soldiers in uniforms of greenish khaki are marching towards the verandah. But no, it is Mubanga, the chief scout in an old topee, and Mukeya, in a beret, come to fulfil their promise. They lead us to the troop. The other boys sport blue shirts, shorts and neckerchiefs of red and blue; with staves and a pole flying the Scouts' flag embroidered with *Unite Dan Crawford Luanza*, at a blast from Mukeya's whistle we set off through town. Two girls in beige dresses and neckerchiefs fall in, bearing bouquets of croton and bougainvillaea. The staves thud, the whistle shrieks, the scouts chant, people wave and call greetings, we try to keep in step up the hill to Kazimuziri. We turn off between houses, half-houses and piles of mud-bricks towards the top of the ridge. A man looks up from his net-making, children try to join us but are shooed away. We drop to a stream shrouded in vegetation, a large-leaved elder tree with orange fruits by the bridge. We thread a path through elephant grass. On a plinth of earth stand a pair of spirit-houses, rough frameworks roofed with bark; each contains a bowl of chalk and a gourd ladle for libations of beer; dead boughs planted in front are thickly hung with jawbones of antelope. Huntsmen's shrines. We look but do not touch. Everyone will be happier that way.

Our leader swings the flag-pole, half marches, half prances uphill to the manioc field at the summit. A log-and-stick trap for civet-cats is set between plants. Breathless, we stop. Staves make an arch. The girls hand us each a bouquet. We pass through and find ourselves facing a line of twelve graves on a hill among hills high above Lake Mweru, an hour's quick march from Luanza.

Dan Crawford's is the third stone in the row. Lufi told me that Konga asked to be buried dressed in his working clothes and wrapped in a grass mat. The elders decided that he should have a coffin as well. Sisi said that he was laid upon the cloth used for the ironing, with his head pillowed upon his Luba-Sanga New Testament. At the graveside the elders made impassioned tributes and Grace encouraged the people, "broken but very brave" as Harry Brown writes. Brown tried to split rock for a gravestone, but in the end he lifted a flag-stone from the spot where Dan's table used to stand on the verandah. He carved "Dan Crawford", his dates, "Konga Vantu", and texts in Luba-Sanga: "Therefore, my beloved, as you have always obeyed, so now, not only as in my presence but much more in my absence, work out your own salvation with fear and trembling," and "He died, but through his faith is still speaking." We stand for a long time at the grave of a small, great man. We place the flowers on the slab. We all relax and the scouts lay down their banner. Some of them dig for sweet manioc and red roots. We eat. The raw sweet manioc tastes like chestnuts, the red roots like sharp refreshing lemon.

Later, the moon was at its fullest, the lake a silver sheet, the grass pewter, trees and scrub ebony. Dan's southern sky. I wanted to launch out for the further shore. A girl came to see Esther, with her mother and a man from across the lake. He'd returned to Luanza, where he was schooled, and found this girl. He would take her home for his son. She smiled at us demurely. She was alight, excited and afraid, facing a thirty-mile journey across moonlit Mweru to Zambia and a man. She said tearful farewells. For love, I'd have gone too. Only for love.

SELECT BIBLIOGRAPHY

Anstey, Roger, *King Leopold's Legacy*, Oxford 1966.
Arnot, F. S., *Garenganze: West and East*, Glasgow 1902.
Axelson, Sigbert, *Culture Confrontation in the Lower Congo*, Falköping 1970.
Badi-Banga Ne-Mwine, *Contribution à l'Étude Historique de l'Art Plastique Zaïrois moderne*, Kinshasa 1977.
Balandier, Georges (trans. Helen Weaver), *Daily Life in the Kingdom of the Kongo*, New York 1968.
Batchelor, John D., "Journey from the Zaïre River Source", *Geographical Magazine*, November 1974.
Bentley, W. Holman, *Pioneering on the Congo*, London 1900.
Birmingham, David & Martin, Phyllis M. (eds.), *History of Central Africa*, vol. 2, London 1983.
Bolamba, Antoine-Roger, *Esanzo: Chants pour mon Pays*, Paris 1955.
Bourne, H. R. Fox, *The Other Side of the Emin Pascha Relief Expedition*, London 1891.
Brown, J. H., *A Missionary in the Making*, Cape Town 1984.
Burrows, Capt. Guy, *The Curse of Central Africa*, London 1903.
Campbell, D., *Blazing Trails in Bantuland*, London n.d.
Carrington, Dr J. F., "Wooden Drums for Inter-Village Telephony in Central Africa", *Journal of the Instituite of Wood Science*, vol. 7, no. 4, November 1976.
Casement, Roger, "Correspondence and Reports from His Majesty's Consul at Boma Respecting the Administration of the Independent State of The Congo", Parliamentary Papers 1904 (Command Paper 1933) LXII.
   "Further Correspondence Respecting the Administration of the Independent State of the Congo" PP 1904 (Cd 2097) LXII.
   The Crime Against Europe (ed. Herbert O. Mackey), Dublin 1958.
   Some Poems of Roger Casement (Intro. Gertrude Parry), Dublin & London 1918.
   MSS notebook and diary, PRO HO 161: 1901 War Office Army Book 153 & 1903 Letts's Pocket Diary.
Conan-Doyle, A., "The Crime of the Congo, London 1909"
Conrad, Joseph, *Almayer's Folly*, London 1895.
   Tales of Unrest, London 1898.
   Youth, a Narrative, and Two Other Stories, London 1902.
   A Personal Record, London 1912.
   Last Essays, London 1926.
Cordeiro, Luciano, *Questãos Historico-Coloniais*, vol. 2, Lisbon 1936.

Cornet, Joseph, *A Survey of Zaïrean Art — The Bronson Collection*, Raleigh 1978.

Crawford, Dan, *Thinking Black*, London 1912.

  Thirsting after God, London 1914.

  The Way Home from the Homeland, Edinburgh & London 1916.

  Back to the Long Grass: My Link with Livingstone, London 1924.

Delcommune, Alexandre, *Vingt Années de Vie Africaine*, Brussels 1922.

Delhez, Charles, *La Bienheureuse Anuarite et le Pape Jean-Paul II*, Kinshasa 1985.

Diallo, Siradiou (trans. Barbara Shuey), "Zaïre Today", Paris 1977, 1984.

Dieu, L., *Dans La Brousse Congolaise*, Liège 1946.

Elebe Lisembe, *Mélodie Africaine: Poems*, Laou 1970.

  Simon Kimbangu ou le Messie Noir, Paris 1972.

Fraser, Douglas, *Through the Congo Basin*, London 1927.

Gide, André, *Voyage au Congo*, Paris 1927.

Gilis, Charles-André, *Kimbangu: Fondateur d'Église*, Brussels 1960.

Glave, E. J., *Six Years of Adventure in Congoland*, London 1893.

Gran, Guy (ed), *Zaïre — The Political Economy of Underdevelopment*, New York 1979.

Greene, Graham, *A Burnt-Out Case*, London 1961.

  In Search of a Character, London 1961.

Gunther, John, *Inside Africa*, New York 1955.

Harmes, Robert Wayne, "Competition & Capitalism: The Bobangi Role in Equatorial Africa's Trade Revolution, c1750–1900", Wisconsin-Madison (Ph.D. Thesis) 1978.

Haveaux, G. K., *La Tradition Historique des Bapendes Orientaux*, Brussels 1954.

Hird, Frank, *H. M. Stanley: The Authorized Life*, London 1935.

Hinde, S. L., *The Fall of the Congo Arabs*, London 1897.

Hochegger, Hermann *et al*, *Dieu Dessécha le Fleuve*, Bandundu 1978.

Hone, Joseph, *Children of the Country*, London 1986.

Inglis, Brian, *Roger Casement*, London 1973.

Jean-Aubry, G., *Joseph Conrad: Life & Letters*, London 1927.

  "Joseph Conrad in the Congo" in *Bookman's Journal*, London 1926.

Johnston, H. H. *The River Congo, from its Mouth to Bolobo*, London 1884.

Johnston, Sir Harry, *George Grenfell and the Congo*, London 1908.

Kaboke Kolomoni, *Chroniques Katangaises*, Paris 1976.

Kadima-Nzuji Mukala (Dieudonné), *Les Ressacs*, Kinshasa 1969.

  Preludes à la Terre, Kinshasa 1971.

Kalb, Madeleine G., *The Congo Cables*, New York 1982.

Kaplan, Irving (ed), *Zaïre: A Country Study*, Washington 1979.

Karl, Frederick R., *Joseph Conrad: The Three Lives*, London 1979.

Karl, Frederick R. & Davies, Laurence (eds), *The Collected Letters of Joseph Conrad, Vol. 1 1861–1897*, Cambridge 1983.

Kawata Ashem Tem, *Des Cendres et Des Flammes*, Kinshasa 1980.

"La Littérature Zaïroise", *Notre Librairie*, no. 63, Paris 1982.

Livingstone, David, *The Last Journals*, London 1874.

Livre Blanc du Gouvernement Katangais sur les Événements de Septembre et Décembre 1961, Elizabethville n.d.

Lomami-Tshibamba, Paul, *N'Gobila des M'Swata*, Kinshasa 1972.

Lumumba, Patrice, *Congo, My Country* (foreword by Colin Legum), London 1962.

Masegabio Nzanzu Mabelemadiko (ed.), *Le Zaïre Écrit*, Tübingen/Kinshasa 1976.

La Cendre Demeure, Kinshasa 1983.

McBride, Ruth Q., "Keeping House on the Congo", *The National Geographic Mazagine*, Vol. LXXII, no. 5 Nov. 1937.

Moloney, J. A., *With Captain Stairs to Katanga*, London 1893.

Morel, Edmund D., Red Rubber: *The Story of the Rubber Slave Trade Flourishing on the Congo in the Year of Grace 1906*, London 1906.

Muamba Kanyinda, *La Pourriture*, Kinshasa 1978.

Mulago Gua Cikala Musharhamina, *Mariage Traditionnel Africain et Mariage Chrétien*, Kinshasa 1981.

Mwamb'a Musas Mangol, *Muenz et Autres Contes*, Kinshasa 1981.

Naipaul, V. S., "A New King for the Congo", *New York Review of Books*, 26 June 1975.

A Bend in the River, London 1979.

Najder, Zdzislaw, *Joseph Conrad: A Chronicle*, Cambridge 1983.

Conrad under Familial Eyes, Cambridge 1983.

Nkrumah, Kwame, *Challenge of the Congo*, New York 1967.

Nlemvo Way wa Ngombe Ndoadidiki, *Ndonzoao Nlemvo*, Kinshasa 1978.

Norden, Hermann, *Fresh Tracks in the Belgian Congo*, London 1924.

Peres, Damião, *Historia dos Descobrimentos*, Coimbra 1960.

Pigafetta, Philippo/Lopes, Odoardo (trans. Abraham Hartwell), *A Reporte of The Kingdome of Congo, A Region of Africa . . .*, London 1597.

Puleston, Frederick, *African Drums*, London 1930.

Raskin, Jonah, "'Heart of Darkness': The Manuscript Revisions", *Review of English Studies*, XVIII, no. 69, 1967.

Reid, B. L., *The Lives of Roger Casement*, Yale 1976.

Sawyer, Roger, *Casement: The Flawed Hero*, London 1984.

Severn, Merlyn, *Congo Pilgrim*, London 1952.

Sherry, Norman, *Conrad's Western World*, Cambridge 1971.

Singleton-Gates, Peter & Girodias, Maurice, *The Black Diaries*, New York 1959.

Slade, Ruth, *King Leopold's Congo*, London 1962.

Smith, H. Sutton, *Yakusu: The Very Heart of Africa*, London n.d.

Stanley, H. M., *Through the Dark Continent*, London 1878.

The Congo, and the Founding of its Free State, London 1885.

In Darkest Africa, London 1890.

Stanley, Richard, & Neame, Alan, *The Exploration Diaries of H. M. Stanley*, London 1961.

Tchicaya U Tam'si, *Selected Poems*, London 1970.

Tempels, Placide, *La Philosophie Bantoue*, Elizabethville 1947.

Thompson, Robert Farris & Cornet, Joseph, *The Four Moments of the Sun: Kongo Art in Two Worlds*, Washington 1981.

Tilsley, G. E., *Dan Crawford of Central Africa*, London 1929.

Tuckey, Capt. J. K. *et al*, *Narrative of an Expedition to Explore the River Zaïre, Usually Called the Congo, in South Africa, in 1816*, London 1818.

Turnbull, Colin, *The Lonely African*, New York 1962.

Twain, Mark, *King Leopold's Soliloquy*, London 1907.

Vansina, Jan, *Kingdoms of the Savanna*, Wisconsin 1966.

    The Children of Woot, Wisconsin 1978.

Viccars, John, "Witchcraft in Bolobo, Belgian Congo", *AFRICA*, 19, 1949.

Ward, Herbert, *Voice from the Congo*, London 1910.

Weeks, J. H., *Congo Life and Folklore*, London 1911.

    Among the Primitive Bakongo, London 1914.

Widman, Ragnar, *The Niombo Cult among the Babwende*, Stockholm 1967.

Wiedner, Donald L., *A History of Africa South of the Sahara*, London 1964.

Yoka Lye Mudaba, *Tshjra*, Kinshasa 1984.

Young, Crawford, *Politics in the Congo*, Princeton 1965.

Periodicals:

Zaïre, Brussels 1947–60.

Zaïre-Afrique, Kinshasa 1960–87.

INDEX